WESTMAR COLLEGE

ARCHAEOLOGY
AND THE
OLD TESTAMENT WORLD

Archaeology
and the
Old Testament World

JOHN GRAY M.A. B.D. Ph.D.

Professor of Hebrew and Semitic Languages
Aberdeen University

Thomas Nelson and Sons Ltd

London Edinburgh Paris Melbourne Johannesburg
Toronto and New York

THOMAS NELSON AND SONS LTD
Parkside Works Edinburgh 9
36 Park Street London W1
117 Latrobe Street Melbourne C1

THOMAS NELSON AND SONS (AFRICA) (Pty.) LTD
P.O. Box 9881, Johannesburg

THOMAS NELSON AND SONS (CANADA) LTD
91–93 Wellington Street West   Toronto 1

THOMAS NELSON AND SONS
18 East 41st Street New York 17, N.Y.

SOCIÉTÉ FRANÇAISE D'ÉDITIONS NELSON
97 rue Monge Paris 5

———

Preface

THE main purpose of this study is to introduce students, clergy, and interested laymen to the mind of ancient Israel in her historical and cultural environment. The material results of the progressive exploration of the Near East have become increasingly familiar through excellent publications on both sides of the Atlantic and through the medium of television. To repeat this matter is no part of our plan, though it is to a certain degree unavoidable. Our interest lies rather in the texts of Ancient Near Eastern literatures and their affinity with the Old Testament writings, and with the institutions, conventions, and beliefs which they illustrate. I have thus endeavoured to conduct the reader through the museum of the Ancient Near East, not seeking to impress him with the show pieces, but explaining the significance of all that is relevant, both what is spectacular and what is not, in an effort to present the world in which Israel encountered her problems and sought to solve them.

One of the most pleasing features of the archaeological exploration of the Ancient Near East has been the enthusiastic co-operation of eminent scholars of the highest integrity of various races, faiths, and denominations. A cursory glance at the bibliography in the footnotes to this work will indicate how much we owe to the great Dominicans of St Étienne in Jerusalem as well as to Protestant scholars in Europe and America and to Jewish archaeologists in the new state of Israel. This co-operation affords a practical example of those ecumenical aspirations which are a welcome aspect of the contemporary scene. Such a discipline has no place for tendentious sectarian theology, and offers us common ground for a positive reconstruction of the antecedents of our Christian faith unvitiated by denominational prejudice. Archaeology sets the word of God in its proper context so that dogmatic theology may draw neither more nor less from a passage than that context warrants.

In my experience of native life in the East—in Bedouin tent and in town and village of the settled land—I was impressed with the many elements that remained constant in spite of the inevitable changes imposed by history and science ; a knowledge of the native mind and ways, especially in more primitive society, was often the best clue to the interpretation of a text from ancient literature or to the reconstruction of the life of ancient society in Palestine. For this reason this study begins with a sketch of life and conditions as I found them in the modern East before the irruption of brash modernity.

In presenting this work I take the opportunity to express my thanks to all those who have helped in many ways : to the numerous kindly Arabs in black tents and in the villages of Palestine, who gave me their traditional hospitality, and by their company and conversation helped me more than they realised ; to the British Police during the Mandate of Palestine, whom it was my privilege to serve as chaplain and who both shared and stimulated my interest in native life and facilitated many a hazardous journey ; and to the staff of the institutions in Palestine who afforded me library facilities, particularly the Dominican monastery of St Étienne and, more recently, the Pontifical Biblical Institute and the library of the Hebrew University in Jerusalem. I am greatly indebted to my colleagues in the University of Aberdeen who read and corrected my proofs, to the Reverend Professor A. C. Kennedy, whose father the late Professor A. R. S. Kennedy first quickened my interest in the life of the Ancient East, and also to Mr W. R. Humphries Lecturer in Scottish History, who combines a lively and stimulating interest in folklore with the technical efficiency of a schoolmaster. Finally my thanks are due to Thomas Nelson and Sons in Edinburgh, who kindly allowed me to adapt the text of my MS after my recent stay in Palestine, and to their compositors who have so beautifully finished the production of the work.

JOHN GRAY

King's College
University of Aberdeen
October 1961

Contents

List of Illustrations

Acknowledgments

THE publishers wish to thank the following for kindly giving permission to reproduce illustrations :

Plate 1—Éditions 'TEL', Paris ; Plates 2, 4, 15—the Trustees of the British Museum ; Plate 3—A Gaddis, Luxor ; Plates 5, 11, 12—Oriental Institute, University of Chicago ; Plate 6—Cairo Museum, Cairo ; Plate 7—Dr C. F. A. Schaeffer and the British Academy ; Plate 8a—The Museum of the University of Pennsylvania, Philadelphia ; Plate 8b—Dr James B. Pritchard ; Plate 9a—Vorderasiatisches Museum, Staatliche Museen zu Berlin ; Plate 9b—Casa Editrice Felice le Monnier, Florence ; Plate 10—The James A. De Rothschild Expedition at Hazor ; Plate 13a—Palestine Exploration Fund ; Plate 13b—Museo di Antichita ; Plate 14a—Dr Aharoni, Jerusalem ; Plates 14b, 16—the Trustees of the late Sir Henry S. Wellcome ; Plate 17—Pacific School of Religion, Berkeley, California ; Plate 18 (The Seal of Shema)—East and West Library ; (The Seal of Jaazaniah), (Seal of Jotham)—President Nelson Glueck ; (The Seal Impression of Gedaliah), 19—the Trustees of the late Sir Henry S. Wellcome ; Plate 20—Bildarchiv Foto-Marburg ; Plate 21 —Mrs Esther Reifenberg, Jerusalem ; Plate 22—L. H. Grollenberg OP ; Plate 23—Dr Yigael Yadin ; Plate 24—Professeur André Parrot, Paris ; Plate 25—American Schools of Oriental Research.

PART I

THE WORLD OF THE
OLD TESTAMENT

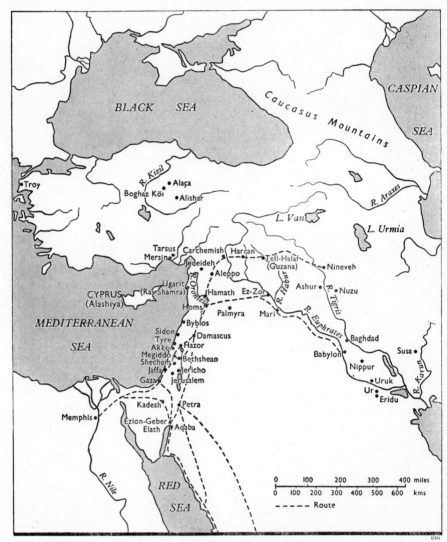

The World of the Old Testament

I The Setting

THE world of the Old Testament in its widest scope extends from the highlands of Iran, where Nehemiah and Ezra knew the courts of the Persian kings, to Athens and Rome, where Paul preached the Gospel to synagogues of Jews. The story of Moses is set in Egypt and Sinai, and the missionary journeys of Paul carry him through the coastlands and uplands of Asia Minor and over the Hellespont to Macedonia. The early history of the Hebrew fathers Abraham, Isaac, and Jacob is set in Mesopotamia, Palestine, and Egypt, though the wars of the nation Israel were fought nearer home and were ultimately confined to the defence of the small kingdoms of Israel and Judah in Palestine. With the collapse of these kingdoms and the dispersion of the people the horizons were again to expand to embrace the Land of the Two Rivers, the royal cities of Persia, the isles and mainland of Greece, and eventually the whole Mediterranean coastland, and Egypt as far south as the first cataract on the Nile. This area of the Jewish diaspora was the field of the Christian mission.

In point of time the events of Scripture must be studied in the context of the history of many races and movements, political, economic, and cultural, of over two millennia. Much of this history has left no trace in written records. It may, however, be recovered by the discovery and patient interpretation of the material remains of vanished peoples, sometimes spectacular, like the monuments of Egypt, and sometimes quite unimpressive, but always clues to the scholarly detective. Some of this history, of course, is inscribed in documents, many of which are themselves archaeological discoveries. These, however, are of varying value. Some are scanty and vague, like Egyptian inscriptions, which give long honorific titles of the Pharaohs, but irritatingly brief, and often quite inadequate, references to historical events ; others again, like the Assyrian historical records, are dry and annalistic, giving events with much detail, but showing no appreciation of the process of history. In this respect the Assyrian historical records stand in direct contrast to the historical books of the Old Testament, which often omit what we know from the former to be important details when these did not relate to the major theme of the divine destiny of Israel. It is obvious that for a true appreciation of history these documents must be studied in relation to one another, and in providing us with the records of Assyria and Babylon particularly archaeology has done a major service. The material remains again show the inter-relation and sequence of cultures in a broad sense, though the science of the typology of weapons, pottery, and utensils has been very highly developed. Here precision is made possible by inscriptions, cuneiform tablets, inscribed scarabs and seals, and, later, coins, which enable the material evidence to be dated and so to serve as a commentary to such documentary remains as there may be from the same period.

The study of the material remains of daily life, sacred and secular, of Israel and her neighbours introduces us to the ecology of the people, that is to say, to their more immediate world in relation to which they developed their character and their faith. Here again material remains are supplemented by inscriptions and written records which limit the field of conjecture and often permit of a great degree of precision in the interpretation of the evidence. In this connection we should note the abundance of ritual texts from Mesopotamia and, to a less extent, from Ras Shamra on the Syrian coast. The myths and sagas from the latter site are of great value as intimate documentation of the fertility-cult of Canaan and of the social system there on the eve of the Hebrew settlement. This last field again is well illuminated by the administrative texts from Ras Shamra, and legal texts from the south and north of Mesopotamia and from Ras Shamra enable Hebrew law and society to be studied in its living context in Near Eastern culture.

Throughout this work we shall have occasion to draw heavily on such documents, but practically every chapter will emphasise that both documents and material evidence are mutually complementary. Both are the discoveries of archaeology which have served to bring the Biblical past out of the mists of antiquity and infuse it again with warm life and fresh vitality.

Such an attempt to recover the past, however, must also take note of the living present. Since the climate of Palestine and the Near East has not changed appreciably in historical times, a knowledge of the cycle of the peasant's year and his various seasonal operations, his implements, and his methods is also of relevance, as may be seen clearly by comparing modern methods and tools with those illustrated by archaeology, both in material remains and in written records. Familiarity with social principles and conventions among modern Arab peasants and tribesmen reveals an astonishing correspondence with principles and conventions implied in Canaanite sagas and in Assyrian and Babylonian law-codes. This suggests that to enter thoroughly into the world of the Old Testament we must, always with care and discretion, use modern sociology as well as the discoveries of archaeology. Thus we may win a sympathetic appreciation of Scripture which will solve many difficulties and, above all, preserve the Old Testament from arbitrary abuse, to which it has been too often subjected, in the interests of homiletic and dogmatic theology.

Before dealing with the specifically archaeological discovery of the world of the Old Testament we must present a picture of that world as it appears to the geographer or sociologist today.

The scene was set at the dawn of history when the northward recession of the last great ice-cap made an arid desert of the rich tropical savannahs of the Sahara and the great Asian deserts, and forced the hunters, whose dainty flint-blades and rock-carvings of tropical game have been found there, to withdraw with the animals to oases and dwindling watercourses. This movement was general in the whole of the land area on the same latitude as the Mediterranean and the northern half of Africa. The great deserts were so formed, the Sahara (' the desert '), the Arabian desert, the high desert of Persia, and those of Baluchistan and Sind. From all those areas there was a gradual migration of animals and their parasite man until the life of both concentrated in the valleys and marshes of the great perennial rivers, the Nile, the Euphrates, and the Tigris, and the Indus and its tributaries. It was the parasite which took possession, finally exterminating the animals or domesticating some and driving others back from his settlements. But with the disappearance of the animals it became necessary for the hunter to supplement his precarious livelihood. So by the industry of his women-folk agriculture developed. When the men were absent on their hunting-quest, ever further afield, the women gathered the self-sown fruit of the earth. Eventually the food-gatherers themselves selected the best grains, planting them in the best earth, keeping them free from weeds and providing water. So agriculture was born, woman's achievement and still largely her province in primitive communities. Naturally he, or rather she, who sowed the seed remained to reap, and so the nomad became sedentary, though

2

only by slow degrees, for such early farming settlements of the Neolithic Age (*c.*7500–4000 B.C.) at Badari and Deir Tasi in upper Egypt and Merimde at the extremity of the western Delta clearly indicated that hunting was still a considerable element of the ancient economy.[1]

Sedentary life and regular provision of food encouraged larger families and communities than was possible in the conditions under which the hunter-nomads lived, which permitted only the survival of the fittest. With the pooling of experience in sedentary communities progress in the technical arts became possible. The rivers supplied water for irrigation, and this in itself was a medium of communal development with far-reaching possibilities. The rivers also eventually facilitated communication between settlements, resulting in the sharing of technical resources, political consolidation, and ultimately conquest. Thus in the world of the Old Testament the great seats of civilisation and empire were the valleys of the Euphrates and Tigris and of the Nile. Here early travellers and later archaeologists found the most impressive remains, many of which, such as the pyramids, temples, and other monuments of Egypt and the *ziggurats* (staged towers) of lower Mesopotamia have always been visible and remain so today. The science and political control which made such achievements possible was the result of the concentration of power in the hands of the kings of Egypt and of the temple-hierarchies of Mesopotamia, both of whom were great monopolists.

In Canaan, which comprised Palestine and Syria, life in historical times was conditioned by the same climatic changes as produced the great deserts and caused the concentrations of life in the great river-valleys of the Middle East. As life was preserved in Egypt, Mesopotamia, and the Punjab in the great desiccation by perennial rivers from sources far beyond these lands, there were intermediate areas in the same latitude watered by clouds borne inland by prevailing winds from seas to inland deserts, which condensed on the mountain escarpments as very heavy dews and seasonal rains. These stimulated immediate growth and percolated the porous limestone rock to gather in caverns and issue in perennial springs. Such regions are Syria, Palestine, the foothills of Anatolia, including Assyria, and the western escarpment of Persia.

In those intermediate areas, however, geographical conditions promoted only a very limited communal development. Those

[1] V. Gordon Childe, *New Light on the Most Ancient Near East* (1935), 49 ff.

were the natural homes of isolated, independent peasant communities, concentrated in necessarily limited numbers about local
springs and pockets of earth, often among mountains. Culturally
they played a role mainly assimilative, depending for their
stimulus upon the great empires and cultures of the Nile and the
Euphrates. Politically they developed slowly and mainly under
external impulse after periodic invasions from the north Arabian
steppes, such as brought the Aramaean kingdoms of Edom and
Moab into being in the end of the 14th century B.C. and Israel
about a century later. The inhabitants of those areas, however,
possessed an inherent toughness evidenced by the military efficiency of Assyria and the continual resistance of the small native
states of Syria and Palestine to Assyrian expansion.

Palestine, geographically and culturally a unit with Syria, is
a land of striking diversity, which is apparent to any traveller
who goes from Jaffa via Jerusalem to Jericho.[1] First there is a
coastal plain of great fertility except where the rich brown earth
has been blanketed under the sand-drift from the shore. This
was never extensively occupied by the Hebrews, but was the
country of the Philistines who took possession about the time that
the Hebrews occupied the interior. Originally a kindred people
of the Philistines, the *Tekel*, occupied Dor (modern *Tantura* on
the coast some fifteen miles south of Haifa) and are mentioned
in the Golenischeff Papyrus *c.*1100 B.C., but in the Old Testament
they are never mentioned, and the Philistines appear to be confined to the coastal plain south of Jaffa. This is corroborated by
the descriptions of the districts under Solomon's fiscal administration. Dor is mentioned (1 Kg. 4:11), but no district in the coastal
plain south of that region.

In modern times this coastal plain produces corn, both wheat
and barley, and olives, and is extensively planted with vines and
particularly citrus-groves. Doubtless vines and olives were grown
there also in antiquity, but the main crop was corn. A Phoenician
inscription from Sidon from the early 3rd century B.C.[2] mentions
the coastal plain behind Jaffa and Dor as a rich cornland. The
mention of those cornlands in Palestine of which the Sidonians

---

[1] The following description refers to the land under the Arabs before the
recent Zionist modernisation, when new methods and crops have been introduced and the density of settlement and the development of the land have
been artificially conditioned by political forces in Europe and the liberal
investment of capital from outside. The natural ecology of Palestine in
pre-Zionist days is much more illustrative of the Biblical past.

[2] G. A. Cooke, *A Textbook of North Semitic Inscriptions* (1903), no. 5, 11, 19

had usufruct by grace of 'the Lord of Kings' is interesting in view of the statement in Acts (Ac. 12:20) that the Phoenicians of Tyre and Sidon similarly depended upon the territories of Herod Agrippa I. As a meeting on this matter took place at Caesarea, it is not unlikely that the business concerned the long-standing privilege of the Phoenicians which the inscription records. The same inscription refers to this area as the Plain of Sharon. The native villages in the coastal plain, particularly south of Jaffa before they were swept away in the Zionist occupation, were featureless conglomerations of mudbrick dwellings. The plain is intersected by several wadis or watercourses, but these are for the most part quite dry except for a few days in the rainy season, when they are raging brown torrents, and even small freshets (*suyūl*) may be dangerous. A case in point is the sudden rising of the Kishon when 'the stars in their courses fought against Sisera' (Jg. 5:20). The present writer recollects his first sight of the Kishon under precisely these conditions when the stream was a heavy flood of liquid mud flowing through a quagmire. The most considerable perennial stream is the Auja ('Crooked') just north of Jaffa, a small but deep stream, which probably formed the boundary between Israel and the Philistines from the time of Solomon.[1]

The southern limit of the coastal plain is the Wadi Ghazzeh, which the Egyptians apparently regarded as the practical limit of the settled land, since they fortified it with a line of fortress-towns, Tell el-Ajjul at the mouth of the wadi, Tell Jemmeh, and Tell el-Farʿa (ancient Sharuhen). In this region the land, prior to the Zionist occupation, was inhabited by semi-nomads who cultivated wide plains of barley but continued to live in tents just as Abraham and Isaac did in the same region, called in the Old Testament the Negeb.[2] South of the Wadi Ghazzeh the rainfall deteriorates until the desert prevails. This is the Wilderness of Paran, sometimes called the Wilderness of

---

[1] This is suggested by B. Maisler in his report of his excavations at Tell Qasileh in the northern suburbs of Tel Aviv, a site which was occupied from *c.*1200 B.C. to the 7th century A.D. If we can credit the evidence of two inscribed sherds this town seems to have been an Israelite trading-post near the coast. These, however, were picked up, it is said, on the surface of the site before excavation, and are therefore not to be admitted as evidence without doubt (B. Maisler, *The Excavations at Tell Qasile; Preliminary Report*, 1951). The strategic significance of the Auja was appreciated by the Hyksos, who had a fortress commanding the fords on the ancient military highway from Egypt at Tell Jerisheh.

[2] Gen. 26:12 explicitly states that Isaac sowed and reaped.

Zin. There is, however, seasonal grass and permanent grazing on low shrubs along the dry watercourses, and there are oases with permanent springs, the most notable being Ain Qadeis in the vicinity of Biblical Kadesh Barnea. Recent exploration by Glueck has revealed much more intensive settlement from the Middle Bronze Age to the Iron Age than was previously suspected, especially in the region of broad cultivable wadis extending from east of Beersheba for some fifty miles in a south-westerly direction, where there were several important towns in the Byzantine period.[1] This was the home of the Biblical Amalekites, with whom the Hebrews contested the region [2] until they occupied a more attractive land in Palestine proper. This steppe-land was also occupied by certain nomad elements with close affinities with the Hebrews, such as the Jerahmeelites, Kenizzites, and Kenites, who were probably the original worshippers of Yahweh.[3]

The coastal plain is broken in the east by the low Judaean foothills, a marked feature of which is the valley running north and south from just north of ancient Lachish (Tell ed-Duweir) to near Beth Horon the Lower (Beit 'Ur et-Taḥta) above the valley of Aijalon. This is known in the Old Testament as the Shephelah ('Lowland') and was definitely occupied by the Hebrews. Besides Lachish at its southern limit, it includes Azekah and Sochoh in the Vale of Elah, where David slew Goliath. Bethshemesh is actually in the valley, and Zorah (modern *Ṣarah*), the traditional home of Samson, is just west of it. This again is a corn-producing area, though less fertile than the coastal plain. The hillsides, terraced to prevent erosion, were planted in Arab times with vines, olives, figs, pomegranates, apricots, and almonds. Though the Arab settlements were fairly numerous, there was little or no sense of solidarity. This narrow local loyalty is a feature of the intermediate areas which we have noted in the Near and Middle East, and has retarded political and cultural development. In Palestine it facilitated the Hebrew occupation in the 13th century B.C. and in the recent Jewish occupation, when the Zionists were able first to buy up land piecemeal and then to occupy more by force of arms without serious native resistance.

[1] For an excellent scientific description of the region see D. Baly, *The Geography of the Bible* (1957), 260 ff.
[2] Exod. 17:8 ; S. Mowinckel suggests that the Amalekites on this occasion were contesting with Israel the control of the Qadesh oasis, which was a most important entrepôt of caravan trade between Egypt and the oases of Arabia, ' Kadesj, Sinai, og Jahve ', *Norsk Geografisk Tidsskrift* XI (1942), 13 ff.
[3] This view is adopted by H. H. Rowley, who states the case, citing the relevant bibliography in *From Joseph to Joshua* (1950), 149 ff.

Jerusalem is approached through a tangle of ravines deeply cut in the limestone mountains and is situated some two thousand five hundred feet above sea-level. Hebron and Bethel are some five hundred feet higher. On these heights corn is cultivated in valley-bottoms and pockets of earth, often quite small, but it is pre-eminently a country of the olive and the vine (cf. the blessing of Judah in Gen. 49:11), and other fruit-trees, which clothe the terraced mountain-sides wherever a patch of earth is found. This again is a country of small farmers, though often the land is common property and farmed on the strip system. The village communities were really kinship units and in social and ethical relationships were for the most part self-regulated, as in the period of the Judges of Israel and the early Monarchy. An absurdly narrow local particularism, however, atomised the population and at all times made them an easy prey to the invader. In the Hebrew occupation, for instance, Jerusalem, Gibeon, and Bethel, three considerable fortress-towns within a radius of less than five miles, made no effort to unite. Jerusalem made common cause too late with four Amorite towns to the south-west, the men of Bethel made a vain stand alone on the ruins of Ai, and the Gibeonites deluded the Hebrews into making a separate peace. Eventually, too, the villages would be torn with internal family feuds, which resulted in burning of crops, barking of fruit-trees, very lively and violent village fights, and often deliberate murder. Another social evil resulting from these conditions of local congestion and lack of opportunities beyond the confines of the village was brigandage, a chronic vice in Palestine and one familiar in the Old Testament (e.g. Prov. 1:10–18). The modern Arab takes light-heartedly 'to the hills', as he says in his local idiom. There brigands and refugees would find cover for ambush and a home for themselves and their associates in the limestone caves, with which the whole country is honeycombed. Many of these are quite capable of housing hundreds of men. Apart from ambush and highway robbery, blackmail would be levied, as in the case of David and Nabal (1 Sam. 25). We wonder the less at the lack of censure on David in the Biblical narrative when we find that the brigand to the Arabs is less of an outcast than a popular hero. Indeed one such brigand, Abu Ghosh, has even attained posthumously to sanctity ; the tomb of Abu Ghosh on the Jaffa road some six miles west of Jerusalem is a *weli*, the shrine of a local intercessory saint. The modern brigand, active in Turkish times, has taken the place of an old *baal*.

The peasant life of Palestine, however, is not without its redeeming graces. Within the narrow compass of the kinship social duties are thoroughly understood. The ethical code operates automatically and is sanctioned by time-honoured custom and public opinion, which few natives care to flout. There are few cases, in fact, in the internal affairs of the village which need be settled beyond the session of local elders in the place of public resort, ' within the gates ' of the Old Testament. Again, charity to widows, orphans, and other helpless persons is a priority charge on the community. With fine delicacy this does not take the form of a locally administered fund like ' parish relief ', but is in kind,[1] a corner or edge of a field or an odd fruit-tree left as if forgotten, and, of course, the poor have the right to glean during harvest. So it was also in Israel (Dt. 29:19 ff. ; Lev. 19:9 ; 23:22).

The hills of Arab Palestine are thickly settled with stone-built villages. Many of these are on or near ancient settlements, which were usually clustered on hill-tops and equipped with fortifications apparently out of proportion to the size of the settlement. The reason for the fortification is double. It reflects the mutual independence of the communities which we have already noted, each providing for its own security against the common enemy and against one another. On the other hand it was a measure dictated by the geographical situation of Palestine, the stepping-stone between the Euphrates and the Nile. Armies of conquest, of course, did not scruple to live off the country which they traversed. It was only when the ancient world of which she was a part was united under the firm rule of Rome that settlements were built in the plains. No doubt in Old Testament times there was seasonal settlement in the plains below the villages. The ploughlands of Arab Nazareth, for instance, used to be about eight miles distant in the great central Plain of Esdraelon, and

---

[1] The Talmud notes five ways of dispensing this charity. A corner of the field or orchard amounting to 1/60 of the whole might be left, the right to glean during harvest was admitted, and to pick up the fruit that fell during picking, and to gather what had been forgotten during the harvest, and to gather grapes which had been unripe at the time of gathering. Besides this there was a levy of 1/10 every three years for the poor and the Levites (Dt. 14:28 ; 26:12 ff.). See further G. Dalman, *Arbeit und Sitte in Palästina* 1, 2 (1928), 585 ff. This poor relief, of course, is standardised within Islam, but among the Syrian peasants in this as in many other particulars local practice is independent of Islam and even of Christianity and, as in the case of the local saint-cult just cited, often quite contrary to the principles of the official faith.

we have met villagers from Beitin (ancient Bethel) who spent the season of spring pasture just west of Jericho. The 'metropolis', however, was the hill-top settlement, the 'city' ('*ir*, so called possibly because it was the place of the vital water-hole, Arabic *ghawr*).[1] The term 'city' is a most misleading one and might more appropriately be rendered 'fortress', or 'burg'. Throughout Palestine certain of those 'fortresses' about a waterhole or spring grew to considerable proportions, though few exceed fifteen acres within the walled perimeter. In the Amarna Tablets, which depict Palestine just after 1400 B.C., there were few such places in the hill-country besides Jerusalem and Shechem. Hence two centuries later in the main phase of the Hebrew occupation this was the area where the Hebrews settled.[2]

Jerusalem stands just east of the watershed of the highlands of Judah. It enjoys a high precipitation of winter rain and summer dew, is cold on winter nights, and occasionally has snowstorms.[3] In an easy morning's walk, however, eastward from the city over the Kidron and the Mount of Olives towards Jericho one soon passes beyond the area of cultivation. East of the watershed there is a very rapid decline in rainfall, so that this illfavoured region sloping towards Jericho and particularly towards the Dead Sea has always been a ready refuge for fugitives from ruling authorities or from fixed conventions, for brigands, patriots, and saints. Here towards the south-west of the Dead Sea is the fortress of Masada, built by Herod the Great on an earlier fortress of the Hasmonaeans, where the Jewish patriots and fanatics made their last dramatic stand against the legions of Titus in A.D. 73. Here, too, farther north, by the oasis of Engeddi David sought refuge from Saul and chivalrously, or with politic foresight, spared the life of 'the Lord's anointed' (1 Sam. 24). In this same locality, a little farther north, 'the Sect of the New Covenant', probably Essenes, who left the now famous Dead Sea Scrolls, had their monastery at Ḥirbet Qumran. No other part of

---

[1] Possible confirmation of this conjecture is 2 Sam. 12:27 if the traditional reading '*ir ha-mayim* is correct.

[2] So A. Alt, *Die Landnahme der Israeliten in Palästina* (1925) ; *Die Staatenbildung der Israeliten in Palästina* (1930), 5–6

[3] In 1936–7 the writer experienced six-foot drifts of snow on the track between Petra and Maan (in Mount Seir), and found that the same storm had blocked the road between Hebron and Jerusalem. On that occasion he witnessed the burial of a man who had perished in his house at Elji near Petra from extreme cold. Readers familiar with T. E. Lawrence's *Seven Pillars of Wisdom* will recall the author's journey through the same region in similar conditions, op. cit. (Jonathan Cape, 1936), 492 ff.

Palestine is dry enough for such documents to be preserved. In this same zone between the desert and the sown lived the prophet Amos at Tekoa within sight of Edom, Moab, and Ammon over the Dead Sea, whose policies fall under his purview. It is not by chance that such a champion of the rights of man is from a region where men are not so far removed from the life of the desert, where within the kinship of the tribe the essential human values were preserved. The austerity of the prophet's message of retribution also seems to reflect this physical and social environment.

Leaving Jerusalem for the Jordan Valley, one descends 3,750 feet to reach the lowest point of the earth's surface 1,246 feet below sea-level by the Dead Sea. We leave a sub-alpine region for a subtropical region. Here where ground-water is available, as at Jericho, vegetation is rank and, as well as the cereals and fruits common elsewhere in Palestine, bananas and date-palms are found. These grow also at the lower, eastern end of the Plain of Esdraelon (the valley of Jezreel), by Bethshan in the coastal strips and plains by the Lake of Galilee, which is also below sea-level. There is a great difference, however, between the Jordan Valley east of the river and that of the west. In the latter region there are but two perennial tributaries of the Jordan, the Wadi Far'a, which flows from Tell el-Far'a (ancient Tirzah) near Shechem and joins the Jordan just south of ed-Damieh (ancient Adamah), and Nahr Jalud,[1] which flows past Bethshan. Generally the western part of the Jordan Valley is waste and desolate. The east bank, however, is fertile, being irrigated from a number of perennial streamlets and considerable rivers such as the Wadi Zerqa (Jabbok) and the Yarmuq, the largest tributary of the Jordan, though unmentioned in the Old Testament, which flows from the eastern plateau by Deraa (Edrei) in the Hauran through an impressive limestone gorge past el-Hammeh under ancient Gadara (Umm Qeis) to join the Jordan just south of the Lake of Galilee. It is probably on one of these wadis, Wadi Yabis, that Jabesh Gilead is to be located. This zone, irrigated by perennial wadis from the escarpment of Gilead, Ammon, and Moab, includes the ' plains of Moab ', which are probably to be located just north-east of the Dead Sea.[2] There must have been many

---

[1] This name is a corruption of Goliath, reflecting the confusion of Arab tradition concerning the Biblical stories of the combats of David with Goliath, and Gideon and the Midianites, which was located about the source of the Nahr Jalud.   [2] Glueck, op. cit., 366–404

from the mountains of Palestine who, like Elimelech and Naomi from Bethlehem, sought relief in that well-watered region when the seasonal rains failed.[1]

The Jordan itself is not an impressive stream. Rushing and cascading from the foothills of Hermon like one of our small Highland torrents, several streams unite and flow into the shallow Lake Huleh among its swamps and tall reed-beds, once the haunt of malaria-ridden Bedouin and herds of cattle and water-buffalo before the Zionist settlement, and very fine shooting country for the Palestine Police during the British Mandate. Between the Lake of Galilee, however, and the Dead Sea the river continues on its swift descent with a strong, even current. It makes some fantastic bends and has cut a deep bed in clay and marl banks. These have been known to collapse and temporarily dam the stream, an occurrence which may be reflected in the tradition of the miraculous crossing of the river at the Hebrew invasion under Joshua. The river itself runs too deep in its bed to be of any use for irrigation, and its immediate banks are overgrown with lush willow and cane-brakes. It is a veritable jungle, and in the British Mandate used to be a fine covert for game, including wild pig. In Biblical times its rankness[2] was proverbial and it was known as the haunt of lions (Jer. 49:19 ; 50:44 ; Zech. 11:3).

In the rift valley from the Dead Sea to the Gulf of Aqaba there are considerable deposits of copper ore, which were worked under the Egyptians already in the middle of the third millennium B.C. Glueck has discovered many such workings and has excavated a refinery at Ḥirbet el-Ḥeleifeh on the northern shore of the Gulf of Aqaba where copper goods were manufactured in the time of Solomon and shipped for trade down the Red Sea to east Africa and south Arabia. The land was indeed one ' out of whose hills thou mayest dig brass ' (Dt. 8:9). Here we should note that it was in the adjacent district of Midian to the east that Moses encountered the Kenites. With these the Hebrews never denied their affinity nor the fact that they were worshippers of Yahweh. Indeed the relationship of their chief Reuel or Jethro to Moses implies that the worship of Yahweh among the Kenites was of longer standing than among the

---

[1] The marriage of their two sons with Moabite girls might reflect a common practice whereby Palestinians secured themselves a right of settlement in this favoured area. The measure would be natural and easy in an age of polygamy, especially if, as was possible then and now among the Arabs in certain cases, the bride might remain in her father's house to be visited periodically.

[2] The ' pride ' of Jordan of the Old Testament

Hebrews.[1] The name Kenite (*qeny*) means simply 'smith' or 'artificer'. Here then we have apparently a caste of smiths attached to the copper-workings, exclusive and passing on the craft from father to son. They till no land, but own herds, and dwell in the desert like the modern desert tinkers, the Nuwwār and Sulayb. Their god is Yahweh, whose theophany, appropriately enough, is smoke and fire. We think that this is probably the origin of the tradition of the 'pillar of cloud by day and pillar of fire by night' which guided the Hebrews in the Exodus. Whatever the relationship of Israel and the Kenites may have been, however, it is not on this aspect of primitive Yahwism that Moses laid emphasis. The alliance between the two folk-groups, with the mutual recognition of definite moral obligations, gave Moses the opportunity to found the religion of his people on a moral basis, and this was ever after the keynote of Yahwism in Israel.

The escarpment east of the Jordan Valley rises to a plateau a mean height of *c*.2,000 feet which shades off into the north Arabian desert. This escarpment and the western part of the plateau has the advantage of precipitation from the rain-clouds from the Mediterranean and at various times has supported sedentary civilisation. This, however, has been intermittent owing to its exposure to the desert with its marauding tribesmen. Here Glueck's surface exploration has revealed such a period of settlement which lasted for most of the third millenium B.C., after which there was a period of recession until settlement was resumed at the end of the Late Bronze Age, *c*.1300 B.C. At that time certain strategic points along natural frontiers were fortified, and Glueck was able to discern the foundation of the kingdoms of Edom, Moab, and Ammon east of the Dead Sea. The frontier between the first two kingdoms was Wadi el-Ḥeṣa (the Brook Zared) which flows into the Dead Sea at its south-eastern extremity. The northern frontier of Moab is less definite, particularly after the establishment of the Hebrew Monarchy, when it fluctuated.[2] For practical purposes, however, we may draw the boundary line

[1] Moses defers to the authority of Jethro in Exod. 18.

[2] In the narrative of the Hebrew invasion Sihon the Amorite king of Heshbon occupied a considerable part of what was later the north part of Moab (Num. 21:21 ff.). By the time of the Judges, however, Moab had recovered all this territory and had actually expanded over Jordan where Ehud slew the Moabite king Eglon near Gilgal and cut off the discomfited Moabites at the fords of the Jordan (Jg. 2:19, 28). Under Omri and Ahab the north part of Moab was occupied but was later recovered by Mesha of Moab according to his inscription (G. A. Cooke, *A Textbook of North Semitic Inscriptions* (1903), no. 1, ll. 5 ff.).

along the Wadi Nimrin, which flows into the Jordan some six miles north-east of Jericho. The kingdom of Ammon to the north of Moab was less defined. It seems hardly to have attained cohesion before the foundation of the Hebrew Monarchy, when Saul first was able to check the Ammonites in the north at Jabesh Gilead (1 Sam. 11), and then David took their capital Rabbath Ammon (modern Amman) and apparently abolished the royal house (2 Sam. 12). North and west of Ammon lay the region of Gilead, which was fairly thickly wooded, as Absalom found to his cost, and which is still well grown with Mediterranean pine and evergreen oak. This land was probably still being colonised from west of the Jordan in the time of the Judges and the Israelite Monarchy. The north part of Transjordan was Debatable Land between Israel and Aram with Ramoth Gilead apparently the key to the possession of this territory, at least from the beginning of the divided Monarchy of the Hebrews.

Edom and Moab, though both had considerable agricultural resources, played an important part in desert-borne trade from the incense-bearing lands and mercantile centres of south Arabia via the oases of the interior. Edom in particular derived great wealth from this commerce through her control of the caravan routes from the South to the land-port of Gaza and so to Egypt and the northern route to Damascus, the metropolis of the north Arabian desert. There are frequent allusions to this caravan traffic in the Old Testament, and Edom is particularly obnoxious for her part in the slave trade (Am. 1:9). Finally the Edomites of Scripture were ousted by commercial rivals, the Nabataeans, who pressed northwards from the oases of the Hejaz in the 5th century B.C. The Edomites found new homes west of the Araba in Palestine itself, where they settled in the land, to a large extent depopulated since the collapse of the Jewish kingdom and the deportation to Babylon.[1] Much of the vituperation against Edom in the Prophets dates from this time before the final compilation of those books. In this way came Herod's family to Palestine, a fact which orthodox Jews never forgot and never forgave.

---

[1] What facilitated Edomite settlement, however, was not so much the depopulation of the land (for a great number of the common people were left) as the indifference of the Jewish peasantry in the absence of leaders or agitators. The Edomite penetration was considerable, since the country about Jamnia, Ashdod, and even Gezer in the foothills of Judah is described in 1 Mac. 4:15 as 'the plains of Idumaea' (so Codex א), and in one passage (*War* IV, § 529) Josephus states that Hebron was in Idumaea.

In the areas we have described the people were for the most part peasants, and any industries, such as dyeing and weaving, which are attested by clay loom-weights and dyeing-vats at Lachish and Tell Beit Mirsim, are the natural adjuncts of peasant or pastoral economy. Today the economy of Arab Palestine is still based on agriculture, and even Jerusalem is a city in the country, while such considerable towns as Hebron and Nablus, and Amman in Transjordan are really just large market villages for rural districts. It is therefore important, especially in view of the understanding of the texts exhumed at Ras Shamra, to understand the cycle of the peasant's year.

Agriculture in Syria and in Palestine may depend on the seasonal rains of winter and the heavy dew of spring and summer, as on the western escarpments of Palestine and Transjordan, or on irrigation from the perennial wadis, as in the Jordan Valley and the valley of the Orontes in Syria. Intensive cultivation is possible by employing both methods. Both are visualised in Deuteronomy 11:10–11, which refers to irrigation in Egypt and agriculture in Palestine 'which drinketh the rains of heaven'. The sources of humidity are comprehensively referred to in David's lament for Saul and Jonathan, when the poet curses the mountains of Gilboa :

> Let there be no dew nor rain upon you,
> Nor welling forth of the lower deeps.[1]
>
> (2 Sam. 1:21)

Hebrew law in the Mishnah draws a distinction between land where agriculture depends upon natural rainfall and that which is irrigated, and Moslem law makes the same distinction.[2] The charity-tax incumbent on every Moslem is lighter on irrigated land ('arḍ 'athur) in consideration of the labour and capital expended. In this connection it is interesting to note that the Arabic term for land watered by natural rainfall is Baal-land ('arḍ ba'al). The Ras Shamra Texts now prove conclusively that the Canaanite Baal was Hadad, the god manifest in the rains and thunder of autumn and winter and secondarily in the vegetation which they promoted.

---

[1] After H. L. Ginsberg's restoration of an obviously corrupt Hebrew text, the emendation being suggested by a passage in the Ras Shamra text (C. H. Gordon, *Ugaritic Handbook*, 1 Aqht 1, 44–5, in a similar situation, *Journal of Biblical Literature* LVII (1939), 209–13

[2] W. R. Smith, *The Religion of the Semites* (1894), 96–7

The peasant's year in Syria and Palestine begins in autumn with the violent rainstorms, the ' former rains ' (*yôreh*), which normally fall in the end of October and the beginning of November The Hebrew New Year is still observed at this time, and the Feast of Tabernacles is celebrated in the same season. The connection of the latter with the ' early rains ' is suggested by the fact that, according to the Mishnah,[1] water was then drawn from the Pool of Siloam, ceremonially brought up to the Temple court, and there poured out. A further Rabbinical reference indicates beyond all doubt that this was a rite of imitative magic.[2] We think we can discern the Canaanite prototype of the Israelite Feast of Tabernacles underlying the Ras Shamra Text describing the building of the ' house ' (temple or palace) of Baal, which took place at this season.[3]

When the heavy rains have softened the crust of the earth, baked iron-hard by the unmitigated heat of summer, the peasant goes forth, ploughing and sowing in one operation. Two main cereal crops are cultivated, barley and wheat, the harvest beginning with the former in April and ending in May or early June with the wheat. In ancient Israel the offering of the first sheaf on the morrow of the Passover, which was associated with the originally distinct rite of Unleavened Bread, marked the beginning of the barley harvest, and the offering of the last sheaf on the fiftieth day after that (Pentecost) marked the end of the wheat harvest. Those rituals were precautionary measures taken by the primitive community to dissociate the new crop with its mysterious life and vitality from the vitalising supernatural power and to make it safely available for common use. Such rites are familiar in primitive communities studied by anthropologists, and such we term ' rites of desacralisation '. These two we have detected in the Ras Shamra Texts. The peasant's year in Palestine about the time of Solomon is outlined in a simple little inscription on a limestone plaque, possibly the exemplar of some apprentice scribe, found in Macalister's excavations at Gezer in 1908. The probable translation is :

Two months of ingathering [4] ;
Two months of sowing ;

[1] *Sukkah* IV, 9
[2] ' Offer water before me on the Feast of Booths, so that the rains of the year may be blessed unto you ' (*Tosephtah Sukkah* III, 18).   [3] See p. 108
[4] The gathering of threshed corn and fruit from the threshing floor into storage is still a grave formality among Arab peasants, being often accompanied with prayer.

Two months of late sowing [1] ;
A month of hoeing up of flax [2] ;
A month of barley-harvest ;
A month of harvest, then festivity ;
Two months of vine-dressing [3] ;
A month of (gathering) summer fruit.

The deserts south and east of Palestine were not without their influence on agriculture in the land. From this quarter came the locusts, before which ' the land is as the garden of Eden and behind them a desolate wilderness' (Jl 2:3). From there the sirocco blew as a blast from a fiery furnace, the ordeal of fire of which Amos speaks, which dried up even the subterranean waters (Am. 7:4). The whirlwind or dust-storm also came from the great empty quarter (Am. 1:14). The ' darkness' or obscuration associated with both sirocco and dust-storm, owing to the fact that the atmosphere is heavily charged with fine particles of dust, is also connected with the desert. Such a darkness obscures the heavenly bodies, and both sun and moon appear ' blood-red'. A prolonged visitation of the sirocco, called in Palestine the *Ḥamsin* (lit. ' fifty'), with drought and famine, causes plague. All these are common manifestations of the presence of Yahweh in the Hebrew prophets. Certain of them have been taken as features of apocalyptic, and they are often, admittedly, elements in that late variety of Hebrew vision. They are not, however, necessarily part of the apocalyptic picture. They are not rare, supernatural phenomena, but are all too common in the experience of dwellers in Palestine in all ages, and to ancient Israel (e.g. Amos) they signified the dreaded presence of Yahweh their desert God.

Though the economy of ancient Israel was largely agricultural, Palestine was a vital link in the land-communication between the Nile and Euphrates, and along this trunk highway with its variant trade-routes there were a number of urban settlements,

---

[1] Possibly for a summer crop, such as millet (*dohan*, Ezek. 4:9, where other summer crops, beans and lentils, are also mentioned)

[2] Hosea mentions flax as one of the main crops of Palestine (Hos. 2:5, 9, Hebrew text 2:7, 11). The stalks were possibly cut at the root with a hoe. Such stalks were spread on the roof of Rahab's house at Jericho where the Hebrew spies of Joshua hid (Jos. 2:6).

[3] The word means strictly ' pruning', probably a late pruning, since the main pruning is done in January–February. G. Dalman attests this as late as March in the Merj Ayun (Biblical Ijon, 1 Kg. 15:20) in Lebanon just beyond the northern frontier of Israel (*Arbeit und Sitte in Palästina* I, i (1928–37), 264 ff.).

small, indeed, in comparison with the cities of Mesopotamia and Egypt, yet foci of a culture which reflected the life of both. We shall now proceed to trace those routes.

The trunk highway from Egypt emerged from the desert at the Wadi Ghazzeh, the line of which was defended by three Egyptian fortresses, Tell el-Ajjul, Tell Jemmeh, and Tell el-Far'a. From this point the traveller might proceed northwards through the coastal plain. We should not visualise a made road, since the route might vary according to local conditions, but generally it was advisable to keep to the east of the coastal plain, partly to avoid the toilsome trudge through sand near the coast or the swamps near the mouths of certain wadis, such as Nahr Rubin, some fifteen miles south of Jaffa, and partly to tap the springs which were more abundant near the foothills of the interior. The main point on this inland road was Lydda, Egyptian *Retenu*,[1] by which the Egyptians actually designated Palestine,[2] and in the same vicinity lay Gezer, which was taken by the Pharaoh, who entrusted it to Solomon when he married his daughter (1 Kg. 9:16). The road continued north along the eastern fringe of the Plain of Sharon until that ever-narrowing coastal plain was barred by the twenty-five-mile-long ridge of Carmel.

The Carmel barrier might either be turned or pierced. The wayfarer might round the southern extremity of the ridge through the gap between Carmel and the hills to the south occupied in the Hebrew period by the tribe of Manasseh. This pass was dominated at the eastern end by the fortress-town of Dothan [3] in the small plain of that name, which is easily accessible from the great Central Plain of Palestine. By this way in the opposite direction the Joseph narrative in Genesis depicts with great verisimilitude the Ishmaelite or Midianite caravan passing down to Egypt. Alternatively the Carmel barrier might be passed by two passes farther north-west. One might use a certain pass to the north-east of the Plain of Sharon which gave access to the great central plain either at Taanach or, a little farther west, at Megiddo, some fifteen miles south-east of Carmel Head. This

---

[1] This was pronounced somewhat like *Letenu*, hence the Hebrew and Arabic *Lod*.

[2] Here history repeats itself, Lydda being now a rail junction and, until the division of Palestine between Arabs and Jews, the airport of the land.

[3] This site is at present being excavated under American direction, the stratification ranging from the Early Bronze Age (third millennium B.C.) to the Byzantine period (J. P. Freer, *Bulletin of the American Schools of Oriental Research* 131 (1953), 16–20 ; 135 (1954), 14–20).

pass first appears in history in the summer of 1479 B.C. when the militant Pharaoh Thothmes III led his army swiftly and secretly through the pass to surprise an alliance of Canaanites from Palestine and Syria who had gathered in the fortress of Megiddo.[1] Here Josiah, making his bid for Hebrew independence and a revival of the glory of the undivided monarchy of David and Solomon after the collapse of Assyria in 612 B.C., sought to anticipate the northward march of Pharaoh Necho and met his untimely end in 609 B.C. The Romans showed their appreciation of the strategic significance of Megiddo by establishing a legionary camp at the head of the pass, the name of which survives in the name of the modern Arab village *Lejjun*. Farther north another pass leads through from the coastal plain to the Plain of Esdraelon, being dominated at its eastern end by the fortress of Jokneam (Tell Qeimun). This plays no role in the ancient record, probably owing to the inaccessibility of the north part of the Plain of Sharon because of marsh and jungle growth. But it was the pass used by Napoleon in his advance to Acre, where his hopes of an Eastern empire were shattered.

The Plain of Esdraelon was traversed by various routes. One led northwards to the Phoenician port of Akka (Hebrew *Akkô*), and others through the hills of lower Galilee to the Plain of Battuf north of Nazareth, and so the Valley of Pigeons (Wadi el-Hammām) [2] to the Plain of Gennesareth and past the north-west end of the Lake of Galilee. The Jordan was forded near the modern *Jisr Banat Ja'qub* (the Bridge of the Daughters of Jacob), where from the Middle Bronze Age (from *c.*1750 B.C.) access to the ford was commanded by the fortress-town of Hazor (*Tell el-Kedah*).[3] So the road led up to the Hauran and eventually to Damascus, the emporium of the north Arabian desert and a vital station on the way to the Euphrates. Alternatively, the way might lead from the head of one of the passes through Carmel eastwards along the Plain of Esdraelon past Jezreel at the western end of Gilboa, and so past Bethshan, the great fortress-town at the east end of the great Central Plain. The Jordan was forded

[1] This movement was repeated in World War I when Allenby threw his cavalry through the pass and barely missed capturing the German Commander-in-Chief, Liman von Sanders, who escaped in his pyjamas.

[2] The cliffs overhanging this valley to the east are honeycombed with caves, which were the last refuge of supporters of the native Jewish royal house, who were actually smoked out of the caves by soldiers of Herod the Great lowered over the cliffs for this purpose (Josephus, *War* i, 310–12).

[3] In the time of our Lord another trade-route ran past Capernaum on the lake shore, where Matthew sat ' at receipt of custom '.

north-east of Bethshan at a ford dominated by the town of Yenoam, possibly to be located at *Ḥirbet Bab el-Munṭar* (the Gate of the Watchpost) by the modern *Jisr el-Majami*.

Along those trade-routes were thus a number of considerable towns, the home of merchants with a keen sense of the value of property rather than of persons. Those towns, such as Hazor, Yenoam, Bethshan, Dothan, Taanach, Megiddo, Jokneam, Gaza, and other such places, however, were originally fortress-towns. They had been strong points on the Hyksos line of communication from the Delta to north Syria, and as such they were the seats of feudal barons and their retainers, as their heavy fortifications and their domestic architecture indicate. The late A. Alt maintained that this system in its strategic and social aspects was adopted by the Philistines when they reached Palestine in the beginning of the 12th century B.C.,[1] and we think that this is very probably the case.

The military tradition of those cities of the plains is reflected in the traditions of the Hebrew settlement in the Book of Judges, which repeat that the Hebrews for long made little headway against the inhabitants of those towns who had ' chariots of iron ' and also, we might fairly add, the organisation and experience to use them to advantage. The role played in Hebrew tradition in the Book of Joshua by the King of Hazor is probably characteristic of the status and activity of those feudal lords who ostensibly held Palestine for the Pharaoh on the eve of the Hebrew settlement.

Owing to the configuration of Palestine, however, the lines of communication through the country between the Nile and the Euphrates were canalised and left large parts of Palestine untouched. Thus in the plains through which the highways of empire and commerce passed there was quite a different way of life from that in the hill-country, where there were no such feudal fortress-towns, except Shechem and Jerusalem. There in the upland villages there was a much greater degree of personal freedom, which was guaranteed to every man through his membership of the kin-group, which was the basis of society there. In the fortress-towns of the plains society was not based on the principle of kinship, but was feudal. From the administrative tablets from the palace at Ras Shamra [2] we know that social

---

[1] A. Alt, ' Völker und Staaten Syriens im frühen Altertum ', *Der Alte Orient* xxxiv, Heft 4 (1936), 31–2

[2] C. Virolleaud, ' Les villes et les corporations du royaume d'Ugarit ', *Syria* xxi (1940), 123–51 ; ' Lettres et documents administratifs de Ras Shamra ', *Syria* xxi (1940), 247–76

privilege in Canaanite society depended largely on military status, and the population was grouped not so much by families as by classes or trade-guilds, an indication, perhaps, of the caste system which we associate with Aryan India.[1]

The situation as we have described it in the fortress-towns of the plains had vital implications for Israel after Solomon endeavoured to incorporate these areas into the state of Israel. This was not successfully done, and the immediate consequence was the disruption of the kingdom. This was not so much owing to the enmity of the northern tribes towards Judah as to the refusal of the kin-groups of Israel to submit to the new social organisation that the king wished to impose on them after the fashion of the Canaanite feudal state. Probably the towns in the plains also felt ill at ease in their superimposed union with the rude villagers and tribesfolk, and the expedition of the Pharaoh Sheshonk seems to imply that Egyptian suzerainty over those towns was taken for granted. In any case, the subsequent history of north Israel does not suggest that the towns were ever really integrated into the life and economy of Israel, whatever Israel's nominal claims may have been.

It was, however, almost impossible that the way of life in Israel should not have been in some degree influenced by that of the cities of the plains. After all, the capitals of the kingdoms, Jerusalem in Judah and Samaria in Israel, from the time of Omri, were not settlements of kin-groups, but rather crown possessions, the personal property of the royal houses.[2] Jerusalem was the conquest of David's sword and Samaria was a virgin site bought by Omri for money. The life in Jerusalem, itself an old Egyptian fief,[3] and in Samaria followed the pattern of that of the Canaanite towns of the plains. The result was that social and economic maladjustment against which the prophets of Israel inveigh from the standpoint of Israelite democracy, which was based on the principle of kinship born in the desert and nurtured in the small hill-settlements of Palestine. The prophets are not agitating for a universalistic recognition of the rights of man, but are rather

[1] The system was possibly introduced to western Asia by the Aryan invaders who brought the horse and light two-wheeled war-chariot to those regions about the beginning of the second millennium B.C.

[2] A. Alt has argued convincingly that it was on the basis of those independent states within states that the dynasties of David and Omri were really founded.

[3] This is clear from the correspondence of Abdi-Ḫepa, the vassal of Egypt in Jerusalem, in the Amarna Tablets (J. A. Knudtzon, *Die El-Amarna Tafeln* (1908–15)).

protesting at the violation of wholesome social principles safeguarded by ways of life where Israel as desert tribes or as closely
knit village communities had known the rights and duties of
kinsmen and had automatically obeyed that primitive social code.

Though the material remains in the various fields excavated
in Palestine show the land as a veritable cross-roads of cultures
and races, they indicate just as clearly that the natives of Palestine
played, in the main, an assimilative rather than inventive role.
There are, however, certain notable exceptions to this rule.

It was the contacts of Palestine and Syria with Mesopotamia
and Egypt that awakened the inhabitants to the advantages of a
convenient way of writing. The respective systems of cuneiform
and hieroglyphics, though great achievements, were yet not the
most expeditious way of communicating men's thoughts. Both
were syllabic, not alphabetic, and the cuneiform might even be
ideographic, a single sign representing a whole word. Thus both
were highly complicated and the medium of specialists. In the
Ras Shamra Tablets we see a great advance in the simplification
of the cuneiform to an alphabetic script of thirty cyphers which,
as may be seen from the private correspondence of one of the
princes of Ugarit with the queen-mother, could be used for short,
informal, personal correspondence. By the middle of the second
millennium a similar experiment was made on the basis of
Egyptian hieroglyphics, and the resulting alphabet was widely
used, evidence being found at Byblos, Gezer, Shechem, and
Lachish and from the Sinai Peninsula, where the Egyptians
mined turquoise and copper. From the Sinai inscriptions, fragmentary and uncertain as they are, a direct line of development
may be discerned to legible alphabetic inscriptions in Syria and
Palestine in the second half of the second millennium B.C. This
group begins with the inscription of the king Shaphat-ba'al of
Byblos, which is dated by Dunand in the 15th century B.C.,[1]
though he does not exclude the possibility of a date two centuries
earlier. From the end of the 14th century come short inscriptions
on a bowl and a ewer from Tell ed-Duweir and an inscribed
potsherd from Bethshemesh, the last of which, however, has not
yet been read. From Byblos c.1000 B.C. come the funerary
inscriptions of the kings Yehimilk and Ahiram and from Gezer
the agricultural calendar, which we have cited, dated about a
century later. From the second half of the 9th century comes
the inscription of Mesha, King of Moab, and by this time the

[1] M. Dunand, *Byblia Grammata* (1936), 146–51

linear alphabetic script had fully established itself in Palestine and Syria. The script of twenty-two signs was adapted not only to monumental purposes but, as we see from ostraca from Samaria [1] and Lachish,[2] it was convenient for daily use. The Egyptian papyrus describing the misadventures of an envoy, Wenamon, to Byblos [3] c.1100 B.C. refers to a consignment of papyrus rolls. So early, then, men in Canaan wrote with pen and ink on papyrus, probably in the linear script. This was the script in which the royal annals and accounts were kept at the court of David by Jehoshaphat the recorder and Shebna the scribe.

It was not, however, primarily for royal annals that the alphabet had been devised. G. R. Driver sees that achievement as the utilitarian device of middlemen. 'In both countries (Egypt and Mesopotamia) a large priestly class devoted itself to the leisurely exploitation of a complicated and esoteric if artistic system of writing. Syria and Palestine could afford nothing of this sort ; but the commercial genius of their peoples went to the very heart of the problem, borrowed what was essential in the Sumero-Accadian or Egyptian systems, and adapted it to their own urgent needs.' [4] Viewed thus, the invention of the alphabet was an important step in the emancipation of the common man from the absolutism of temple or court, leading surely and progressively to the ultimate self-realisation of the individual.

The early traditions of Israel, long supposed to rest on the merely relatively stable authority of oral tradition, must now be viewed in a different light. No doubt much has been incorporated by the earliest hands in the Pentateuch and the Books of Joshua, Judges, and Samuel from the oral traditions of the tribes of Israel, but there were probably written sources too, as, indeed, is apparent from the references to earlier sources such as the Book of the Wars of Yahweh and the Book of Yashar.[5] By the time of the great Hebrew prophets a medium had been devised and perfected whereby, whether they themselves used it or not, their thoughts and oracles and the great message they bore could be

[1] E. L. Sukenik, ' Inscribed Hebrew and Aramaic Potsherds from Samaria ', *Palestine Exploration Fund Quarterly Statement* (1933), 152–6
[2] H. Torczyner, L. Harding, A. Lewis, and J. L. Starkey, Lachish I (1938), *The Lachish Letters*
[3] J. H. Breasted, *Ancient Records of Egypt* IV (1906–7), 576 ff.
[4] G. R. Driver, *Semitic Writing* (1948), 3
[5] This source is from at least as late as the early part of the reign of David, since it contains his lament for Saul and Jonathan at the battle of Gilboa.

conserved and handed on as a testimony to their people and as the permanent heritage of all mankind. Here on the foreland of Asia the Greeks found in the alphabet a rich heritage, the greatest product of the culture of Canaan.[1]

So far we have emphasised the situation of Palestine as the stepping-stone between the culture-areas of Mesopotamia and Egypt. It is no less the foreland of the great Arabian desert. The whole of Syria and Palestine, particularly the lands lying adjacent to the desert, were exposed to periodic invasions of land-hungry tribesmen. This movement occasionally reached large proportions, first in the Amorite invasions about the end of the third millennium B.C., of which Glueck found evidence in Transjordan, then in the Aramaean invasions c.1300 B.C. which resulted in the formation of the kingdoms of Edom and Moab and later of Israel and the Aramaean kingdom of Damascus. In view of the desert antecedents of Israel and her continued contact with the people of the southern desert we must now consider the main features of life in those regions.

First and foremost nomadic economy, precariously dependent on seasonal grazings and the use of rare springs and waterholes, imposes certain security measures. Comparatively small social groups cling together, developing a very high community sense, to defend their grazing lands and their flocks against less fortunate elements driven by drought or poverty to cattle-raiding, or against stronger tribes who seek relief from their precarious living or from the monotony of the desert life by the same measure. Thus the tribe, so isolated and compact, soon becomes and remains a kinship with a high degree of solidarity and splendid loyalty, if somewhat narrowly particularist. Typical of this attitude is the reaction of the Bedouin on descrying a distant figure in the desert. His remark is ' qawm ', which means at once ' people ' and ' enemy '. To the tribesman all are enemies until they are proved friends.

Such a community where the kin-relationship is simple and direct may expand until new grazings and waterholes have to be occupied. If the group is strong enough this occupation is by force. If not, then relief may be obtained from a stronger tribe or confederacy by accommodation. Within such confederacies social rights and obligations are clearly understood. In the

---

[1] The Greeks possibly learnt the alphabet from Phoenician traders in Greece and the islands, who may have used the letters as number-cyphers as the Hebrews did.

narrower kin-group the emphasis is also laid on social relationships. There are certain persons, for instance, whom one may
not marry, and others again whose blood one must avenge.
There are others again whom it is desirable to marry in order to
preserve the integrity of the family, such as first cousins, a practice
which was rigidly observed by the patriarchs in Hebrew tradition,
Isaac marrying Rebeka and Jacob Leah and Rachel. Moreover,
since the welfare and often the very existence of the tribe depends
on those correct social relationships, it is of great importance to
the tribesman to know precisely his relationship to various tribal
elements ; hence the importance of genealogy among the Bedouin,
a particular in which ancient Israel closely reflects the life of the
desert.

Those kin-groups are democratic in their constitution. Where
social duties are a matter of family relationships they are automatically recognised and discharged. Thus there is no need for
a law-code formulated and imposed *ab extra*. It is only when
two such groups enter into formal alliance that a formulation of
social obligations becomes necessary. This occurred in the history of Israel when the Hebrew kin-groups led by Moses were
brought into alliance with the Kenites, the people of his father-
in-law, in Midian. The consequence was the ethical conditions
of the Covenant, though the experience of modern Bedouin
tribes in similar conditions makes it very unlikely that we have
to visualise a written code in the time of Moses.

In such a society there is no need for an official executive to
enforce moral obedience to the code of social conduct. Any
anti-social tendency is held in effective check by the force of
public opinion and the power of ostracism, very potent in such a
particularist society where all outside are enemies. Each tribe,
of course, has its sheikh, but there is nothing autocratic about his
status. The name simply means ' elder '. He is *primus inter pares*,
a natural leader marked out by courage, success in war, sagacity
in council, generosity, or by the popular belief that his family
enjoys the favour of Providence, the ' blessing ' (*baraka*). The
office, however, is not necessarily hereditary. It is noteworthy
that the sheikh is not elected or formally invested with the office ;
he owes his position to his natural dignity, ability, or personal
grace and the popular acclaim which these may evoke. In this
respect his informal office is like that of the Hebrew ' judges ',
who were natural leaders called to the front by some crisis in the
history of their people to which they responded with heroic *élan*

which won them a spontaneous following, their success sealing their office. The sheikh may command in war, and it might be expedient to obey, but his command is not bound to be obeyed, nor has he power to enforce obedience. This situation again is in a manner illustrated in the case of the Hebrew judge Gideon, who is abused by the Ephraimites, who resented being excluded from his exploit against the Midianites ; to them Gideon resorts to a soft answer to turn away wrath (Jg. 8:1–3). In the light of such antecedents we may well understand the cry of the men of Israel under David, ' To your tents, O Israel ! ' We agree with Alt that in north Israel the majority of men never accepted the claim that the king was in effect other than a judge, to be obeyed or not at will, who, after he had done the work to which he was specifically called, need not necessarily be succeeded by his son. Such a theory well accounts for the instability of the dynasties in north Israel. Again, though the sheikh might be mature and astute in counsel, this is not his monopoly. The council of the desert is the public sederunt (*majlis*) of the adult males of the tribe around the open coffee-hearth of the sheikh. There tribal affairs are openly discussed and all tribesmen have a voice. The coffee-hearth, incidentally, is the university of the desert, and many a ragged tribesman we have met who has astounded us by his real grace of speech and his shrewd insight into life's philosophy. Against such an ultimate background we begin to understand the courage and self-possession of Amos at the royal shrine of Bethel and the freedom with which Nathan and Elijah rebuked kings.

In such disputes as may arise within the narrow confines of the kin-group the sheikh's counsel is often sought. This is not bound to be followed, though it often does happen that he is held in such regard that the contending parties accept his decision. This is as far as his authority reaches, and the successful appellant is his own executor. In more grievous offences, such as adultery and bloodshed, the tribe may act collectively in punishing the guilty party, or the head of the family of the culprit may act for the community. An adulteress may be put to death by the whole community, as in Israel (Dt. 22:20 ff.), a practice which survived in Israel until the time of our Lord (Jn. 8:4–7). Another instance of this communal executive in Israel is that in the fictitious case cited by the wise woman of Tekoa where, irrespective of her wishes, the community of kinsmen insist on putting the fratricide to death (2 Sam. 14:4). In the Bedouin tribe again a father may put his own daughter to death if she is guilty of adultery, and an instance of this *patria potestas* in the Old Testament is that of the contumacious son, who may be handed over to common justice by his father, whereupon he is stoned to death by the community (Dt. 21:18–21).

Though the basis of the nomad way of life is wholly ethical in a sense which it never was in the settled life of Canaan, it is obvious from what we have said that that ethic was not at all individual but communal. Nothing illustrates this fact more than the law of blood-revenge, the grim *lex talionis*, the old Israelite principle of ' an eye for an eye, a tooth for a tooth, life for life '. Briefly stated this means that if A kills B, the family of B automatically claims a life from the family of A. If one out of the actual family, i.e. the tent, of the victim, a father, son, or brother, takes the life of A, so much the better, and, unless the family of A is particularly strong or proud, or has a prior grievance, the matter may rest there, at least in practice. On the other hand, any kinsman of the slain man, near or remote, may remember his social duty and, seeing his occasion, level the score by slaying any one of the kinsmen, near or remote, of the homicide. Those generally held liable, however, are kinsmen to the fifth generation. This communal responsibility for the act of one of the kin-group was a feature of early Israelite morality, as is obvious from the case of Achan after his breach of the taboo in appropriating part of the forbidden spoils of Jericho. Not only was Achan put to death, but his family also suffered (Jos. 7:24, 25). The grim practice of blood-revenge, however, may be mitigated. By common agreement the two kin-groups may decide upon a commutation of the blood-due. A certain amount of money or real property is fixed as a price and so peace (*sulḥ*) may be made.[1] This course is now, in effect, usually followed, but the general opinion of Bedouin in north Sinai with whom we discussed the problem was that the *sulḥ*, far from being a measure of progress and enlightenment, was a declension from the wholesome sim-plicity of the *lex talionis* ; it savoured too much of commercial justice, where the licence to kill one's enemy with impunity might be bought by him who could afford it.[2] This attitude, inci-

---

[1] The principle of life for life, however, is often observed by the inclusion of women in the blood-price. Jaussen cites one case in Transjordan where the blood-price was two girls, a hundred ewes, two asses, two rifles, and a piece of ground (*Coutumes des Arabes au pays de Moab* (1908), 223).

[2] The negotiation for payment of the blood-price, however, begins by the nominal agreement of the homicide to pay all his goods and more, and from

dentally, is expressed in the Old Testament where Samuel
declares that he has never admitted commutation for the sterner
application of the *lex talionis*.[1]   There is substance in the Bedouin
argument.   The law of blood-revenge, involving as it does the
kinsmen of the homicide to the fifth generation and even the
whole tribe, is a potent deterrent to homicide, and life is certainly
not more cheap than in the cities of the East or in the ' enlightened '
West.   This is also the opinion of J. L. Burckhardt, who states :
' I am inclined to believe that this salutary institution has contributed to a greater degree than any other circumstance to
prevent the warlike tribes of Arabia from exterminating one
another.   Without it their wars in the desert would be as sanguin-
ary as those of Mamelukes in Egypt. . . .' [2]

A further mitigation of the stern simplicity of the blood-feud
is the right of sanctuary.   Every Arab tent is a sanctuary where a
fugitive from this rough justice may claim sanctuary for three
days and four hours.   Even if the avenger of blood is on the very
heels of the fugitive, let the latter but seize the tent ropes or poles
of the flimsy goathair shelter, saying, ' I come as thy refugee '
('*ana daḥîluk*), and the owner of the tent is in honour bound to
defend him.[3]   This right of sanctuary is the ground of one of the
most striking figures in the Old Testament, in Psalm 23, where
the harassed sufferer is depicted as such a fugitive who has found
sanctuary in the very face of his enemy.   The same passage
depicts also the hospitality of the desert, which is still a conspicuous feature of Bedouin life.   The good offices of the host,
however, must not be strained to his own prejudice beyond the
space of three days and four hours.   On the other hand the host,
if powerful, may consider it a point of honour to afford the
refugee permanent protection.   According to inter-tribal politics,
again, he may consider such a course expedient.   At any rate
there are few tribes in the Arabian desert which have not their
quota of refugees from the avenger of blood.   This practice of
refuge may lead to a formal alliance between tribes and a formal

---

[1] 1 Sam. 12:3.   The word translated in the AV by ' bribe ' signifies money
to cover the offence.
[2] J. L. Burckhardt, *Notes on the Bedouins and Wahabys* (1830), 84
[3] Jaussen states that among the Faiz east of the Dead Sea the area of
sanctuary was extended to double the distance which a strong man could
throw a heavy-headed camel stick from the tent (op. cit., 214).

---

this the blood-price is reduced to a reasonable sum.   The fact that the blood-
price is the liability not only of the individual but of the community is also a
deterrent of crime.

acceptance of social obligations between them. Such may well have been the genesis of the relationship between Moses and the Kenite tribe into which he married and to relationship with whom he eventually brought the Israelites. This may well have led to the articulate formulation of social obligations in the Covenant, those having up till that time been tacitly admitted within the kin-group. The principle of temporary refuge from the avenger of blood finds its expression in Israel in the appointment of certain ' cities of refuge ' where, if the matter was adjudged an accident, a homicide might live permanently unharmed. Here Hebrew law shows an advance on the simplicity of desert justice, which admits no distinction between deliberate and accidental homicide.

Those then are the main features of the nomad way of life in the north Arabian and Sinai deserts to which Palestine was open in the east and south. There the Israelite tribes had been bred, and there lived the Kenites, Kenizites, and Jerahmeelites, with whom they were affiliated. On their southern frontier, too, lived the Amelekites, the inveterate enemies of Israel. Israel's relationship with those tribal elements and her proximity to the desert might retard cultural development, but it served to keep alive in Israel a sense of ethical values which were so vital in the life of the desert. With the desert in such close proximity Israel was never allowed to forget her nomadic past. This is illustrated in her law, in the democratic attitude which men adopted to the kingship, particularly in north Israel, and in the moral emphasis which the great prophets laid on the religion of the people.

II   The Land of the Two Rivers

MESOPOTAMIA, where the Tigris and the Euphrates facilitated intercourse between settlements, which were developed by irrigation from the two rivers, was the home of an urban culture from the fourth millennium B.C.   The land was a refuge in times of drought to nomads from the north Arabian steppes, and the productive fields and rich palm-groves were a continual attraction to the hungry tribesmen, who periodically over-ran the settled country and even succeeded in establishing dynasties, the most notable of which in our period were at Babylon and in Assyria. The cultural pattern was set by non-Semitic Sumerians, probably from the Iranian plateau, who first built the cities of southern Mesopotamia.   To this high culture the Semitic invaders were obliged to defer, but inevitably they left their own impress. Since the Hebrews and the Semites of Mesopotamia, who were dominant in the later historical period, were ultimately of common stock and, in the case of Abraham and Jacob at least, shared a common habitat in north Mesopotamia, the culture of Babylon and Assyria is of great importance in elucidating many aspects of Hebrew culture which, particularly in their origins, are often obscure.

Material remains discovered in this ancient cradle of civilisation since the expedition of Sir Henry Layard in 1849 make a very impressive record, though the material imposes its own difficulties of interpretation ;   a clearer and fuller picture of the general culture of the people is given in the cuneiform inscriptions and especially in the durable clay tablets which are found in immense numbers at most sites which have been excavated.   The recovery and decipherment of these is itself an interesting story, but the scope of this work demands that we limit ourselves strictly to their content.   Before concentrating on the documents, however, we must, in a necessarily selective manner, cite certain material evidence of archaeology which bears directly on Hebrew history and tradition.

The city of Ur in southern Mesopotamia, with which Hebrew tradition connects Abraham, was excavated by Sir Leonard Woolley, who found, especially in the royal tombs, art treasures and a wealth of precious metal which indicated the splendour of Ur and the wide ramifications of her influence at least a millennium before the time of Abraham. The Hebrew records, however, give no indication that the Hebrew fathers were influenced by the advanced Sumerian culture, and it is probable that their contact with Ur was only slight, probably, as Woolley suggests, as conductors of trading caravans. Their real affinities were with the Aramaean tribes of northern Mesopotamia, where their associations with Harran, like Ur a centre of the cult of the Moon-god Sin, were probably of the same nature as with Ur.

In soundings at Ur, Woolley found that life had been interrupted by a flood, which had left a deposit between two strata of occupation some time in the fourth millennium B.C. As to the relevance of this to the Biblical Flood-tradition, however, we must accept it with grave reserve. Woolley reports that his water-laid stratum was a mean depth of eight feet.[1] The material remains above and below show a cultural break, not sufficient, however, to suggest the total destruction of mankind. Similar evidence has been claimed from other Mesopotamian sites, but the dates of none of these correspond with the evidence from Ur, except certain pluvial layers of scarcely three feet at Nineveh.[2] E. Dhorme claimed similar evidence from Kish and dated the cataclysm c.3300 B.C. (*Revue Biblique* XXXIX (1930), 484). This claim, however, was somewhat premature, since the excavators Watelin and Langdon distinguished one decisive ' Flood ' stratum, which was, however, the last of four. This they date c.3000 B.C., almost a millennium after the Ur stratum. ' Flood ' strata of various depth which are roughly synchronous with the Kish stratum were found at Warka (ancient Uruk and Biblical Erech) and at Tell Fara (ancient Shuruppak, the home of Ut-Napishtim, the Sumerian Noah). To counteract any rash conclusions which may have been drawn from Woolley's evidence from Ur it may be stated that at El-Ubaid, some four miles from Ur, no such stratum was found, though it was keenly sought. This corroborates the tradition that there was a flood, or rather floods, in Mesopotamia, but certainly does not indicate the single universal cataclysm of the Book of Genesis. The Flood in the Old Testament has a significance of its own, but that is not as the record of ancient history.

[1] Sir L. Woolley, *Antiquaries' Journal* IX (1929), 329
[2] R. C. Thompson and M. E. L. Mallowan, ' The British Museum Excavations at Nineveh, 1931–32 ', *Annals of Archaeology and Anthropology* XX (1933), 130–4

The flood, not an unusual occurrence in the low flat land between the two rivers, is a theme of Sumerian tradition in the ancient king-lists, mythology, and glyptic art. In the king-lists the ' Flood ' demarcates between historical dynasties and the early ages, where historical ignorance was covered up, as in the narratives of the Hebrew patriarchs, by the mention of few names and long ages. Indeed in comparison with the Sumerian ante-diluvians Methuselah himself is a mere youth. The fullest account of the ' Flood ' is contained in the Gilgamesh epic, known from the version in Ashurbanipal's library at Nineveh and from other fragments from Nippur, the ancient religious centre of the Sumerian South. In this account the survivor of the Flood is Ut-Napishtim. There is another tradition where the hero is named Zius-udra, Xisuthros of Berossus, who wrote in Greek in the 3rd century B.C. In another account the hero is named Atraḥasis. Yet another version of the Gilgamesh epic has survived among the Hittite literature from Boghazköi, and this has a special interest in so far as the hero is named Na-aḥ-mu-u-li-el, of which the Hebrew Noah is a possible abbreviation. This version, in Hurrian and so probably known in the area occupied by this Armenoid people in north Meso-potamia, was probably the source from which the Hebrews drew the tradition, and in this connection we note the association of the Hebrew patriarchs with north Mesopotamia which the Pentateuchal traditions unanimously attest.

Babylon was excavated by Koldewey between 1899 and 1912, but proved somewhat disappointing. The remains illustrated mainly the neo-Babylonian period after the fall of the Assyrian Empire at the end of the 7th century B.C. The most impressive remains were the foundations of the *ziggurat* on which the temple of the city-god Marduk once stood and the Processional Way and the Gate of Ishtar with its lions, bulls, and dragons in low relief in moulded brick and coloured glazed tiling such as is, incidentally, the distinctive feature of exterior decoration of the mosques and minarets of Baghdad at the present day. A relic of the greatness of Ḥammurabi's Babylon is a stele of black diorite bearing a code of laws claimed by the king to be a revelation by Shamash the Sun-god. This monument, however, was found not at Babylon but at Susa (Biblical Shushan), where it had been removed as a trophy of war after some victory of the Iranian Kassites.

The poverty of the remains of the Babylon of Ḥammurabi's

age was compensated by the excavations at Tell Ḥariri on the west bank of the middle Euphrates by A. Parrot from 1933 and resumed since the war. The history of the place (ancient Mari) goes back to the third millennium, but the most interesting period is that of the Amorite occupation in the second millennium B.C. The extensive palace of Zimrilim, the contemporary of Ḥammurabi, was found with statuary and bright, even elegant, wall-frescoes and over 20,000 cuneiform tablets. From diplomatic texts it is possible to reconstruct the contemporary political scene. The great Ḥammurabi is mentioned, his older contemporary Shamsi-Adad I of Ashur, and other rulers of city-states such as Larsa, Eshnunna, and Isin in Mesopotamia, Yamḥad in the region of Aleppo, Qatna in the Orontes Valley in Syria, Ugarit (modern Ras Shamra) on the north Syrian coast, and Hazor near the upper Jordan in Palestine. These rulers disposed of armies tens of thousands strong, preserving a very delicate balance of power until Ḥammurabi was able by subtle diplomacy to detach and strike down his rivals in Mesopotamia, including Mari.

It used to be held that Ḥammurabi ruled a Babylonian empire of which Palestine was a province, and the Mesopotamian influence in the Pentateuch was explained on this assumption, the Creation and Flood narratives being taken to reflect the mythology of Mesopotamia known from texts from Ashurbanipal's library, and the legal codes being regarded as embodying the principles of the code of Ḥammurabi. Apart, however, from the fact that the significant differences in the Mesopotamian and Hebrew material are no less striking than the common elements, the tablets of Mari show that the idea of a Babylonian empire embracing Palestine at this early age is without a basis. Palestine, however, was in the orbit of Mesopotamian cultural influence in the patriarchal period. The use of the Akkadian language and cuneiform script in the correspondence of local chiefs of Syria and Palestine with Egypt in the Amarna Tablets (c.1400 B.C.) is clear indication of this, and this evidence has just been amplified by the surface find in the hills near Megiddo of a fragment of the Mesopotamian Gilgamesh Epic, the palaeography of which suggests the Amarna age.[1]

The Mari Tablets show Ḥammurabi to be the younger contemporary of Shamsi-Adad I of Ashur, so that he and his dynasty

[1] A. Goetze and S. Levy, 'A Fragment of the Gilgamesh Epic from Megiddo', 'Atiqot II (1959), pp. 121–8

can be brought into the scheme of Assyrian chronology. On
the basis of the *limmu*-canons and an Assyrian king-list from
Khorsabad [1] it has been calculated that Shamsi-Adad reigned
from 1744 or 1734 to 1724 B.C. and Ḥammurabi from 1724 to
1682 B.C.[2] It is quite possible that a phase of the Hebrew
penetration of Palestine in the patriarchal period occurred
at this time, but this cannot be demonstrated by the simple expedient of the very questionable identification of Amraphel
of the Abraham narrative (Gen. 14) with Ḥammurabi of
Babylon.

It has been stated that the Mari Texts contain references to
the Hebrew tribe of Benjamin.[3] Beni-iamini are indeed mentioned as very troublesome neighbours from the western desert.
There are, however, others called Beni-shamali, ' Sons of the
Left Hand ', i.e. Northerners. Here clearly is a case not of tribal
designation, but of a purely geographic appellative, Beni-iamini,
' Sons of the Right Hand ', signifying, according to the general
Semitic orientation, Southerners. The Israelite tribe Benjamin
may be so called because it occupied the southernmost district of
the north Israelite confederacy. The texts mention also the
leaders of those peoples and others from the desert and the
sown land by the term *dawidum*. The meaning of this word is
probably ' general ', and we think that it had the same significa-
tion in the case of David, who became king after first having
been a professional soldier under Saul and under Achish of
Gath.[4]

Work has proceeded steadily in Mesopotamia, and, if the
spectacular results of Layard, Rassam, and Woolley have not
been achieved, much valuable information on the prehistory of

---

[1] See p. 39
[2] P. van der Meer, *The Chronology of Ancient Western Asia and Egypt* (1955),
25–31. Before the publication of the Khorsabad king-list, Sidney Smith had
proposed the date 1792–1750 B.C. for Ḥammurabi on the basis of the Mari
Texts, archaeological material from Mesopotamia and north Syria and
recorded observations of the Venus-star (*Alalakh and Chronology* (1940)). The
worth of the first two categories of data, however, is relative only, and the last
inconclusive by Smith's own admission.
[3] G. Dossin, ' Benjaminites dans les Textes de Mari,' *Mélanges syriens offerts
à M. René Dussaud* (1939), 981–96
[4] We believe that the term is used with this connotation in the inscription
of Mesha of Moab (mid-9th century B.C.) (G. A. Cooke, *A Textbook of North
Semitic Inscriptions* (1903), no. 1, l. 11). We translate this passage, ' . . . and
I brought back from there Ariel its commander, and I dragged him before
Kemosh in Qeriyyoth.' That ' David ' was not the proper name, but the title,
of the king of Israel is suggested by the fact that no other person in ancient
Israel was called David.

Mesopotamia has been gathered by stratigraphic excavation of various sites in the north. The excavations of the Americans Chiera and Speiser at Yorghan Tepe (ancient Nuzu), a hundred miles north of Kirkuk, bore directly on the Old Testament. A mass of cuneiform documents in Akkadian were found dating c.1400 B.C. These were chiefly domestic archives, and reveal certain legal peculiarities which are reflected in the patriarchal narratives.[1] The case of Abraham and Sarah's maid Hagar (Gen. 16) is exactly paralleled in the legal texts of Nuzu. The legislature of Hammurabi indeed had already provided for licensed concubinage in the event of childlessness. Another indication of the importance attached to progeny was the common practice of adoption. A childless person might adopt a son to perpetuate his name and preserve the family property, to provide for his old age and to perform due funeral rites at his death. One of the household slaves, who was, according to the ancient social convention, one of the family, might be thus formally adopted, as Abraham apparently contemplated leaving his status and his goods to his confidential slave Eliezer (Gen. 15:2). Though the birthright of the eldest son was strictly established, it is interesting to note that one of the Nuzu Tablets attests the cession of a birthright to a younger brother in return for livestock. Though this man drove a better bargain than Esau, the transaction in principle is the same, though in the sale of the birthright of Esau, the ancestor of Edom (' red '), for a mess of ' red pottage ' we see a deliberate reflection on the historical relations of the nations Israel and Edom rather than the faithful reproduction of an actual social transaction between two individuals. The same may be said of the blessing cunningly secured by Jacob from Isaac on his deathbed. It is none the less interesting to note the binding force of a deathbed blessing admitted in Nuzian law, where on a certain tablet a man claims a wife by appealing to his father's deathbed blessing and oral disposition. Rachel's theft of her father's *teraphim* (Gen. 31:19) is also explicable in the light of the social conventions of the Hurrian community of Nuzu, where the possession of these household gods apparently gave the son-in-law the right of inheritance even where there was already a son and heir. Such a case as this, which, so far as we know, is peculiar to the Hurrian community, indicates the association of the Hebrew fathers with north Mesopotamia in the middle of

[1] C. H. Gordon, 'Biblical Customs and the Nuzu Tablets', *Biblical Archaeologist* 3 (1940), 1-12

4

the second millennium B.C.[1] Here it must be noted that the
Old Testament tradition represents the Hebrew patriarchs as
maintaining close links with that area through personal sojourn
and intermarriage with their Aramaean kinsfolk.

Still the most significant discovery of Mesopotamian documents is that of Hormuzd Rassam, the native assistant of Layard,
of the vast royal library of Ashurbanipal, a great patron of
culture, who had the temple libraries of his empire ransacked for
their literary treasures and had copies made of the ancient
documents in Sumerian and Akkadian on clay tablets, which, of
course, barring abuse, are indestructible. These documents,
distributed in museums in various countries, have occupied
scholars until the present time and continue to be the source of
fresh discoveries in ritual, mythology, liturgy, history, and law.

The knowledge of cuneiform has been of the greatest importance to field archaeologists as more sedentary scholars, since it
often provided a clue to the nature and date of buildings as well
as the identification of different kings who left their record on
stelae, reliefs, and the less spectacular, but no less important,
foundation-tablets. These give a list of the exploits of the royal
founders including, for instance, Tiglath-Pileser I (1115–1076 B.C.),
Sargon II (722–705 B.C.), the conqueror of Samaria, Sennacherib
(705–681 B.C.), who ravaged Judah in the days of Hezekiah and
the prophet Isaiah, Esarhaddon (681–669 B.C.), his son, and
Ashurbanipal (668–626 B.C.), who effectively reduced Egypt. In
the south foundation-tablets of the neo-Babylonian, or Chaldaean,
kings Nabopolassar (625–605 B.C.), Nebuchadrezzar (604–562 B.C.),
and Nabona'id (556–538 B.C.) have been found, and also one of
the Persian conqueror Cyrus the Great.

The bearing of these and other historical documents on the
Bible is immediately apparent. They are contemporary records,
objective evidence often of the same events and conditions, and
occasionally even of the same persons. As such they help us to
appreciate the peculiar viewpoint of the writers of the Old
Testament. In short, while the interest of the Assyrians in

---

[1] E. A. Speiser, who regards the Hurrians as an important element in the
Hyksos invasion of Palestine and Egypt c.1730 B.C., would connect the penetration of Abraham with the Hyksos ('Ethnic Movements in the Near East
in the Second Millennium B.C.', Annual of the American Schools of Oriental
Research XIII (1933), 43–52). It is unnecessary, however, to make this assumption since there is nothing except Genesis 14 to suggest that Abraham was
involved in such political events. The common elements of culture may have
been shared by the Hurrians and Hebrews in Upper Mesopotamia rather than
in Palestine.

history is that of the exact annalist, the Hebrew interest is that of the philosopher of history, to whom individual political events are secondary to the historical process as an unfolding of the purpose of God. In the historical books, notably Kings in their present literary form, we are never left in doubt as to the real interest of the writers ; for history objectively recorded in the manner of the Assyrian annals we are referred to other works such as ' the Books of the Chronicles of the Kings of Israel ' and those of Judah. Hebrew tradition significantly classifies the ' historical books ' Joshua, Judges, Samuel, and Kings as ' the Former Prophets ', indicating at once the peculiar value and the limitation of these works.

Among the Assyrian records are lists of officials, *limmu*, who, like the Greek *archon eponymos*, gave their names to the year. In addition there are *limmu*-annals, which note not only the names and titles of the officials, but certain events which occurred in their term of office. Cross-references may thus be made to royal annals, enabling us to introduce dates into the sequence of annual *limmu*-offices. This chronological material is supplemented by king-lists giving the sequence and duration of reigns. The most significant of these is that found by the expedition of the Oriental Institute of the University of Chicago in 1932–3 at Khorsabad, ancient Dur-Sharrukin (' the Fortress of Sargon '). It is dated in 738 B.C. and gives a complete list of Assyrian kings down to Ashurnirari V (755–745 B.C.). In the earlier periods, however, only the names of the kings are given without the duration of their reigns.[1] From the beginning of the Hebrew monarchy, however, the duration of each reign is given, so that this material provides a chronological framework for the history of Old Testament times. The key to the situation is the note of an eclipse of the sun in the month Simanu in the *limmu*-ship of Pur-Shagale. This may be astronomically calculated and fell on June 15th, 763 B.C. Now the *limmu*-ship of Pur-Shagale coincided with the ninth year of Ashur-dan III. Thus with the combined aid of king-lists and *limmu*-chronicles we may reckon back and forward and, for the period with which we are immediately concerned, establish a firm chronology. The period covered by the

---

[1] For a description of the tablet and a discussion of its significance see A. Poebel, ' The Assyrian King List from Khorsabad ', *Journal of Near Eastern Studies* I (1942), 247 ff., 460 ff. ; II (1943), 56 ff. The accuracy of this list is corroborated, in spite of minor variations, by another king-list bought in Mosul and now in the Seventh Day Adventist Seminary of New York, published first by I. Gelb, ' Two Assyrian King Lists ', *Journal of Near Eastern Studies* XIII (1954), 209–30.

Khorsabad king-list and the somewhat longer period to which the *limmu*-canons extend are overlapped by the canon of Ptolemy, the Egyptian astronomer, geographer, historian, and chronologist. Within this framework we shall find certain synchronisms between the history of Israel and Assyria, Babylon, Persia, and the Greek dynasties which succeeded to the empire of Alexander the Great in Egypt and Syria, so that in making possible a sound Hebrew chronology from David to Herod the Great this statistical material is not the least significant acquisition from the mounds of ancient Assyria.

Life in Mesopotamia is well illustrated by legal rescripts from the time of Ḥammurabi and from his celebrated law-code. This, though not the only code nor even the earliest,[1] gives a very comprehensive picture of society in the Babylonian city-state in the 18th and 17th centuries B.C. The picture is one of an urban society where the status of freemen and slaves, sacred and secular, is clearly defined. There are also traces of feudalism in regulations governing military classes. Both freemen and slaves had their privileges, but there was discrimination in favour of the former, and for the same crime the freeman might be discharged with a fine, whereas the slave was put to death. There was, however, no *apartheid* in ancient Babylon and, in spite of legal discrimination, the classes were free to mix and even intermarry, provided that the slave to be married was bought from his or her owner. The ancient Babylonians had a keen commercial sense, and this is strongly emphasised in Ḥammurabi's code and in the laws from Qalʿat Shergat (ancient Ashur) in the Middle Assyrian period (*c.*13th century B.C.).[2] Helping a runaway slave to escape, for instance, was a capital offence even where the guilty party was a freeman.[3] This commercial interest comes out again in the various laws of damages in the case of tenant-farmers of fields, date-groves, and orchards, of boatmen who act as haulage-contractors, and of herdsmen who lose some of their beasts except by proven accident (cf. Exod. 22:9 ff.). This property sense

---

[1] The code of Lipit-Ishtar, known from excerpts from tablets from Nippur, is about a century older than that of Ḥammurabi (F. R. Steele, *American Journal of Archaeology* LII (1948), 425–50 ; S. N. Kramer in J. B. Pritchard, *Ancient Near Eastern Texts relating to the Old Testament* (1950), 159–61). From about the same period comes the code of the city of Eshnunna from Tell Abu Hirmil in the Diyala region east of Baghdad (A. Goetze in Pritchard, op. cit., 161–3). Older still is the code of Ur-Nammu, founder of the IIIrd Dynasty of Ur (*c.*2050 B.C.), found in 1952.

[2] G. R. Driver and Sir John Miles, *The Assyrian Laws* (1935)

[3] Pritchard, op. cit., 166, § 15, cf. Dt. 23:15–16, where one is obliged to harbour such a slave.

often led to extreme severity, as in the case of housebreaking, where the thief was walled up on the scene of his burglary,[1] and of fire-raising with intent to steal, where the culprit was thrown into the fire he had kindled.[2] Here we notice one of the major differences between Mesopotamian and Hebrew law. In view of the Hebrew laws of damages (e.g. Lev. 6:1–7) it would be wrong to say that the Hebrew legislation showed no property sense, but the property-motive does not obtrude itself in Hebrew as in Babylonian law. The Hebrews emphasised the essential rights and obligations of a man and framed their laws to preserve moral values.[3] Here, however, the Hebrews were not unique in the ancient East, for they but reflected the characteristic tribal socialism of the desert. No matter how serious a view is taken of crime in Hebrew law, there is no case of cruelty or infringement of the dignity of the individual as in Middle Assyrian law, where facial mutilation, castration, merciless flogging, and impalement are among the penalties. In Hebrew law flogging was limited to forty strokes to be carried out before the judge, ' lest if one should exceed and beat him above these with many stripes, then thy brother should seem vile unto thee ' (Dt. 25:3).[4]

In principle and execution Hebrew law is much closer to its tribal antecedents than Mesopotamian law. In the oldest Hebrew code, for instance, the Book of the Covenant (Exod. 20:22–23:33), no mention is made of judges, and in the time of Ahab (874–853 B.C.) it was the local elders and notables who condemned Naboth at Jezreel (1 Kg. 21). So in the time of David the kin-group was the legal executive, with whose application of a traditional principle of justice even the king scrupled to interfere on appeal, as we see from the case, fictitious though it was, cited by the wise woman of Tekoa (2 Sam. 14:4).

In the Babylonian code justice is in the hands of the judges and local governors appointed by the king. Periodic inspections by the king and appeals to him are possible, and many royal directives are extant. Cases were normally decided by judges on the evidence of witnesses, and sometimes there were written attestations, as in the case of marriage, which was in fact invalid without such a contract. Adoption was similarly attested in deed, as well as conveyance of property, commercial transactions, and leases, and many such documents are recovered in excava-

---

[1] Pritchard, op. cit., 167, § 21   [2] ibid., p. 167, § 25
[3] This was true even where the Hebrews adapted existing Canaanite laws.
[4] cf. 2 C. 11:24, where Paul says that five times he had received forty stripes save one.

tions in all Mesopotamian sites, many of them still intact in their clay envelopes. Where the evidence of witnesses was not available the accused could take an oath of purgation at a shrine, as also among the Hebrews (Exod. 22:7–10). In Babylonian and Assyrian law, as in Hebrew law, trial by ordeal was possible. In Mesopotamia parties accused of adultery or sorcery might be thrown to sink or swim in the river, which is always preceded in Akkadian writing by the determinative cuneiform sign for ' divinity ', a vestige of primitive animism, which is the origin of the primitive Hebrew belief in the significance of springs in connection with justice, as in the case of the wells of Massa (' trial '), Meribah (' contention at law '), and Mishpat (' judgment '). In Babylon and Israel the ultimate sanction of law was religion, a fact which was formally recognised in the respective codes by their ascription to divine authority and the addition of formal blessings and curses (e.g. Dt. 27:11 ff.). This same convention is observed in Ḥammurabi's code.

There is abundant evidence for the religious life of Sumerians, Amorites, Assyrians, and Aramaeans in Mesopotamia from the third millennium to the 6th century B.C. in the great myths, hymns, ritual texts, glyptic art, and particularly the less pretentious texts such as the incantations, counter-incantations, and psalms of lamentation, in which we certainly have our finger on the pulse of the people. In all such texts we gain a welcome insight into the life and literature of the Hebrews in the context of the living Near East.

The influence of Mesopotamian on Hebrew thought is apparent in the use, particularly in the poetic parts of the Old Testament, of the imagery and theme of the triumph of Cosmos over Chaos expressed in Creation, as in the Babylonian myth *enuma elish* (' When on high . . .' [1]). In this myth, which we believe to be functional, expressing articulately and making doubly effective the rites of the fertility-cult which it accompanied, the element of Creation is but one in a larger context. The text describes how the high gods were threatened with the enmity of the powers of Chaos under Tiamat, the deification of the subterranean waters, a feature which reflects natural conditions in Mesopotamia, the land of two rivers and swampy lagoons, perpetually menaced by the uncertain flood-waters from the

[1] This text was recovered from Ashurbanipal's library at Nineveh. No extant text antedates the first millennium B.C., but the myth is believed on grounds of language and literary style to date from early in the second millennium.

highlands of Armenia which could only be controlled by a well-organised system of canals. Dismay reigns in the divine court until Marduk, the young god of Babylon, undertakes to champion the order of Providence against the powers of Chaos, first making his bargain that if victorious he would be acknowledged as king. He overcomes the powers of Chaos and his kingship is eventually established. Up to this point the myth has a counterpart in the Canaanite myth of the conflict of Baal and the unruly waters and his assumption of the kingship.[1] The Mesopotamian myth, unlike its Canaanite counterpart, goes on to describe how Cosmos was established by the victorious god :

> The lord [2] trod on the legs of Tiamat,
> With his unsparing mace he crushed her skull . . .
>
> . . . .
> He split her like a shell-fish into two parts ;
> Half of her he set up and ceiled it as the sky,
> Pulled down the bar and posted guards.
> He bade them to allow not her waters to escape.
> He crossed the heavens and surveyed the regions,
> He squared Apsu's [3] quarter, the abode of Nudimmud,[4]
> As the lord measured the dimensions of Apsu,
>
> . . . .
> He constructed stations for the great gods,
> Fixing their astral likeness as constellations.
> He determined the year by designating the zones ;
> He set up three constellations for each of the twelve months.
>
> . . . .
> The moon he caused to shine, the night to him entrusting,
> He appointed him a creature of the night to signify the days :
> ' Monthly, without ceasing, form designs with a crown.
> At the month's very start, rising over the land,
> Thou shalt have luminous horns to signify six days,
> On the seventh day be thou a half crown.' [5]
>
> E. A. SPEISER

Man is then created out of the blood of Kingu, the chief ally of Tiamat, the purpose of his creation being to give the gods their due service.

Here it will be noted that the order of creation, culminating

[1] *v. infra*, p. 106   [2] i.e. Marduk   [3] i.e. the Deep
[4] One of the names of Ea, the god of earth and water
[5] Pritchard, op. cit., 67 ff.

in the creation of man, is not that of Genesis 2:4, which is from
the earlier literary source J, but of Genesis 1:1–2:3, which is
from the Exilic compilation P. In this Hebrew adaptation of
the Mesopotamian creation theme there is much that reflects the
late date of its appropriation. The culmination of creation in
the Sabbath day's rest has no counterpart in the Babylonian
myth, and obviously reflects the observance of the weekly Sabbath, which became an institution among the Jews in the Exile,
when the Temple and its cult were no more.[1] In the Babylonian
myth the stuff of creation is the carcass of Tiamat, and man is
created out of the blood of Kingu. In the much more mature
Hebrew version of P creation is by the divine fiat.

At this point a problem emerges. In the Mesopotamian myth
the essential feature is the conflict of Marduk, the champion of
Cosmos, and Tiamat and her monstrous allies, the powers of
Chaos. Conscious of the absence of this conflict motive in the
accounts of creation in Genesis, Hermann Gunkel sought for it
elsewhere in the Old Testament and found it expressed sporadically in the poetic portions, the Psalms (e.g. Ps. 89), Prophets
(e.g. Isa. 51:9 ff.), and the Book of Job (e.g. 26:12–13), etc.[2]
Except where there is specific use of the imagery of the Babylonian myth, however, we would regard this theme in the Psalms
and Prophets particularly as the Hebrew adaptation of the local
Canaanite myth appropriate to the autumnal New Year.[3]

As the formal religion of Mesopotamia revealed in the myths
was naturalistic, the pantheon consisting of deified natural forces
and elements, the people moved about in a world peopled by a
host of such forces which had not succeeded in winning a regular
status in public religion. All sufferings and even minor mishaps,
such as headache or personal quarrels, were attributed to these
demons. The desert is their proper home, a belief which probably
reflects the peasant's dread of the Bedouin ; they lurk in ruins,
a belief to which the Old Testament alludes in depicting the ruin
of Edom (Isa. 34:14). Again the demons might be personified,
as Namtar or Ashakku, the demons of plague or wasting disease,
and depicted as stalking the streets like the Hebrew ' pestilence
that walketh in darkness '. There are many names of those

---

[1] From such passages as 2 Kg. 4:23 ; Isa. 1:13 ; Am. 8:5 ; and Hos. 2:11
it is apparent that the Sabbath was a lunar festival in pre-Exilic Israel. In
these passages the Sabbath is associated only with the *new* moon, and it is not
apparent that the four lunar phases were observed as in Mesopotamia.
[2] H. Gunkel, *Schöpfung und Chaos in Urzeit und Endzeit* (1895)
[3] *v. infra*, 104–5

demons by which the lives of the ancient Mesopotamians were ridden, and certain of them, such as the common noun *shedu* and *lilîtu* (the Night-hag) have passed into Hebrew (*shēdh* and *lîlîth*). In God's admonition to Cain that sin would lurk (*rôbhēṣ*) at the door of the sinner there is probably an allusion to the Mesopotamian demon *rabîṣu* (he who lies in wait). As this demon was particularly active in nightmares the passage in Genesis may refer to a bad conscience.

In such a milieu we naturally find the belief that there were certain persons capable of controlling the demons, either in directing their evil potential or in checking it. The priests naturally were relied upon to exercise this control. Alongside the priests, however, in Mesopotamia as in Israel, there were unofficial sorcerers, or more usually sorceresses, since women in Mesopotamia and elsewhere in the Near East and in primitive societies were generally regarded as the medium of demonic influence.[1] This power was usually sinister, and the witch was conspicuous in ancient Mesopotamia. Such persons indulged in their nefarious practices on the principle of imitative magic. By tying knots or making the image of their victim in wax, fat, clay, or some such substance, piercing it or melting or dissolving it with due incantation they sought to influence the powers of evil by auto-suggestion. Against such malpractices, which in primitive societies often succeed through the credulity of the victim, the ancient Mesopotamians resorted to various antidotes. Like the modern Arabs they had great faith in amulets and written texts used as charms. They kept, besides, little families of household gods (cf. Hebrew *teraphim*) usually buried in their houses, particularly below the threshold, which for them as for the ancient Hebrews, as we see from the Passover rite, was a ' danger zone '.[2] Often, however, the apprehensive man had to resort to the priest, who in his simplicity or wisdom undertook counterspells in rite and incantation, specimens of the latter of which are extant :

[1] In this connection we should note the role of females in rites appropriate to seasonal crises, e.g. goddesses in the Râs Shamra mythology, Ishtar in her search for Tammuz in Babylonian mythology, Isis for Osiris, and Demeter for Kore. Women, too, led mourning rites. Such superstitious regard for women was probably due to their nature as the mysterious source of life, they being regarded as open to influences beyond the normal range of society. Again in exogamous societies women were technically intruders into the families of their husbands, and all kinds of prophylactic rites were observed to guard against the possible evil influences which came in with them.

[2] The affixing of small cylinders containing texts from the Law to the doorposts (*mezûzôth*) of orthodox Jewish homes has probably such an origin.

But I by command of Marduk the lord of charms,
By Marduk the master of bewitchment,
Both sorcerer and sorceress
As with ropes I will entwine,
As in a cage I will catch,
As with cords I will tie,
As in a net I will overpower,
As in a sling I will twist,
As a fabric I will tear,
With dirty water as from a well I will fill,
As a wall throw them down.

after M. JASTROW, *The Religion of Babylonia and Assyria*

Here we note an essential feature of the counter-incantation, the accurate repetition of the words of the spell which had been cast on the same principle of imitative magic on which the spell was based. This element was carried over into a much higher type of religious exercise, the psalms of lamentation, a feature of which is the precise enumeration of the evils from which the sufferer seeks relief.

The sufferer is not always the victim of witchcraft. He may have fallen directly under the power of some demon of disease or misfortune by the positive or permissive will of one or other of the high gods. In this case the priests had help for him in rite and incantation which involved a long and, in fact, exhaustive confessional of all possible sins, both ethical and ritual, against all possible deities. Here again texts are to hand, e.g. :

Has he sinned against a god ?
Is his guilt against a goddess ?
Is it a wrongful deed against his master ?
Hatred towards his elder brother ?
Has he despised his father or mother ?
Insulted his elder sister ?
Has he given too little ?
Has he withheld too much ?
Has he for ' No ' said ' Yes ' ?
For ' Yes ' said ' No ' ?
. . . .
Has he used false weights ?
. . . .
Has he taken an incorrect amount ?

Not taken the correct sum ?
Has he fixed a false boundary ?
Not fixed a just boundary ?
Has he removed a boundary, a limit, a territory ?
Has he possessed himself of his neighbour's house ?
Has he approached his neighbour's wife ?
Has he shed the blood of his neighbour ?
Robbed his neighbour's dress ?

. . . .

Was he frank in speaking ?
But false in heart ?

after M. JASTROW, *The Religion of Babylonia and Assyria*

From such texts it seems that the personal sense of sin was not strong. What is fundamental, however, is that the ancient Mesopotamian believed in the principle of divine retribution, suffering implying sin, which might, however, be a ritual rather than a moral lapse. The same conception dominated Hebrew thinking throughout the period of the great prophets. The author of the Book of Job, for all his moral vigour, could not effectively refute it, and the author of the poem of the ' Suffering Servant ' in Isaiah 52:13–53:12, though he could discern the positive purpose of suffering, which was an unsolved problem to Jeremiah, argues back from the suffering of the innocent Servant to the sin of the community he represents. Apart from the recognition of the causal connection between sin and suffering, these Mesopotamian confessions indicate, though in a negative way, social morality in ancient Mesopotamia, and so provide a criterion by which we may assess the moral development of the Hebrews.

We have already indicated the value of the Mesopotamian law-codes as illustrating the life and problems of the various strata of ancient society. There are other, royal, texts which demonstrate that, contrary to the common misapprehension, the ancient Eastern kings were no tyrants living beyond the pale of common morality, but had generally a very high sense of duty and responsibility as the representatives of their peoples before their gods. A case in point is the prayer of Nebuchadrezzar on his accession to the throne of Babylon :

O Eternal Ruler, Lord of the Universe,
Grant that the name of the king whom thou lovest,

Whose name thou hast mentioned, may flourish as seems good
   to thee.
Guide him on the right path.
I am the ruler who obeys thee, the creation of thy hand.
It is thou who hast created me,
And thou hast entrusted to me sovereignty over mankind.
According to thy mercy, O Lord, which thou bestowest upon all,
Cause me to love thy supreme rule.
Implant the fear of thy divinity within my heart,
Grant to me whatsoever may seem good before thee,
Since it is thou who dost control my life.

after M. Jastrow

This does not fall far short of the tone of Solomon's prayer in
his dedication of the Temple (1 Kg. 8).

To be reckoned in this category of royal texts, which give us
a more intimate view of the status, function, and problems of the
king, are the psalms of lamentation. Many of these give clear
indication of their occasion, a great public disaster, such as
defeat in war, drought, famine, locusts, plague, or when the
prognostications of the astrologers were particularly unfavour-
able. Again, as in the incantations, there might be no particular
consciousness of sin, nor might it be known what deity was
offended, and other elements of the popular counter-incantation
texts are present, though more fully developed in the psalms of
lamentation. As in counter-incantations there is a detailed list
of sufferings, often in hyperbolic terms. There is also prayer, in
which the subject was much more intimately related to his god
than in the counter-incantations. Some of these obviously
express the experience of the people in face of some great public
disaster. Others again, in the first person singular, seem rather
to be the expression of personal grief. The difference, however,
is more apparent than real, and, though some of the latter do
relate to personal grief, we must always reckon with the possibility that such were declared by the king in the first person
singular, he being a ' societary ' figure representing in his sole
majesty his people before their god. Thus those psalms of
lamentation give us a fuller and truer picture of life in the ancient
Mesopotamian state than the official inscriptions, which are a
record of uniform success. The king in antiquity, for ' all his
homicidal glory ', had to walk the *via dolorosa*.

A formalistic study of this literary type with its clearly marked elements of invocation to the deity, detailed recitation of suffering, assurance of faith in the deity, and often a vow, suggests that here is the prototype of certain psalms in the Old Testament, e.g. Psalm 44, where verse 9 indicates that Israel was making humble supplication before God in the hour of military defeat. Detailed study of such texts reveals also striking affinities with the phraseology and even the theology of Hebrew psalms of this nature, and here we may cite a Psalm of Lamentation to the goddess Ishtar from the Neo-Babylonian period, which is true to type. The psalm begins with the invocation of the goddess by all her epithets and by allusion to all her attributes, which finds its counterpart in the Psalms in the Old Testament in allusions to the mighty acts of God, such as Creation or the Exodus, by which He had revealed His nature. Then the sufferer appeals to the goddess :

I have cried to thee, suffering, wearied, and distressed, as thy
    servant.
See me, O my Lady ; accept my prayers.
Faithfully look upon me and hear my supplication.
Promise my forgiveness and let thy spirit be appeased.
Pity ! For my wretched body which is full of confusion and
    trouble.
Pity ! For my sickened heart which is full of tears and suffering.
Pity ! For my wretched intestines (which are full of) confusion
    and trouble.
Pity ! For my afflicted house which mourns bitterly.
Pity ! For my feelings which are satiated with tears and
    suffering.
O exalted Irnini, fierce lion, let thy heart be at rest.
O angry wild ox, let thy spirit be appeased.
Let the favour of thine eyes be upon thee.[1]

. . . .

As in the Hebrew Psalms the suffering of the mourner is aggravated by the gloating of his adversaries, and his afflictions are recounted in hyperbole and figurative language, certain of which is familiar from the Old Testament :

How long, O my Lady, shall the crippled and weak seek me out ?
One has made for me long sackcloth ; thus have I appeared
    before thee.

[1] F. J. Stephens in Pritchard, *Ancient Near Eastern Texts relating to the Old Testament* (1950), 384–5, ll. 42–53

The weak have become strong ; but I am weak.
I toss about like flood-water, which an evil wind makes violent.
My heart is flying ; it keeps fluttering like a bird of heaven.
I mourn like a dove night and day.[1]

. . . .

Since it was an axiom in Mesopotamia as in ancient Israel that
suffering implied sin, sin is admitted, though in a general and
almost perfunctory way :

To thee I have prayed : forgive my debt.
Forgive my sin, my iniquity, my shameful deeds, and my offence.[2]

This is also a feature which is apt to surprise the Christian reader
of certain of the Psalms of the Old Testament, where confession
of sin is often cast in a negative mould, which is tantamount to
exculpation.   So in the Prayer to Ishtar the sufferer asks :

I—what have I done, O my god and my goddess ?
Like one who does not fear my God and my goddess I am
    treated ;
While sickness, headache, loss, and destruction are provided for
    me ;
So are fixed upon me terror, disdain, and fullness of wrath,
Anger, choler, and indignation of gods and men.[3]

. . . .

But I have payed heed to thee, my Lady ; my attention has been
    turned to thee.

This penitential psalm is by all appearances that of a private
individual, but others which are just as obviously of public
import employ the same conventions and imagery.   The Old
Testament gives clear evidence of occasions in ancient Israel to
which such liturgies were appropriate.   The prayer of Solomon
at the dedication of the Temple (1 Kg. 8:33–40) indicates that
national disasters such as defeat in war, drought, famine, or
plague occasioned solemn fasts when the people abased themselves before God, the implication being that they confessed the
sins which they believed to be the cause of the disaster.   Nor are
such liturgies confined to the Psalms in the Old Testament
(e.g. Ps. 44, 61, 133, 144, etc.), but appear also in the Prophets
(e.g. Jl 1:13–14 ; 2:12–17), which is a liturgy on the occasion

---

[1] ibid., ll. 56–64   [2] ibid., ll. 80–1   [3] ibid., ll. 67–71, 79

of a drought and locust plague, and probably Habakkuk 1 and 2 in the dark days before the final collapse of Judah in 586 B.C. The classic example of this literary form in the Old Testament, of course, is Lamentations, which is, in fact, read by orthodox Jews on the ninth of the month Ab at the great fast for the destruction of the Temple. There is no reason to doubt that in Lamentations we have liturgies used at such fasts immediately after the fall of Jerusalem. Such fasts in pre-Exilic times were apparently *ad hoc*, but from Zechariah 7:5, which alludes to fasts in the fifth and seventh months, it is apparent that after the Exile there was a tendency to regularise the fast as a ritual practice.

In the light of the public nature of the Mesopotamian psalms of lamentation, even those in the first person singular, we cannot absolutely dismiss the possibility that certain of the Hebrew psalms of this type may be the plaint of a cultic official or even the king himself representing the community. Nevertheless in such a small nation as Israel, strong as she was in her democratic tradition, the trials and sufferings of the common individual as well as those of the community must have been consciously voiced by such spirits as Jeremiah, who uses this literary type, and by the authors of the psalms which we have noted.[1] There was in Israel a democratisation of the public liturgy, especially after the destruction of the royal house and the nation in 586 B.C. Thus in the providence of God those psalms of lamentation, so stereotyped in their original form, became infused with life in the mouths of the prophets and psalmists of Israel until eventually they become the fitting expression of the feelings of spiritual sufferers in all generations.

Having considered the content and form of Mesopotamian religion in its most important aspects, we now turn to the study of the sacral personnel, priests, prophets, and the king.

In the complex urban civilisation of Mesopotamia, where the state was theoretically, and to a great extent actually, the estate of the god, the priesthood was much more departmentalised than in the simpler economy of Israel. All attached to the cult, of

---

[1] e.g. Jer. 11:18–20 ; 15:15–21 ; 17:12–18 ; 18:18–23 ; and 20:10–13 ; Ps. 22, 73, etc. W. Baumgartner, though recognising the conventional type of the lamentation used by Jeremiah, emphasises the marks of the prophet's individuality ('Die Klagedichte des Jeremia', *Zeitschrift für die Alttestamentliche Wissenschaft*, Beiheft 32 (1917)). A thorough analysis of the formal elements, motives, and diction of this literary type in Babylonian and Hebrew psalms is undertaken by G. Widengren, *The Accadian and Hebrew Psalms of Lamentation as Religious Documents* (1937).

course, were in 'holy orders'. Holiness (*qôdhesh*) here as among
the Hebrews denotes physical relationship to the deity or his
property rather than a moral or spiritual state.[1] Among the
priests of Mesopotamia were many functionaries who would not
have been so regarded among the Hebrews. Besides the priests
proper, who officiated at the great seasonal festivals and public
sacrifices, there were others who performed rites of exorcism and
pronounced the accompanying incantations (*asipu*), while others
were experts in augury (*baru*) divining by entrails, stars, or by
patterns assumed by oil dropped in a bowl of water, a means of
divination apparently familiar to the Hebrews also (Gen. 44:5, 15).

Other cultic officials were media of revelation in a more
personal way which is reminiscent of the Hebrew prophets.
These are termed *maḫḫe*. They are, in the first place, attached
to the cult [2] and the subject of their revelation often concerns
cultic arrangements.[3] Occasionally, however, they intervene, like
the Hebrew prophets in affairs of state. A tablet from Mari in
the Amorite period (*c.*18th century B.C.) refers to their intervention in negotiations between the king and certain desert tribes,[4]
and a late-Assyrian tablet from Nimrud (ancient Kalḫu) records
how the intervention of the *maḫḫe* affected a campaign of Tiglath-
Pileser III in 734 B.C.[5] It is now being more appreciated that
the Hebrew prophets had a more regular place in the cult than
was formerly realised,[6] and in this connection the clear evidence
of the cultic status of the Mesopotamian *maḫḫe* is particularly
significant. Again, the etymology of *maḫḫu* suggests ecstatic
experience,[7] and this too has been taken as an essential feature

---

[1] Thus in pre-Exilic Palestine the sacred prostitutes, of both sexes, of the
fertility-cult were technically 'holy'.

[2] A. von Soden, 'Verkündigung des Gotteswillens durch prophetisches
Wort in der altbabylonischen Briefen aus Mari', *Die Welt des Orients* (1950),
396–403

[3] e.g. D. D. Luckenbill, *Ancient Records of Assyria* ii, §§ 658 D, 989

[4] von Soden, op. cit., 398

[5] D. J. Wiseman, 'Two Historical Inscriptions from Nimrud', *Iraq* XIII
(1951), 21–6

[6] S. Mowinckel, 'Kultprophetie und prophetische Psalmen', *Psalmen-
studien* III (1923) ; A. Causse, 'L'ancienne poésie cultuelle d'Israël et les
origines du Psautier', *Revue de l'Histoire et de Philosophie Religieuse* VI (1926), 1–37 ;
A. R. Johnson, 'The Prophet in Israelite Worship', *Expository Times* XLVII
(1935–6), 312–19 ; *The Cultic Prophet in Ancient Israel* (1944) ; A. Haldar,
Associations of Cult Prophets among the Ancient Semites (1945). The significance
of the prophet in the cult had already been recognised by W. R. Smith (*The
Prophets of Israel* (1882), 85) and by A. C. Welch (*Prophet and Priest in Old Israel*
(1936)).

[7] J. Gray, 'The Period and Office of the Prophet Isaiah in the Light of a
New Assyrian Tablet', *Expository Times* LXIII (1952), 264 ff.

Plate 1   Victory Stele of Naram-Sin of Akkad, from Susa

Plate 2   Shalmaneser III receives the submission and tribute of Jehu,
' the son of Omri ' ; a fragment from Shalmaneser's Black Obelisk

of Hebrew prophecy. With this view we cannot agree without qualification, but the issue is still sufficiently open for any fresh material on the subject to be important. The *maḫḫe* are, in our opinion, rather analogous to the prophetic guilds, ' the sons of the prophets ' of the Old Testament, who might intervene in affairs of state, as in the case of the prophet who rebuked Ahab for releasing the king of Damascus (1 Kg. 20:42 ff.), or the prophet (' this mad fellow ') who anointed Jehu king at Ramoth Gilead (2 Kg. 9:1 ff.). Such, however, like the *maḫḫe*, were closely bound to the cult [1] and submitted to the limitations of their office, like Zedekiah ben Chanaanah and the four hundred prophets who favoured Ahab with auspicious oracles on the eve of his expedition to Ramoth Gilead (1 Kg. 22) and those contemporaries of Jeremiah whose oracle was ' Peace ! Peace ! ' [2] The great Hebrew prophets, in spite of their possible cultic status and the extremes of behaviour to which they often resorted in their prophetic symbolism, like the ecstatic ' sons of the prophets ', were never circumscribed by their office. They had been admitted to God's intimate council and they retained a firm grasp of the purpose of the Almighty, and that redeemed even their most extravagant symbolism from meaningless eccentricity. Moreover, in their life-mission there was a consistency which was, so far as we know, quite lacking in the *ad hoc* activity of the ' sons of the prophets ' in Israel or the Mesopotamian *maḫḫe*. The situation is well summed up by Martin Noth. ' The prophetical literature deals with guilt and punishment, reality and unreality, present and future of the Israelite people as chosen by God for a special and unique service, the declaration of the great and moving contemporary events in the world as part of a process which, together with the future issue of that process, is willed by God. Even where the prophets give practical directions in a concrete situation, they keep this larger connection in view.' [3]

Kingship, wherever it is found in primitive society, is the keystone of the social order, and as such it merits especial notice in our study of life in ancient Mesopotamia. The institution is invested with a certain sanctity, which invites closer investigation, whether one's interest is political or religious. The latter fact has led a number of scholars to assume that the ancient king was

[1] They are found in the Elijah saga at the sanctuary of Bethel and at Jericho (2 Kg. 2:3 ff.).   [2] Or, better, ' All's well ! All's well ! '
[3] M. Noth, ' History and the Word of God in the Old Testament ', *Bulletin of the John Rylands Library* xxxii, ii (1950)

5

regarded as divine.[1] In ancient Egypt the Pharaoh was certainly
so regarded.   In the syncretistic religion of the united kingdom
he was worshipped as the incarnation of Re, the sun-god, and
as Horus, the son of Osiris, the fertility-god.   When dead he was
regarded as Osiris, who thus incorporated all dead Pharaohs.
Thus as giver of light and fertility the Pharaoh was indeed a
Messiah.   In the Semitic world, however, the evidence is against
the view that the kings in Babylonia and Assyria, much less in
Syria and Israel, were regarded as divine.   In the Sumerian
city-states of southern Mesopotamia the third millennium B.C.
saw the emergence of monarchy from an oligarchy of elders via
the expedient of occasional dictatorship.[2]   The officer thus
appointed *ad hoc* eventually regularised his office, and was known
as LU-GAL, ' the great man ', a title which hardly suggests the
supernatural status of the Pharaoh.   In sculpture the ' great man '
is depicted as singled out among his fellows certainly, but still
only as man among men.   He is not ' hieratically scaled ' to the
proportions of a god like the Pharaoh, who is always depicted as
many times larger than men.   Nor does he bear divine insignia.
In the whole of the records of the Sumerians, Amorites, Assyrians,
and Aramaeans who ruled in Mesopotamia for over two millennia
there are significantly few exceptions to this rule, the most
notable being the great imperialist Naram-Sin of Akkad, who is
so depicted on his famous stele of victory.   Again, before the
names of deities in Akkadian cuneiform the cypher, known as
the determinative, for deity was invariably written.   This is used
before the names of certain kings, to be sure, in remote antiquity,
but in Assyrian and neo-Babylonian times it is never found.
Thus there is no evidence of the obvious type that the king in
ancient Mesopotamia was as such normally regarded as divine.
He was rather one of the people and as such their representative.

In antiquity there was no such thing as a secular community.
The community, and in later times the state, was a religious unit ;

---

[1] Sir J. G. Frazer was the first to formulate the theory of divine kingship
by a rather indiscriminate use of miscellaneous evidence in *The Golden Bough IV*
(*Adonis, Attis, Osiris*) (1914).   It is elaborated in English by A. M. Hocart,
Kingship (1927), and in *Myth and Ritual* (1933), and *The Labyrinth* (1935), both
edited by S. H. Hooke.   The most extreme statement of the case is by the
Swedish scholar I. Engnell, *Studies in Divine Kingship in the Ancient Near East*
(1943).   It is significant that S. Mowinckel, who had earlier held similar views,
modifies them considerably in his work on the Messiah, *Han som Kommer* (1951),
where he accepts the arguments and conclusions of H. Frankfort, *Kingship and
the Gods* (1948), where a radical difference is noted between the status of the
Pharaoh and kings in the Semitic East.
[2] T. Jacobsen, *Journal of Near Eastern Studies* v (1943), 159 ff.

its *raison d'être* was the service of its god or pantheon ; its worship not only renewed and preserved the unity of the community and god, but was vital to the coherence of the community itself (hence the charge against the early Christians of disloyalty to the state and society). Thus the king as the representative of the people stood in especially close relationship to their god. This was particularly so at the great seasonal occasions, such as the New Year festival, which was celebrated in Babylon at the vernal equinox, but the king fulfilled a similar function in other crises, both natural and social, such as a time of drought, plague, or similar national disasters. As the agent of the rites whereby the community survived such crises the king was the channel of divine blessing to his people. As such and as one who was habitually in ceremonial contact with the divine the king was no doubt in popular thought invested with divinity, that divinity which doth ' hedge a king '. This conception is fostered by the phraseology of Mesopotamian royal inscriptions, where the kings claim to be fore-ordained by their gods, to be called ' from the womb ' (Frankfort, op. cit., 238), and even to be suckled by goddesses (ibid., 300), a conception which was current also in Canaan. In *The Keret Text in the Literature of Ras Shamra* (1955) I have suggested that the text is a ' social myth ', i.e. the articulate expression of certain social conventions and institutions with the purpose of keeping these in currency. The same may be said of the phraseology of these Mesopotamian royal inscriptions, such as the claim to divine sonship, though this presented no difficulty in Mesopotamia, where legal adoption was a familiar practice. In this connection the formal language of the Hebrew royal psalms 2 and 110 re-echoes the formula of adoption.

The Mesopotamian king, as one habitually in contact with the gods, was a priest, as he was also in Canaan [1] and Israel.[2] There was a sense in which he was also a prophet. He is the recipient of oracles from his god, which he may receive in dreams, possibly in ritual incubation at the sanctuary, as Solomon at the shrine of Gibeon (1 Kg. 3:4), or on cultic occasions, as the Hebrew king received the reassuring oracle in Psalm 2 and 110, or when he intercedes for the community in great distress. This office, however, as well as the office of priest and leader in war

---

[1] J. Gray, ' Canaanite Kingship in Theory and Practice ', *Vetus Testamentum* II (1952), 203 ff.

[2] Saul personally officiated at sacrifice (1 Sam. 13:9 ; 14:35) ; David officiated at the installation of the Ark in Jerusalem (2 Sam. 6) ; and Solomon at the dedication of the Temple.

tended to devolve from the king to specialists, and the prophetic
office was that in which the king would be most likely to defer
to such as showed obvious signs of prophetic proclivity. Nevertheless it is interesting to find that in Mesopotamian texts as well
as Aramaean texts from Syria [1] there is still a close association
between king and prophet. Thus in Israel, besides the figure of
the prophet Samuel by the side of Saul, Nathan and Gad were
' king's seers ' to David, a situation which explains, in our
opinion, the ready access which Elijah and Elisha, Isaiah and
Jeremiah had to the king.

The theory of the divinity of the king, apart from the Egyptian
data, was really based upon the part he was presumed to play in
the Babylonian New Year festival. On that, the greatest occasion
of the whole year, the king was taken into the temple of Marduk
on the fifth day, there to undergo a veritable ' passion '. He was
stripped of his royal insignia, which the officiating priest laid
before the god. He was buffeted in the face by the priest and
subjected to treatment quite other than the deference due to
royalty. He then knelt before the god and made confession of
all sins of which he was conscious and other lapses which were
merely possible. After this penance and prayer he was granted
pardon and re-invested with the royal office. He for his part
promised to discharge seriously his divine commission to rule his
people and care for the city of Babylon and particularly for the
temple of Marduk, while the god promised to punish all his
enemies. This renewal of the right relationship, conceived among
the Hebrews in terms of a covenant between God and the king,
and the discomfiture of the enemies of Israel and her king, is a
feature of certain Hebrew psalms which are almost certainly to
be related to the New Year festival, which, in Palestine and Syria,
fell in the autumn. In the essential features of the Babylonian
New Year festival it is not difficult to recognise those of the
Hebrew New Year in spite of the fact that the former was a
spring and the latter an autumn festival. We do not suggest
that there was direct borrowing, but that both were local varieties
of the same experience, the sacramental participation of the
community in the conflict of Cosmos and Chaos at the most
critical juncture of the peasant's year. The Hebrew New Year
festival is essentially an adaptation of the native Canaanite

---

[1] Zakar-Baal of Hamath in Syria apparently had a staff of prophets who
communicated the will of Baal Shamaim to him. M. Lidzbarski, *Ephemeris für
semitische Epigraphik* II (1909–15), 3.

festival at the autumnal equinox on the eve of the vital ' early rains '. In the penitential rites of the Hebrew Day of Atonement which is associated with the New Year ceremonies, we seem to have an element elaborated in the Exile under the influence of similar penitential rites native to the Babylonian New Year ceremonial.

The Mesopotamian king at this stage received back his royal insignia and was honoured as a king ought to be. In this ritual it is supposed that the king represented the god of vegetation in his death and annual revival. Of this, however, we are doubtful. Up to this point Marduk was not suffering and dead, but was triumphant. He had been engaged in a fierce struggle with Tiamat and her monstrous allies, but he was undaunted and victorious, as the relevant myth *enuma elish* indicates.[1] So far Marduk is a cosmic figure, of much greater proportions than the vegetation-spirit, called in Mesopotamia Tammuz. Later in the New Year festival Marduk seems to be treated as this dying and rising deity, but here we have probably a case of religious syncretism. At this stage of the festival, significantly enough, the king undergoes no humiliation which would suggest that he was identified with the god, but plays the role of a mere master of ceremonies, as Frankfort indicates.[2]

The truth is that here the king represents the community. The anthropologist A. van Gennep [3] has familiarised us with the reaction of primitive societies in passing the crises of individual or social life or in passing from one phase of nature to another. In those periods of ' passage ' the whole community is particularly susceptible to sinister external influences. Hence it spends a period of suspension, refraining from normal activities, staple foods, regular dress or toilet, as, for instance, at death, when the ' bread of affliction ' was eaten, sack-cloth was worn, people went unwashed, and regular places of resort were avoided by the mourner, who sat, like Job, on the village midden. Now the equinoctial season, whether in autumn or in spring, was such a period of ' passage ', when the community must walk with the utmost circumspection. This it did in the person of the king, who submitted in Mesopotamia to the various indignities we have described in order that by divesting himself of royalty he might rob the apprehended evil forces of their objective, like Ahab in disguise at the Battle of Ramoth Gilead, or that he might let them have free play in his ' passion ' in order that for the

[1] *v. supra*, 42 ff.   [2] op. cit., 321 ff.   [3] *Les Rites de Passage* (1909)

coming year their virulence might be exhausted. This interpretation of the experience of the king as the embodiment of the
community at this most critical season finds support in restrictions
imposed upon the king at other times when there was no question
of fertility-ritual or of the king representing the god, namely the
Babylonian Sabbaths, the seventh, fourteenth, nineteenth, twenty-
first, and twenty-eighth days of the month. Those days were
obviously related to phases of the moon and so were periods of
' passage ', hence they were deemed unlucky, and the king for the
good of the community could not eat bread prepared by fire, nor
don his royal dress, nor ride in his chariot, nor hold court. In
pre-Exilic times in Israel the Sabbath was associated with the
new moon. It seems, however, to have been an occasion of
somewhat riotous rejoicing (Hos. 2:11).

When a public disaster, such as plague, drought, locusts, or
the like, was experienced or apprehended, or when the stars were
particularly inauspicious, or at an eclipse the king was obliged
to undergo penitential rites on behalf of the community, which
made the lot of royalty in ancient Mesopotamia no sinecure.
Besides the pressure of tedious ceremonial, such occasions might
demand even painful rituals, such as when the king was obliged
to shave literally every hair from his body, a particularly harsh
sentence when one possessed no more delicate instrument than
an iron razor, which must have made even normal shaving the
greatest inconvenience of antiquity.[1] In such circumstances even
the life of the king might be menaced, and, if so, a substitute (*puḫi*)
for the king (*sharru*) was appointed.[2] The king went into obscurity
until the crisis was past, the substitute meanwhile being treated
as king, as we see from a certain text from the late-Assyrian
period, where the substitute king (*shar puḫi*) was actually furnished with a court lady as his consort. At the end of his ' reign ',
however, the *shar puḫi* and his unfortunate consort were put to

---

[1] This rite is referred to in an Assyrian text (Frankfort, op. cit., 260) and
in Isa. 7:20.

[2] The evidence for this rite is not abundant. There are a dozen letters
from the time of Esarhaddon (681–669 B.C.), all of which refer to the rite in
Babylon. It is not certain that these do not all refer to one occasion, an eclipse
(for discussion and bibliography see G. Goossens, ' Les Substituts Royaux en
Babylonie ', *Analecta Lovaniensia Biblica et Orientalia*, Ser. II, fasc. 13 (1949), 389
and n. 26). From a much earlier period and uncertain circumstances in Isin
in the south comes another instance (L. W. King, *Chronicles concerning Early
Babylonian Kings* II (1907), 12–14, ll. 8–13 ; 15–16, ll. 1–7). It is suggested
by Frankfort that the ' royal ' tombs at Ur, unique so far in Mesopotamian
archaeology, may be those of a substitute king and his ' court ', a view quite
possible but not yet demonstrable.

death and buried in a special tomb. There is, however, no evidence that this was an annual or seasonal festival as Frazer supposed.[1] In the person of the *shar puḥi* the king as the representative of the community exposed himself in exceptional crises to the extreme of suffering. The rite was not connected with the seasonal fertility-cult, but had a purely social significance.

We must state plainly that we do not believe that we can explain the institution of the kingship in Israel simply by analogy with the institution in Egypt or Mesopotamia. There are, in the first place, as the late A. Alt recognised,[2] two patterns of kingship among the Hebrews. In Israel the dynastic principle was never freely admitted. Attempts were made, as, for instance, by Omri and Jehu, but the Israelites never abandoned the idea that the king was simply a judge called to leadership in some particular crisis. In Judah David succeeded in founding a dynasty on the basis of Jerusalem as a crown possession, a state within a state. Here a more mature ideal of kingship developed, more analogous to the Babylonian type. In royal psalms like 2 and 110 we find language which recalls the exaggerated language and royal titulary and address of Mesopotamian royal inscrip-

---

[1] Frazer (*The Golden Bough VII, The Scapegoat* (1913), 355 ff.) assumes that such a rite is indicated in the Babylonian *Sacea* mentioned by Berossus (cited by Athenaeus, *Deipnosophist* XIV, 44), and in the *Sacea* noted by Strabo (XI, viii, 4–5) in the north of Asia Minor, and by Dio Chrysostom (*Oratio* IV, 69), who regards it as of Persian origin. Frazer assumes that this rite involved the sacrifice of the substitute king and was an element in the Babylonian New Year festival. Berossus says nothing about the sacrifice of one who impersonated the king, but simply that there was a general saturnalia, the roles of servants and masters being reversed for a space of five days, one of the servants being arrayed in robes resembling the king's. A domestic festival is obviously visualised with 'gangs' of slaves headed by one singled out as leader by his tawdry regalia, like an English May Queen or the Abbot of Unreason in medieval times. Dio Chrysostom is the authority for human sacrifice as an element in the *Sacea*, stating that a condemned criminal was released and treated as king, being given the amenities of the royal harem, and then put to death. This may or may not be identical with the Babylonian *Sacea* of Berossus. Against Frazer's identification of the latter with the humiliation of the king at the Babylonian New Year festival is the fact that Berossus explicitly dates the *Sacea* in autumn (16th of the month Loos), whereas the Babylonian New Year festival was in spring. Goossens (op. cit., 396–7) concludes that the Babylonian and Persian *Sacea* were distinct, the former being a domestic saturnalia where certain elements of an autumnal New Year festival, the temporary abdication of the king in the spring New Year festival, and the occasional rite of substitution in exceptional crises were popularly degraded from their public significance. The *Sacea*, then, may be regarded in the same light as English mumming or Scottish 'guizing' at Christmas, New Year, and Hallowe'en. A Jewish analogy is the Purim festival in spring, to which the Book of Esther is relevant.

[2] 'Das Königtum in den Reichen Israel und Judah', *Vetus Testamentum* I (1951), 1–22

tions. Nevertheless the Hebrews, even in Jerusalem, were much nearer their nomadic origins, and the constitution was much more democratic than in Mesopotamia, thanks, no doubt, to the wisdom and tact of David the founder. This situation is emphasised particularly by the independent importance of the prophet in Israel, which contrasts markedly with the strictly subordinate role he played in Mesopotamia.

In providing such abundant evidence of the obligations and functions of the king as the embodiment of the community and of the sacramental unity of both in suffering, death, and triumph, Mesopotamian archaeology has done a great service to Old Testament scholarship and also to Christian thought in helping us to a fuller understanding of the Son of Man as a societary figure, a redeemer in whom all he has redeemed have sacramental fellowship.

Apart from legal and religious texts from Mesopotamia, there are certain myths which we may best appraise as documents of Mesopotamian humanism, in particular the myths of Adapa and Gilgamesh.

In the former, extant in three fragments from Ashurbanipal's library and in one fragment from the Egyptian archives from the early 14th century B.C. at Tell el-Amarna, the theme is man's loss of eternal life. Adapa, an ancient hero of Eridu, the southernmost of the cities of Mesopotamia, caught in a storm while out fishing for the temple of Ea, the god of the earth and waters, curses and cripples the South Wind, thereby incurring the wrath of Anu, the sky-god. Summoned to appear and answer before Anu, he is prompted by his patron-god Ea, who advises him that on his appearance he will be offered bread and water which are the bread and water of death ; these he must refuse. He is further advised how to placate the two divine ushers Tammuz and Gizzida.[1] In this he is so successful that they secure the favour of Anu, who offers Adapa the bread and water not of death but of life. Rigidly adhering to the advice of Ea, however, Adapa rejects the elements and so loses the opportunity of eternal life. It is hard not to see a certain cynicism on the part of the author, who makes man the victim of divine bungling.

The loss of eternal life is also the central theme of the greatest extant Mesopotamian myth. This is the epic of Gilgamesh, in

---

[1] cf. the angels with the flaming swords who guarded the garden of Eden (Gen. 3:24)

twelve tablets, totalling about one-third of the length of the Odyssey. The epic tells how the hero, the King of Uruk,[1] finds a match for his superabundant force and virility in the wild man Enkidu, possibly the type of the native Semite from the adjacent desert who, tamed by his contact first with a harlot from the town and then with civilisation, becomes the *fidus Achates* of the king in a number of heroic exploits.

The first of these is the conquest and slaughter of Huwawa,[2] the wild guardian of the cedar forests, which reflects the interest of the powers of treeless Mesopotamia in the famed forests of Lebanon and Amanus. The hero then excites the desire of Ishtar, the redoubtable goddess of love and war, but repulses her advances. Thereupon the goddess persuades the high-god Anu to send a pestilent monster, ' the Bull of Heaven ', to earth. Gilgamesh and Enkidu champion suffering mankind against this prodigy and actually slay it, to the great chagrin of the slighted goddess, who voices her resentment in a curse. Enkidu replies by tearing off the bull's hindleg and throwing it with insult in her face, truly a heroic gesture ! The gods go into council, however, and Enkidu is marked down as a victim of plague. He dies and is mourned by his comrade Gilgamesh, who, in his exuberant confidence and physical strength, is more than half incredulous of the fact of death until ' on the seventh day ' a worm crawls out of the nose of the dead man. Thus dramatically the fact of human weakness is borne in upon Gilgamesh, who is now obsessed with the desire to escape death as the ultimate limitation to human endeavour.

With this end in view the hero undertakes the formidable journey to ' the confluence of the two streams '[3] to consult with Ut-Napishtim, the primeval hero who had survived the Flood and had been invested with eternal life. Throughout the myth, of course, the philosopher speaks, but it is none the less an epic, with many miscellaneous elements from ancient Mesopotamian tradition worked in for diversion. Now comes what to most readers is the most interesting part of the text, the digression of the Flood.

The great gods determined to destroy the ancient city of Shuruppak by flood. Ea, however, secretly informed Ut-Napishtim and advised him to build a huge vessel into which he should take ' the seed of all living things '. The construction of

---

[1] Biblical Erech, modern Warka, some forty miles from Ur on the left bank of the Euphrates

[2] The Assyrian version gives the name Humbaba.

[3] i.e. the upper and the lower waters of Mesopotamian cosmology

the craft is then described. She was seven-decked, with floor-space of an acre, well caulked with bitumen, with which the land abounds. At length after ' seven days' ' work the vessel is launched. Ut-Napishtim then loads his possessions aboard, silver, gold, his family, his domestic animals, ' the beasts of the field, the wild creatures of the field '. He includes the craftsmen who made the vessel.

The deluge is graphically described. Indeed it is sufficiently violent to dismay the gods themselves, who ' cowered like dogs against the outer wall '. After the conventional ' seven days ' the storm abates ; Ut-Napishtim sees ' all men turned to clay '. A mountain-top, however, is visible, Mount Niṣir (' Salvation '), and here the vessel grounds. On ' the seventh day ' Ut-Napishtim releases a dove, which, finding no resting-place, returns. A swallow is released and similarly returns. Then a raven is sent out and, finding food, does not return. Then Ut-Napishtim lets out the inmates of the vessel and offers libation and sacrifice on the mountain, the gods crowding ' like flies about the sacrificer '. Nor is the rainbow motive lacking, for Ishtar lifts up her necklace, which is identified in Mesopotamian myth with the rainbow, and swears by it that as she will ever remember the ornament about her neck so she will never forget the days of the Deluge. The storm-god Enlil, however, realises when he sees the vessel that he has been cheated, and a turbulent scene ensues. He is eventually placated and so far relents as to bless Ut-Napishtim and his wife, conferring immortality upon them.

Ut-Napishtim endeavours to dissuade Gilgamesh from seeking physical life merely for its own sake. With all the ardour of youth, however, Gilgamesh refuses to abandon the quest and is accordingly advised by Ut-Napishtim to dive to the bottom of the sea and pluck the plant of immortality which grows there. He ties large stones to his feet and makes the plunge, emerging with the plant. As often in human experience, what is won with so much persistence and strenuous effort is lost in a moment of negligence. So as Gilgamesh sleeps the serpent steals from him the plant of immortality and nullifies all his high endeavour.

By its very nature comparative religion is interested in con-trasts as well as similarities, and often it is the former which are the more significant, as in the case of Babylonian and Hebrew traditions. This is notably the case in the Mesopotamian Flood narrative in the Gilgamesh epic, where the affinity in motives with the Hebrew Flood narratives serves to emphasise the difference in details and in the main purport of the Hebrew adaptation of the Mesopotamian prototype. In the latter the flood is an isolated episode without moral or historical context. The Hebrew narratives, on the other hand, subserve the double purpose of emphasising the moral government of the one living and true God and of delimiting mankind to the progenitor of peoples known to the Hebrews. Furthermore, the oracles on Shem, Ham, and Japheth (Gen. 9:25–7) make it quite plain that the interest is narrowing down from mankind to the immediate neighbours of Israel and eventually to the Semitic group and ultimately to the Hebrew kinship through Jacob. Quite obviously the Hebrew writers who adapted the Mesopotamian Flood-story are anticipating the eventual election of Israel and the covenant at Sinai. They are essentially theologians ; they use Babylonian mythology as historical sources are used in the Books of Samuel and Kings, namely as the basis of a theological interpretation of history, *eine Heilsgeschichte* (' a history of salvation ').

The Flood-story in Genesis is compounded of two parallel and often discrepant traditions belonging to the J (early monarchic) and P (Exilic) sources of the Pentateuch. The latter, though incorporating older material from Canaan, was compiled in Mesopotamia and so is more likely to include direct adaptations of Mesopotamian mythology. Mesopotamian traditions in J may have also come into Hebrew literature directly, since from the 15th century at least Mesopotamian cuneiform was the diplomatic medium between Palestinian rulers and the Egyptian court, and fragments of the Adapa myth among the Amarna texts indicate its use as a scribal exercise. Thus with the art of the scribe the content of Babylonian literature may have been disseminated in the West. Such tales as the Gilgamesh epic, in spite of its primarily speculative character, may have been the stock-in-trade of professional story-tellers, like the Arab *rāwi*, who used to recite the Arabian Nights until the gramophone and radio drove him from the coffee-halls of the East.

In the Adapa and Gilgamesh myths Mesopotamian philosophy is conscious of the age-long antithesis of human endeavour and the limitations of the flesh. Is this limitation to be a ban to enterprise ? In the bitterness of death Enkidu is tempted to say so, but the nobler sentiment finally prevails that

> ' 'Tis better to have loved and lost
> Than never to have loved at all.'

Adapa misses the opportunity of eternal life by over-astuteness ; Gilgamesh loses the hard-won plant of immortality while he sleeps. In both cases comedy is mixed with tragedy and man was even then recognised to be

> ' The glory, jest, and riddle of the world.'

In the great antithesis of human life the sages of ancient Mesopotamia were too wise to dogmatise. It is noteworthy that the antediluvian Ut-Napishtim has nothing to say in recommendation of eternal life, and the real sentiment of the philosopher seems to be expressed in the homely advice of the ale-wife whom Gilgamesh encounters on his adventures :

> Gilgamesh, whither rovest thou ?
> The life thou pursuest thou shalt not find.
> When the gods created mankind,
> Death for mankind they set aside,
> Life in their own hands retaining.
> Thou, Gilgamesh, let full be thy belly,
> Make thou merry by day and by night.
> Of each day make thou a feast of rejoicing,
> Day and night dance thou and play !
> Let thy garments be sparkling fresh,
> Thy head be washed ; bathe thou in water.
> Pay heed to the little one that holds on to thy hand,
> Let thy spouse delight in thy bosom !
> For this is the task of mankind.[1]

---

[1] E. A. Speiser, *Ancient Near Eastern Texts relating to the Old Testament* (ed. J. B. Pritchard) (1950), 90 (Gilgamesh Tablet x, col. iii)

III   Egypt : Land of Bondage and Land of Refuge

DISCOVERIES in Egypt are of less significance than those in Meso-potamia for the understanding of life and culture in ancient Israel, since in the period contemporary with the history of Israel the dominant element in Mesopotamia was of kindred Semitic stock. The Hebrews, however, knew Egypt in the days of the patriarchs, and from the collapse of Judah in 586 B.C. Egypt was the home of an influential Jewish community. At all times, moreover, Egypt was vitally interested in Palestine, and it is not by chance that almost as soon as a Hebrew state emerged the Pharaoh should have married one of his daughters to King Solomon (1 Kg. 9:16). In short Egypt claims our attention as part of the world of the Old Testament.

The great past of Egypt has always been more obvious than that of Mesopotamia. The pyramids of vast two-ton blocks of limestone, sphinxes, colossal statues, obelisks, and temples of hard granite have defied the hand of spoilers through the ages and have excited the wonder and curiosity of sages and travellers from the writer of the Book of Job (3:14) and Herodotus to the present day.

Systematic research on Egyptian antiquities began with the Eastern expedition of Napoleon in 1798, when savants and specialists in various sciences accompanied the general. As a result an archaeological survey of the land was made and a collection of antiquities assembled, which, by the hazard of war, found their way to the British Museum. These monuments and the reports of French scholars served to awaken interest in the ancient civilisation of Egypt. In the next phase of the explora-tion of ancient Egypt, French scholars were particularly active as directors of the antiquities service in Egypt. The most note-worthy were Champollion and Mariette, the latter being most vigilant and energetic in suppressing exploitation by the natives and in preserving the monuments under proper care in Egypt. His zeal for the museum in Cairo, however, led him often to separate monuments and lesser remains from their context so that, while they were safely preserved, their scientific value was seldom fully appreciated and would have been lost but for the inscriptions they often bore and the comparative work of later archaeologists.

The key to the secret of the hieroglyphic inscriptions had already been found in the celebrated Rosetta Stone, discovered fortuitously by one of Napoleon's officers in repairing the fortifications of Rosetta (Rashid) in the Delta. This stone, from the Ptolemaic period,[1] was inscribed in two languages and in three different scripts, the ancient hieroglyphics of the monuments, the later demotic, used chiefly in papyri, and Greek. The last was a ready clue to the solution of the problem of the native scripts, which is associated chiefly with the name of Champollion.

The Egyptians were not nearly so meticulous in their records as the Babylonians and Assyrians. Nevertheless it is possible to trace at least the outline of Egyptian history from the first half of the third millennium by means of various inscriptions from monuments. These were often the clue to tombs in the vicinity. Many of these had been rifled in antiquity, but inscriptions and often mural paintings were left untouched. These in themselves, apart from objects and pottery, so indispensible in other fields of archaeology, give a comprehensive picture of life in Egypt in various ages.

By grace of the Pharaoh nobles and high officials were buried with provisions for their continued existence similar to, but on a much less sumptuous scale than, the elaborate funerary preparations of the Pharaoh, such as is illustrated by the tomb of Tutankhamen. In these tombs, or ' houses of eternity ',[2] there are detailed pictures of life in ancient Egypt, since in the security of the Nile Valley men believed the after-life to be a replica of the here and now. The paintings and sculptures show how the nobles spent their less serious moments fowling and fishing from their reed-punts and enjoying informal garden-parties on the river-front. Other high officers record and sometimes depict, by permission of the Pharaoh, their public services. On the tomb of the noble Uni at Abydos[3] we read how he led a punitive expedition into Palestine against the Bedouin, who were harrying

---

[1] The inscription records a decree by the priests of Memphis in honour of the benefits of Ptolemy V (203–181 B.C.) to temples. The names of the king and his family supplied the clue to the meaning of the hieroglyphic and demotic signs.

[2] The Hebrew of man's ' long home ' (*beth 'ōlam*) in Ec. 12:5 is possibly a literal translation of this Egyptian expression.

[3] J. H. Breasted, *Ancient Records of Egypt* I (1906–7), §§ 490 ff.

mining operations in Sinai in the time of Pepi I (c.2600 B.C.), and proceeded by sea to the ' Land of the Gazelle-nose ', perhaps Carmel Head or some promontory farther north en route to Byblos, the timber port of the Lebanon.[1] Others describe how they led expeditions to Punt down the Red Sea or prospected in the desert for gems and precious metals. Others again in the strenuous days of the XVIIIth Dynasty describe the stirring exploits of the Pharaohs who expelled the Hyksos, or Asiatic, invaders from Egypt in the second quarter of the 16th century B.C. Ahmes the son of Ebana, called the Admiral, in his tomb-inscription at El-Kab describes the actual expulsion of the Hyksos by Ahmes I (1580–1557 B.C.) after a naval battle on a branch of the Nile and a siege at Sharuhen in southern Palestine [2] which lasted three years. The subsequent Asiatic campaigns are described similarly on the tomb of another Ahmes pen Nekhbet, also at El-Kab. The campaigns of the great Thothmes III, the conqueror of the Asiatics at the first battle of Megiddo (1479 B.C.) [3] are supplemented by the tomb-inscriptions of his officer Amen-em-het at Thebes,[4] while the inscriptions and sculptures from the tomb of the noble Rekhmare from the same period record the receipt of tribute from Keftiu (Biblical Caphtor, or Crete).[5] Paintings in the same tomb depict brick-making and building by Semites and Negroes under Egyptian taskmasters. These and other such records depicting the life in Egypt and Egyptian enterprises abroad indicate the foreign influences brought to bear on the native culture of Egypt, and suggest in turn the extent of the influence of Egypt on her neighbours. From the sculptures and inscriptions of Ramses III (1168–1137 B.C.), who halted the invasion of the Philistines and their kindred ' Sea-peoples ' on the Asian coast early in the 12th century B.C., we have a good representation of the various racial types with whom the Egyptians were brought into contact, the Hittites, Amorites, Bedouin, and the various races among the Aegean invaders of

---

[1] From here G. Contenau attests a hieroglyphic seal which he dates in the beginning of the Old Kingdom c.3000 B.C. (La Civilization Phénicienne (1949), 120–1, pl. 1). The copper axe-head of an Egyptian lumberman with an inscription of Cheops, the builder of the great pyramid at Gizeh, was found in 1911 near the mouth of the River Adonis (Nahr Ibrahim) near Beyrout (A. Rowe, A Catalogue of Egyptian Scarabs in the Palestine Archaeological Museum (1936), Addendum A, 283).

[2] Breasted, op. cit., II, §§ 6 ff. Sharuhen is identified by W. F. Albright with Tell el-Far'a, one of the three Egyptian fortresses on the Wadi Ghazzeh, c.14 miles south-east of its mouth (The Archaeology of Palestine (1949), 39).

[3] Breasted, op. cit., II, §§ 26 ff.   [4] ibid., II, §§ 406 ff.

[5] ibid., II, §§ 574 ff.

Palestine and the Delta.[1]   To this abundant evidence of the life
and external relations of Pharaonic Egypt the treasures of the
unplundered tomb of Tutankhamen come simply to corroborate
and illustrate that which is already known.

An even more intimate picture of Egyptian life is presented
in the numerous papyri, literary and non-literary, which have
been preserved in the dry soil of Egypt.   The older specimens,
from the third millennium B.C., such as the ' Dialogue of a Man
with his own Soul ',[2] illustrate thought in ancient Egypt concerning life and the hereafter, while the Teachings of Kagemni,[3]
Duauf,[4] and Anii, all of which antedate the first millennium B.C.,
indicate the contemporary scene from the standpoint of a successful official.   These and similar documents, which served as
exercises for prospective scribes, reveal many intimacies of life in
ancient Egypt.   The Teaching of Duauf depicts, not without
humour, the hard lot of the manual worker as an incentive to
the young scribe.   We see the smith at his forge, his hands callous
and rough as the skin of a crocodile ; we almost feel the body-
aches of the stone-hewer.   We accompany the barber from street
to street seeking customers ;   we shiver to think of the brick-
moulder, his shirt stiff and clammy from the mud of his calling.
The weary lot of the weaver is to sit in the house, more confined
than any woman, ' his thighs in his belly ', crouched before his
loom ;   the arrow-maker, on the other hand, must risk his ass,
and indeed his life, in his long, lonely journeys in the desert
seeking for flint.   The lot of the fisher is the worst of all ;   he
stinks of mud and dead fish and runs the continual risk of himself
furnishing a meal for the crocodiles.   A similar scribal exemplar
from the New Kingdom [5] warns the student against the distrac-
tions of the liquor and the ladies, *communia vitia* of students in all
ages !   Like the Teaching of Duauf too it depicts the distresses
of other callings as an incentive to success.   Here we have a vivid
picture of the husbandman's trials.   His growing crop is menaced
by worms, mice, locusts, sparrows, and the hippopotamus.
Thieves raid the grain on the threshing-floor ;   and finally the
fiscal official lands on the canal embankment to claim his toll,
with his ominous retinue of porters with their measuring-rods
and Negro police with palm-ribs.   The soldier fares no better.
Flogged by his officers, he is loaded on the march like a pack-

[1] From Medinat Habu (Breasted, op. cit., IV, §§ 62 ff.)
[2] A. Erman, *Egyptian Literature* (English translation, A. Blackman, 1927),
86 ff.   [3] ibid., 66 ff.   [4] ibid., 67 ff.   [5] Erman, op. cit., 188 ff.

Plate 3 Palestinian and Syrian towns captured by Sheshonk, the 'protector' of Jeroboam I, on the wall of the Temple of Amon at Karnak, ancient Thebes. Note the 'hieratic scaling' of the Pharaoh

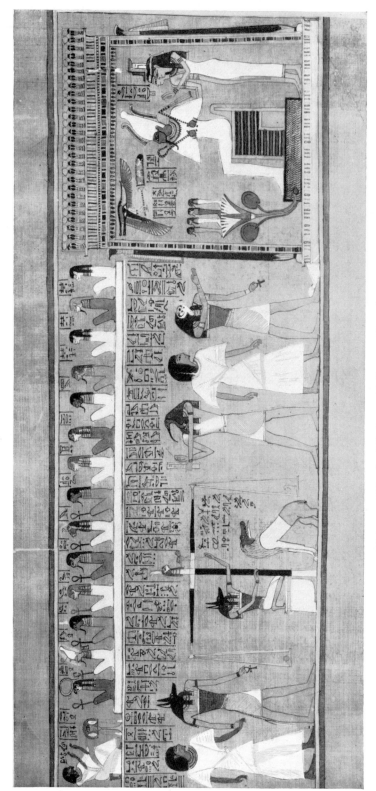

Plate 4 'The Last Judgment', from an Egyptian papyrus

horse, and knows the rigours of a campaign in Palestine and Syria with its grim preliminary of long desert marches. The charioteer, too, for all his brave show and nominal privileges,[1] finds that his fief is not sufficient to maintain his equipage, and he is forced to draw even on his mother's dowry. The good preceptor finishes this melancholy catalogue with a humorous description of the baker, who reaches so far into his conical clay oven that his boy must hold his feet with the perpetual hazard of his pitching head-foremost into the blaze.

Nor are we confined in these scribal exercises to life in Egypt. One Hori, who was attached to the cavalry in the time of Ramses II (1292–1225 B.C.), uses his reply to a rival scribe Amenemope as a scribal exercise [2] primarily for the purpose of familiarising his pupils with the technical terms of his calling. Here we have a sketch of the routes of Egyptian armies through Syria and Palestine and of the various strategic points there, Raf'a, Gaza, Jaffa, Shechem, Megiddo, Bethshan,[3] Tabor (Deper), Hazor commanding the fords of the upper Jordan, Achshaph and Akko in the coastal plain of Galilee, and other sites the identity of which is less certain. Hori depicts the muster of the Egyptian army with its various auxiliaries including the western Shardanu, who were associated with the Philistines and other ' Sea-peoples ' in invasions in the Delta and in Palestine, but were also employed as Egyptian mercenaries. The provisioning of the force on the desert frontier is also described. The scribe, as he goes about his duties, excites the wonder of the Bedouin, who characteristically prowl in the offing like jackals. ' Sôpher yôde' ', they remark in their native dialect, ' A knowing scribe ! ' The scribe, however, may bungle, and Hori depicts the troops hungry and clamorous for their morning rations at midday. Here and in other documents of the kind the hardships of a campaign in Syria are noted. The mountains present many difficulties to the Egyptians. Chariots had to be dismantled for transport ; the rocks cut the sandals to pieces ; the thorns tear the clothes to shreds, and the scrub harbours hardy guerillas. The Bedouin are constantly pilfering and night raids are made on the camp,

---

[1] This class of equestrian feudatories (mariannu), whose status depended directly on the king, was a feature of the Middle and Late Bronze Ages in Syria and Palestine, having been introduced by the Indo-Iranians c.1800 B.C. The information of the Egyptian text is supplemented by the administrative texts from Ras Shamra.   [2] Erman, op. cit., 227 ff.

[3] The text has Beth-sha-el, which, if accurate, would mean Bethel. The name, as the context suggests, may be an Egyptian rendering of Bethshean.

suggesting the exploit of Gideon and his servant in the camp of
the Midianites (Jg. 7:9 ff.). The Egyptian troops are also
familiar with local ladies of easy virtue, like Rahab of Jericho
(Jos. 2:1), though in these amorous adventures the warrior runs
the risk of being isolated and made to pay heavily for his escapade.
The sapient Hori obviously knew the expedient of seasoning his
lecture with the spice of humour, and he depicts the unfortunate
victim of all these mishaps having his equipage clouted up and
renewed to play the doughty warrior in Egypt when the campaign
is over.

From another letter used as a scribal exemplar [1] we have a
very realistic picture of an Egyptian officer weary with the
tedium of holding a desert post of the Sinai frontier. Under
barren palms, beset by a host of pariah dogs by day and mos-
quitoes by night, he gazes at the vast emptiness of desert and sky
like many a service-man since, casting wistful eyes northward to
Palestine and Syria, the land of adventure. To crown his misery
he has the company of a wretched scribe afflicted with ophthalmia
and grimacing with toothache.

Without such texts it is obvious that our knowledge of the
world of the Old Testament would be very much poorer. In
this wealth of evidence is there any particular trace of the Hebrew
patriarchs?

There is a certain panel from the tomb of Khnumhotep at
Beni Hassan from the time of Sesostris II (1906–1887 B.C.) which
is often cited as illustrating the coming of Abraham to Egypt.
Indeed the leading figure among the thirty-seven men, women,
and children represented has been taken as Abraham himself.
The inscription, however, gives the name of the chief as Abshai
and there is little if anything in the scene to suggest the Abraham
of Scripture apart from the fact that the party are Semites.
Abraham, however, was a pastoral nomad, whereas the Beni
Hassan group are warriors or possibly hunters armed with bow,
spear, and scimitar. The inscription tells us that they brought
the ancient equivalent of *kuhl*, the mineral eye-cosmetic commonly
used in ancient Egypt. This they procured probably from Sinai.
The party, with their arms and what is apparently bellows and
an anvil on the backs of asses, and a harp, strongly suggests metal-
workers and artisans. In fact all these details and the captive
ibex and gazelle give the group the exact appearance of Sulayb,
or desert tinkers, who are found throughout the Near East today

[1] Erman, op. cit., 203 ff.

as nomads, owning no camels but asses, and combining the craft
of the smith and the hunter, to say nothing of the mountebank.
To judge by the diversified fabrics of their robes the Beni Hassan
group were also weavers of skill and imagination. It is possible
that they may have been Kenites, or smiths, from the vicinity of
the Araba, the people with whom Moses was later associated
(Exod. 2:16–22 ; Jg. 1:16).

Certain texts from a little later give us an insight into the
condition of Palestine in the latter half of the 19th century B.C.
and indicate the political interest of Egypt in Asia. These are
the Execration Texts. The first of these documents (c.1850 B.C.),
written in hieratic script on potsherds, were bought by the
German scholar Schaefer at Luxor and deciphered by the great
Egyptologist Kurt Sethe of Berlin.[1] The latter were on clay
figurines in the guise of prisoners. They were found in a dealer's
shop in Paris and identified by Posener with similar inscribed
figurines which he had seen and appraised in the Museum in
Cairo on the eve of his own departure from Egypt in 1939.[2]
They were traced by means of photograph and register to the
later XIIth Dynasty level at Saqqara near Cairo, and proved,
like the 'Ächtungstexte' of Sethe, to be curses on various
enemies of the Pharaoh pronounced [3] with solemn magic rites.[4]
The significance of these texts is that they name chiefs and
localities in Palestine and southern Syria. The localities, including Jerusalem, Askalon, Jaffa, and Akko, can be for the most part
identified, and the names of the chiefs prove to be of the same
theophoric form and contain the same divine elements and
attributes as Amorite names of the First Amorite Dynasty of
Babylon, collected and published by E. Dhorme. We are thus
introduced to the pantheon of Palestine in that period and know
the relation in which men stood to their gods. The texts, moreover, throw a definite light on the political and social organisation
of the inhabitants of Palestine in the 19th century B.C. In the

---

[1] K. Sethe, 'Die Ächtung feindlicher Fürsten, Völker, und Dinge auf
alt-ägyptischen Tongefäßscherben des Mittleren Reiches', *Abhandlungen der
preussischen Akademie der Wissenschaft, Phil.-hist. Klasse* (1926)

[2] G. Posener, 'Nouveaux Textes hiératiques de Proscription', *Mélanges
syriens offerts à M. René Dussaud* (1939), 313–17

[3] ibid., *Princes et Pays d'Asie et de Nubie, textes hiératiques sur des figurines
d'envoûtement du Moyen Empire* (1940)

[4] This does not necessarily mean that the enemies were beyond reach of
the effective power of the Pharaoh. They may have been retained for their
economic value as prisoners of war, their individuality being destroyed by the
magic means suggested.

earlier texts, from Luxor, a noteworthy feature is that in any one locality there may be several chiefs. Jerusalem has two chiefs and Askalon three, surely an indication that tribal organisation prevailed,[1] a view strikingly corroborated by the discovery of Dr Kenyon and her colleagues that the invaders who destroyed the last Early Bronze Age settlement at Jericho used no fewer than five different modes of burial.[2] In our opinion these texts reflect the situation depicted in the Book of Genesis, where Abraham and Isaac, nomad sheikhs encamped by Gerar, are potential rivals of Abimelech, the ruler of the town. The texts seem to illustrate the condition of the land into which Abraham or his kindred may have come, possibly in the wake of Amorite penetration from the north and east, which reached the Delta at the end of the third millennium B.C. There is, however, nothing in Hebrew tradition, except the problematic Genesis 14, to suggest that Abraham or Isaac were connected with any large folk-movement.

The eclipse of Egyptian power in Asia, and indeed in the homeland, as the result of the Amorite invasions was succeeded by a period of revival and peaceful penetration of Syria and Palestine, possibly by the intermarriage of the Pharaohs of the XIIth Dynasty (2000–1788 B.C.) with native princesses,[3] a policy which we know definitely to have been pursued later in the XVIIIth Dynasty (1580–1350 B.C.). To judge from material and literary remains, particularly from Ras Shamra on the north Syrian coast, the influence of Egypt did not pervade the native Semitic culture very deeply. These relations, however, were rudely interrupted by the invasion of Egypt from Asia by the foreigners known to the Egyptians as the Hyksos.

Hyksos is really a corruption of two Egyptian words *hyk* and *khwsht* meaning ' rulers of foreign lands ', and thus gives no clue to the identity of the invaders. To judge by their material

---

[1] W. F. Albright, ' The Egyptian Empire in Asia in the 21st Century B.C.', *Journal of the Palestine Oriental Society* VIII (1928), 223–56. A similar view is held by A. Alt, who sees in the plurality of chiefs various waves of fresh invaders (' Herren und Herrensitze Palästinas im Anfang des zweiten Jahrtausends vor Chr.', *Zeitschrift des deutschen Palästina-Vereins* LXIV (1941), 38).

[2] K. M. Kenyon, *Digging Up Jericho* (1957), pp. 194–209

[3] These relations are suggested by royal sphinxes and votive inscriptions at Ras Shamra and at Qatna in the interior, fifteen miles north-east of Homs on the Orontes. The most conspicuous of the sphinxes were of queens of the Pharaohs (C. F. A. Schaeffer, *Ugaritica* I (1939), 20–2, pl. V ; R. du Mesnil de Buisson, ' Les Ruines d'El Mishrefeh au Nord-Est de l'Homs ', *Syria* VII (1926), 1).

remains and from the names of their rulers,[1] which occur on scarabs, various racial elements were united in the great enterprise against Egypt, including both Semites and non-Semites. The invasion of the Delta was probably the culmination of ethnic movements in Syria and Palestine of Amorites from the north Arabian steppes, of Hurrians from the Zagros and the highlands of Anatolia, and of Aryans from Iran, who introduced the horse and two-wheeled war-chariot to western Asia. From their base at Avaris, later Zoan or Pi-Ramesse (Ramses of Exod. 1:11), the Hyksos dominated Egypt and secured their lines of communication with Asia by means of a close series of strong fortresses rather reminiscent of the Crusaders' defensive system in Palestine or the network of police-posts in the latter period of the British mandate. Albright has shown that the architecture of the Palestinian towns of this period indicates a feudal system of administration, and the whole system, though not, we believe, the personnel, was taken over by the Pharaohs of the XVIIIth Dynasty when they reasserted their power in Palestine. This urban system, established along the main lines of communication through the coastal and central plains of Palestine, conditioned the particular development of that area, which was quite independent of development in the mountains.

It has been thought that this period of foreign domination of Egypt was the very time when men such as Joseph might rise to power there. On no reckoning, however, on the basis of Hebrew tradition can Joseph be brought into the Hyksos period. On the evidence of 1 Kings 6:1, which dates the Exodus 480 years before the foundation of the Temple, and the numerical statements of the length of the Sojourn in Egypt the descent of Jacob and his sons would be dated early in the 19th century B.C., and the tradition of Scripture is that Joseph was already there. Reckoning on the basis of tribal genealogies, which bring us as near to accuracy as we shall probably ever get in the patriarchal traditions of the Hebrews, we get a much reduced scale of dates which can be much more easily reconciled with such external evidence as we possess, both from Egyptian records and from excavations in Palestine, and on this reckoning the *floruit* of Joseph is long after the Hyksos period.

Here we may cite one of the papyri recently discovered in

---

[1] e.g. Jaqob-har and Anat-har. Josephus grossly exaggerates the association of the Semites with the Hyksos in his pro-Jewish reply to Apion (*Contra Apionem* I, § 73).

Brooklyn Museum, New York.[1] In this legal document, accurately dated between 1842 and 1742 B.C. a number of Asiatics with Semitic names are listed. These may have been prisoners of war or descendants of such, who may be mentioned in the Execration Texts, or they may, like Abraham (Gen. 12:10), have been seasonal immigrants from Palestine who had elected to stay in Egypt, or had been detained there, perhaps for debt or misconduct, real or alleged, like Joseph's brothers (Gen. 42:24 ; 44:14 ff.), or they may have been sold into slavery like Joseph. Semitic women are mentioned also, some of whom were married to Egyptians. This indicates the verisimilitude of the narratives of the patriarchs, which visualise such intermarriage in the traditions of Sarah and Rebekah.[2] In view of the story of Joseph in Egypt it is interesting to note that this document mentions persons with Semitic names who were chamberlains in Egyptian households. Though we cannot agree to date Joseph in the Hyksos period (1730–1580 B.C.), we admit that his case may well have been paralleled by some Semitic personality such as we have mentioned, or by someone who rose high in the service of the Hyksos rulers of Egypt.

In our opinion it is vain to expect particular evidence from archaeology for any particular Hebrew patriarch. It is but natural to see in the final form of the narratives in Genesis the fusion of various traditions of various elements of the early Hebrews. The Egyptian records suggest that the experiences recorded of Abraham, Isaac, Jacob, and his sons were historically possible, but were not confined to one age or limited to certain individuals. On the question of the Exodus too our conclusion will be that there were many descents of Semites to Egypt and also many cases of exodus.

The power of Egypt under native rulers revived in the 16th century B.C. and the Hyksos were expelled. Eventually Thothmes I (1531–1501 B.C.) cleared Palestine and reached ' the land of the inverted river ', i.e. the Euphrates. The Hyksos invasion, however, had brought many foreign elements to Palestine, among others the Hurrians, probably the Horites of Scripture. These various Asiatic peoples gathered to challenge the power of Egypt, rallying on Megiddo, the key to one of the main passes through the Carmel range from the coastal plain to

[1] G. Posener, ' Les Asiatiques en Egypte sous le XIIᵉ et XIIIᵉ Dynasties ', *Syria* xxxiv (1957), 145–63
[2] We should not, however, particularise here in view of Sarah's advanced age.

the Plain of Esdraelon. In 1479 B.C. Thothmes III (1501–1447 B.C.) moved swiftly to the attack. He struck at the Asiatic confederacy by a sudden advance through the pass and dealt a crippling blow. He did not, however, succeed in reducing the fortress until some months later, after which he swept on to the Euphrates. Thothmes III has left a very full account of these events on the wall of the temple of Amon at Karnak (Thebes), this being one of the most valuable records of the inhabited localities in Palestine in this period. In his enumeration of the booty taken at Megiddo he gives a picture of material wealth and culture which quite amazes us. Costly dishes of silver and gold are noted as local products. On this, however, we may be justly sceptical. Such elegant and costly wares in pottery, ivory, and precious metals were certainly known in the land, as the excavations of Ras Shamra and, to a less extent, Megiddo and Bethshan have shown. This, however, was just the period when there were close cultural and economic contacts with Cyprus and the Aegean,[1] so that the precious vessels recorded by Thothmes may well have been imports from the West. Chairs and carved objects in ivory are recorded, with ebony and precious woods overlaid with silver and gold. In the same list we read of an elaborate statue of one of the most notable chiefs in the coalition defeated by Thothmes, and this indicates a high degree of material culture and a political organisation which gave security for art to flourish. There is likewise mention of gold and silver in rings,[2] which suggests intense commercial activity, the metal rings anticipating stamped coinage, which appears in Palestine a millennium later under the Persians. The land thus bears a far different aspect from that in which, according to the patriarchal narratives the Hebrew fathers ranged so freely with their flocks.

Once victor, Thothmes III never relaxed his hold on Palestine, which now appears in Egyptian records as Ḥaru, or the Hurrian land. He records regular expeditions through Palestine, which was occupied by garrisons posted at strategic points throughout the land, a feature of Egyptian control of Palestine for the

---

[1] This is well illustrated by the permanent settlement of Aegean traders at Minet el-Beida, the seaward quarter of Ras Shamra. A similar settlement of this period, which was probably a trading ' factory ', was Tell Abu Hawam at the mouth of the Kishon some fifteen miles from Megiddo.

[2] The saga of King Keret in the Ras Shamra literature compares tears falling to shekel-pieces, probably rings of regular weight being told off on a stick.

next two centuries.[1] Thothmes seems also to have anticipated the Roman expedient of training the sons of provincial notables at the imperial court. Certain features of the saga of Joseph or even of Moses may preserve reminiscences of this practice.

A certain development of the policy of Egypt in Asia is noted as the power of the XVIIIth Dynasty was established, and Amenhotep II (1448–1420 B.C.) and Amenhotep III (1411–1375 B.C.), the 'Grand Monarque' of the dynasty, intermarried with Asiatic princesses and favoured Syrian settlement in Egypt.[2] Akhnaten (1375–1358 B.C.), the bold reformer who dared to oppose the age-long authority of the priesthood of Amon at Thebes in favour of solar monotheism and a more liberal, universal faith, apparently continued this policy of conciliation in Asia. From the Amarna Tablets, the correspondence of the Egyptian 'Foreign Office' in the time of Amenhotep III and Akhnaten, we see that the connection between Egypt and Palestine was a close one. The power of Egypt in Asia was not so strong as it had been, but still Syrian chiefs might visit the court of Egypt by choice or compulsion.[3] Again, Horemheb (1350–1315 B.C.) records in one of his inscriptions that he admitted Semitic refugees into Egypt in time of famine ' after the manner of their fathers' fathers from the beginning '. This reference to repeated coming and going on the part of Semites suggests that in Hebrew history we may well expect to find in the references to the sojourns in Egypt and in the Exodus the conflation of traditions of different ages. Finally in this connection we should cite the Harris Papyrus from the time of the Pharaoh Siptah (1215–1209 B.C.), which mentions a Syrian administrator in Egypt, one Arisu,[4] an exact parallel to the case of Joseph, on the basis of which the Dutch scholar B. D. Eerdmans ventured to suggest 1130 B.C. as the date of the Exodus.[5]

The picture of pre-Israelite Palestine is completed by inscrip-

---

[1] The relic of such garrisons are four temples at Bethshan dedicated to local deities indeed, such as Mekal, the god of pestilence, and Anath, the fertility-goddess, but by Egyptians, as the sculptures and hieroglyphic inscriptions show. The four temples of Bethshan are now dated almost a century later than they were dated by the excavator (A. Rowe, *The Four Canaanite Temples of Bethshan* (1940)). They range from the 14th to the 12th century B.C.
[2] Circumstances again which might be reflected in the Joseph or Moses tradition
[3] A notable example is that of the Syrian chief Aziru, who was obliged to obey such a summons to Egypt (Knudtzon, *Die El Amarna Tafeln* (1915), 169 etc.).   [4] J. H. Breasted, *History of Egypt* (1906), 474
[5] B. D. Eerdmans, *Alttestamentliche Studien* II (1908), 67–76

tions from the XIXth Dynasty (1350–1205 B.C.). Seti I (1313–
1292 B.C.) in a stele which was found at Bethshan,[1] the great
fortress guarding the east end of the Plain of Esdraelon, mentions
the 'Apiriw. They were active in the vicinity of Bethshan,[2] but
whether as allies or as enemies it is hard to determine. These
were probably the same as the Ḥabiru of the Amarna Tablets, a
class of homeless, restless people rather than a race, of whom the
Hebrew fathers were but one element. With this reservation, it
is possible that the Apiriw of Seti's Bethshan inscription were
those Israelites who were eventually to settle in Galilee, specifically Naphtali. On the other hand the corridor of Esdraelon
was a common way of access to raiders from the desert, such as
the Midianites in the time of Gideon, who would also be classi-
fied by the Egyptians as Apiriw. Here again it is not permitted
to particularise.

From the reign of Ramses II (1292–1225 B.C.) an important
inscription has survived, unique among Egyptian historical
inscriptions for its details.[3] This is an account of a battle at
Kadesh on the Orontes against the Hittites and their allies, when
Ramses succeeded in retrieving a situation which should have
been disastrous. The battle was drawn and a *modus vivendi*
was reached with mutual recognition of the respective spheres of
Egyptian and Hittite influence. In spite of all that has been
supposed concerning a Hittite occupation of Palestine, there is
no actual evidence of the Hittites in force any farther south than
Kadesh on the Orontes. A cache of Hittite arms from about this
time was found under the altar of a temple at Bethshan (A. Rowe,
The Topography and History of Bethshan (1930), pl. xxxv, figs. 2
and 3), and taken as evidence of Hittites in Palestine. If the
Hittite occupation were considerable it is remarkable that there
should be so little material evidence of them. The Hittite arms
at Bethshan may have belonged to Egyptian mercenaries or may
have been a votive offering of the Egyptians.

Israel is mentioned by name for the first time in history on a
stele of Merneptah[4] in 1223 B.C., who mentions also the Hittites
and the ' Sea-peoples '. Thus the Pharaoh commemorates the
pax Aegyptica :

[1] A. Rowe, *The Topography and History of Bethshan* (1930), 29 ff.
[2] Rowe read the location as ' the mountain of Jordan ' and referred it to
Transjordan. B. Grdseloff read the name not ' Jordan ' but ' Yarmuth ',
which he located north of Bethshan.
[3] J. H. Breasted, *Ancient Records of Egypt* III, §§ 288–327
[4] Breasted, op. cit., III, § 602

Libya is laid waste,
Heta [1] is at peace ;
Plundered is Canaan with every evil ;
Carried off is Askalon,
Seized upon is Gezer,
Yenoam is made a thing not existing,
Israel is desolated,
His seed is no more ;
Ḥaru [2] is become a widow for Egypt.
All lands are united in peace,
Every adversary is fettered.

This has been taken as evidence that Israel was already established in Palestine and that the Exodus had been effected long before the time of Merneptah. The matter, however, is by no means so simple as that, and ' Israel ' in the inscription begs the question of how many of the Hebrew kindred and confederacy were so denoted at the time of the inscription, and how many of the Hebrews were actually in Egypt, questions which we shall discuss later.

Finally in the period between the Exodus and the establishment of the Hebrew monarchy there is the celebrated inscription of Ramses III (1168–1137 B.C.) describing the invasion of the ' Sea-peoples ',[3] including the Philistines, who were halted as they advanced southwards in a great folk-movement by sea and land along the Syrian coast. After a battle, which the details of the inscription suggest took place in Syria rather than in Palestine,[4] the invaders were allowed to occupy the coastal plain of Palestine under the suzerainty of Egypt, or, at least, so Ramses claims, stating, ' I settled them in strongholds bound in my name.'

For all her proximity to Palestine and her keen interest in the land as a sphere of political influence, Egypt had little effect on the cultural life of the natives, apart from the influence in official circles at important coastal cities such as Ras Shamra and Byblos in Syria and in urban centres along the arterial highways, such as Gaza, Bethshan, and Megiddo, where Egyptian influence is apparent in sculpture and relief-work in gold and ivory. The

---

[1] i.e. the Hittites   [2] i.e. Palestine   [3] Breasted, op. cit., IV, §§ 62 ff.
[4] The reference (ibid., § 65) to the blocking of harbour mouths by the Egyptians suggests the Syrian rather than the Palestinian coast, where such an operation would be impracticable south of Akko since there are no natural harbours in Palestine but only open roadsteads.

warlike Pharaohs of the XVIIIth and XIXth Dynasties did not
thoroughly occupy the land, but ruled it, as the Amarna Tablets
show, through native chiefs or mercenary commandants and a
few Egyptian commissioners with very small garrisons, mere
platoons, posted at strategic points throughout the country. The
Egyptians were a pleasure-loving, peaceful people ; their home
was in the secluded garden-land of the Nile Valley, and the
garrison-duty fell more and more to the share of mercenaries
from the Sudan, from Libya, and latterly from among the sea-
rovers such as the Shardanu and possibly also the Philistines.
Such Egyptian temples as have been found at Bethshan and
Lachish are small, and are little more than garrison-chapels, and
were in any case dedicated to local deities. The main influence
which that military minority mediated from Egypt was apparently the veneration of minor deities such as Bes, Ptah-Soker,
Isis with Horus, and Bast, the cat-deity, which, with sundry
figurines of apes, crocodiles, and the jackal-headed Anubis, and
the eye of Horus, were found in the form of amulets as late as
the 7th century at Lachish.[1] This, however, in the general
development of culture in Palestine is negligible. The invective
of the prophets of the Old Testament, though directed
against the pro-Egyptian politics of certain of the kings of
Israel and Judah, is significantly confined to the apostasy
of their people not to the idolatry of Egypt, but to the fertility-
cult of the native Canaanite Baal and the goddesses Astarte and
Asherah.

Nevertheless, though ' the manner of the gods of the land '
meant more to the peasantry of Palestine than the religion and
culture of Egypt, there was a more mature class acquainted with,
and more appreciative of, the thousand-year-old culture of Egypt.
Such were to be found in the courtly circles in Jerusalem certainly
from the time of Solomon, who numbered a lady of Pharaoh's
family in his harem. In the rather extravagant language in
which the king is addressed in the Psalms [2] we may have a trace
of the influence of Egypt where the Pharaoh was regarded as the
god incarnate.

Actually in the only explicit description of the accession of a
king to the throne of David, that of Joash (2 Kg. 11), there is

---

[1] J. L. Starkey, ' Tell Duweir ', *Palestine Exploration Fund Quarterly Statement* (1933), 195 ; O. Tufnell, *Lachish* III (1953), pls. 34–6

[2] e.g. Ps. 45:6 (Hebrew text v. 7), where the king is apparently addressed
as ' god ' ; cf. Lam. 4:20, where the king is ' the breath of our nostrils '.

sufficient, taken in conjunction with phrases in the royal psalms, to suggest that the influence of Egypt was felt in the ideology of kingship in Israel, at least as far as courtly convention was concerned. This has been the subject of a special study by G. von Rad,[1] who has made felicitous citations from Egyptian coronation texts. From 2 Kings 11 we learn that the king manifested himself to his people at his accession in a certain place in the sanctuary, either by a certain pillar or, as the variant text in Chronicles suggests, a special platform or podium. This is attested in Egypt too in the XVIIIth Dynasty. On this occasion the officiating priest handed to the king the crown (*nēzer*) and what is known as ' the testimony ' (*ʿēdūth*). The content of the latter is indicated by the association of the crown (*nēzer*) with ' the covenant ' (*bᵉrīth*) in Psalm 132:12, by which it seems that ' the testimony ' (*ʿēdūth*) was a copy of the covenant, probably that of Yahweh with the Davidic House (2 Sam. 7:12 ff.), though possibly also an epitome of the moral law. Another word which is used with ' covenant ' (*bᵉrīth*) in this connection is ' legitimation ' (*ḥōq*) in Psalm 105:10. The latter is found again in Psalm 2:7, where it is amplified by a citation of the assurance of divine adoption in connection with the covenant with the House of David. Now in Egyptian royal inscriptions cited by von Rad it is apparent that with the diadem the Pharaoh received a protocol, purporting to be divinely written. The significance of this is plain from an inscription of the Queen Hatshepsut which refers to the writing of her protocol formally declaring that she is the daughter of the god and that he is her father, words which recall the adoption formula of Psalm 2:7, ' Thou art my son ; this day have I begotten thee '. The Egyptian analogy too fairly entitles us to infer that the protocol legitimising the ruler contained a new honorific name which was tantamount to a divine oracle investing him with new power and assuring him of divine support. The assumption of throne-names by the kings of Judah is appreciated by A. M. Honeyman,[2] and this is surely the significance of the acclamation of the young prince of the Davidic House in Isaiah 9:6, ' Wonderful Counsellor is God the Mighty, Covenanted Father, Prince of Peace '.

With the new institution of the monarchy there came into

[1] G. von Rad, ' Die judäische Königsritual ', *Theologische Literaturzeitung* LXXII (1947), cols. 211–16

[2] A. M. Honeyman, ' The Evidence for Regnal Names among the Hebrews ', *Journal of Biblical Literature* LXVII (1948), pp. 13 ff.

being a new class of officials, a royal bureaucracy apparently modelled to a large extent on the Egyptian system. The scribe now became very important in administration. In Egypt we know a great deal about the status and training of scribes, not the least part of which consisted of a thorough training not only in the technique of writing but also in administration and conduct, which ranged from the details of provisioning an army to empiric moral philosophy. The latter might vary from quite lofty ethics to the most blatantly utilitarian worldly wisdom. Here there is an affinity in literary type as well as in content with the Book of Proverbs, much of which probably took its origin for this purpose of training young scribes in Jerusalem. This we believe to be the substance of the tradition which ascribes the book to Solomon, though, to be sure, only two of the seven collections of proverbs in the book (1:1–9:8 ; 10:1–22:16) are actually ascribed to him, and of these the first section is certainly very much later than Solomon. We are fortunate in the possession of exemplars and copies used by young Egyptian scribes. Here we find that the concern of the teacher was not only with subject-matter, but, at a certain stage, rather more with vocabulary. So we have texts so constructed as to include long lists of technical terms. If we suppose the education of young administrators in Jerusalem to have been based on the Egyptian model this may well be the origin of the tradition which says of Solomon ' he spake of trees from the cedar which is in Lebanon even unto the hyssop that springeth out of the wall ; he spake also of beasts, and of fowls, and of creeping things, and of fishes ' (1 Kg. 4:33). Apart from this, which is a matter of plausible speculation, there is no denying that the prototype of the ' thirty items [1] for counsel and knowledge ' of Proverbs 22:20 (Prov. 20:17–24:22) is the Egyptian Teaching of Amenenope,[2] a document which is to be dated probably c.1000 B.C.

Thus in the Psalms and Wisdom literature in the Old Testament the influence of Egyptian culture is most direct. The story of Joseph's temptation in the house of Potiphar, however, has a direct prototype in the Egyptian Tale of the Two Brothers,[3] which indicates that Egyptian influence extended to the narra-

---

[1] According to a different vocalisation of the Hebrew consonantal text, as suspected by the Hebrew scribes themselves
[2] On a papyrus in the British Museum. The most recent translation is by J. A. Wilson (Pritchard, *Ancient Near Eastern Texts relating to the Old Testament* (1950), 421–5)
[3] op. cit., 23–5, from a papyrus of the late 13th century B.C.

tives also, and the love-songs published by Erman [1] certainly suggest by form and imagery the Song of Solomon. In addition to the borrowed motive in the Joseph-saga which we have just mentioned, a passage in the Complaint of the Eloquent Peasant, where, in spite of actual good intent, the high steward Rensi puts the poor man to painful trials at court, suggests Joseph's agonising trial of his brothers in similar circumstances. In the Exodus narratives too there are features which seem to be suggested to the authors by passages in Egyptian literature. In a certain papyrus of the Old Kingdom containing the disasters suffered by Egypt at the end of the third millennium B.C., when the Amorites broke into the Delta,[2] the prophet Ipuwer complains that the river is blood.[3] A similar description by Nefer-rohu [4] declares that ' the sun is veiled and will not shine that men may see '. Statements like this, originally figurative, may be used in the saga of the Exodus in the description of the plagues of Egypt. All the plagues of Egypt, it is true, cannot be thus explained, but the coincidence of such themes in Egyptian literature and Hebrew tradition suggests that the purely miraculous element in the Exodus was perhaps much less than superficially appears. From the papyrus of Ipuwer which we have just cited, for example, it is stated that ' gold and lapis-lazuli, silver and turquoise, cornelian and bronze are hung about the necks of slave-girls ', [5] which suggests the spoiling of the Egyptian ladies by the Hebrew women in the Exodus narrative (Exod. 20:35–6). So superfluous is this incident to the narrative, indeed, and so improbable that it can hardly be other than such borrowing.

In admitting the affinities of Hebrew and Egyptian literature in form and content, we must insist that in Proverbs, where those affinities are strongest, the stamp of Hebrew genius is beyond doubt.[6] Here, as everywhere in the Old Testament, it is most illuminating to study a passage from its origins, but an Old Testament book cannot be properly assessed by the appraisal of the nature of its component parts studied in isolation and only with reference to its origins in the general cultural complex of the ancient Near East. A book of the Old Testament must rather

---

[1] A. Erman, op. cit., 243–51   [2] ibid., 92–108
[3] ibid., 95   [4] ibid., 110 ff.   [5] ibid., 96
[6] In his study of the Wisdom of Amenemope and the parallels in Prov. 20:17–29:22 and elsewhere in the Old Testament (*Zeitschrift für die Alttestamentliche Wissenschaft*, Neue Folge I–II (1924–5), 272–96) H. Gressmann concludes that the relative length of the Egyptian and the Hebrew collections indicate that Israel borrowed from Egypt, but borrowed only what suited her ethos and adapted even that.

be assessed by the relevance which by the intention of the editors the whole book had to the religion of Israel.

It would be strange, however, if after two thousand years of political and cultural development the sages of Egypt had failed to win certain insights in the realm of the spirit to which the comparatively primitive Hebrews attained. On the contrary, in one most important respect, in the confident expectation of an afterlife, Egyptian faith ranged far beyond the hope of Israel in pre-Exilic times. In the late period of the Exile, the earliest date to which the Book of Job is assigned by critical scholarship, a life beyond the grave where the innocent sufferer might expect vindication is a wistful hope which, had it been common belief, would have rendered the agonised questionings of the Book of Job meaningless. In Egypt, however, men had lived and died for more than a thousand years in the hope of personal survival and divine judgment. The office of the Pharaoh and even his person were held as divine, and the reigning Pharaoh as the living Horus and the incarnation of the Sun-god Ra, became at his death the beneficent god Osiris. It was but natural for men to transfer the activity of Osiris in the yearly revival of nature to the needs of society and of the individual for a comparable renewal. What was obviously granted to the lower forms of life must surely not be denied to the highest order of creation. Hence the ancient Egyptian hoped that like the Pharaoh he might appropriate the experience of the dying and rising god Osiris. To be sure, commoners, like the ancient Pharaohs in the pyramids, took precautions to be buried with an abundant stock of magic spells known in the latter half of the second millennium B.C. as the Theban Book of the Dead, which is a farrago of formulae from the many local cults in the composite religion and culture of Egypt. Nevertheless this hope was soberly qualified by ethical considerations. Osiris was regarded as the judge in the hereafter, before whom all men had to appear. The heart of the deceased was weighed against the feather of Mat, the divine principle of what was right and true, by the jackal-headed deity Anubis, the physician of the dead, and the measure is recorded by the ibis-headed Thoth, the scribe of the gods, while by the side of the scales the monstrous ' devourer of the dead ' watched Thoth's record in order to destroy the delinquent.[1] The mythological crudities of this conception should not blind us to the salutary

[1] See Plate 4, from a papyrus of the Theban Book of the Dead from the XVIIIth Dynasty

faith in a conditional immortality, which must have been the nerve of a sound ethic in ancient Egypt.[1] We marvel the more that, with the opportunity of familiarity with this conception, Israel never seriously reckoned with judgment in the afterlife and personal survival until so very late, in the Persian period after the Exile.

[1] The relevant text from the Book of the Dead consists of a denial of forty-two sins before judges. These sins include stealing, hypocrisy, lying, blaspheming, conspiracy, defiling the river, laziness, cruelty, land-grabbing. adultery, murder, false-dealing. Virtues claimed are ritual devotion, piety to the dead, giving bread to the hungry, water to the thirsty, and clothing to the naked. The negative confession is reminiscent of Hebrew and Mesopotamian Penitential Psalms and of the prohibitions of the Decalogue.

IV   The People of the Land

ONE feature which strikes the reader of the narrative of the Hebrew conquest is the apparent diversity of races in Palestine. No fewer than seven peoples are said to have been dispossessed, 'the Canaanites, the Hittites, the Hivites, the Perizzites, the Girgashites, the Amorites and the Jebusites'.   In such a widely diversified land as Palestine, where subtropical conditions vary with mountain and steppe in a comparatively limited space, the apparent diversity of peoples may well be thought to be due to ecology rather than to race, or may be due to the fact that the Hebrews settled the land piecemeal and at various times and were not all familiar with the same opponents.   Yet, in view of the situation of Palestine between Asia and Africa, it is natural to expect a mixture of races, and this assumption is confirmed by the history of the land as known from the Egyptian records of pre-Israelite times and by the material evidence of archaeology.

The first definite clue to the ethnology of the Levant is the nomenclature of chiefs of Palestine and southern Syria in the Execration Texts from Luxor and Saqqara.   The names, being theophoric, consisting of a divine name and a predicate, which is a noun, adjective, or verb, may be certainly identified according to their linguistic affinity, and are without exception Semitic. More precisely the deities and their attributes are identical with elements in theophoric names in documents of the First Amorite Dynasty of Babylon (1826–1526 B.C.).   Here then, at least on the horizon of the age of the Hebrew patriarchs, the strong points in Palestine were in the hands of the virile Amorites.   On the evidence of the later Saqqara Texts, as compared with the Luxor Texts, they were able to consolidate their power within half a century, and possibly after another century combined with non-Semitic elements from the north, employing the new tactical armament, the horse and two-wheeled chariot, to effect the conquest of Egypt.

The next definite information on the population of Palestine is in the Amarna Tablets, the correspondence of the native chiefs and Egyptian deputies in Palestine and Syria with the suzerain power in the reigns of Amenhotep III (1411–1375 B.C.) and his son the 'heretic' Akhnaten (1375–1358 B.C.) found at Tell el-Amarna, Akhnaten's capital.   On the criterion of nomenclature the situation is quite different from that in the Execration Texts and a diversity of races is indicated, a situation which is confirmed by contemporary documents from Ras Shamra in Syria and from Taanach and Shechem in Palestine.   The Amorites are represented by Mut-Ba'lu and Milkilu of Aijalon, Shammu-Adda of Shamḫuna and Yabni-ilu of Lachish, whose names correspond in type to those of the Execration Texts and of Babylonian documents of the Amorite period.   Just as strongly represented is a non-Semitic strain, which may be, again on the basis of proper names, associated with the region of upper Mesopotamia occupied at this time by the kingdom of Mitanni. Such names as Biridiya, Widia, Tadua, Shuwardata, and Yashdata find parallels in form with names from the north-east. The chief who holds Jerusalem for the Pharaoh is named Abdi-Ḫepa, the servant or devotee of Ḫepa, a goddess venerated in the kingdom of Mitanni.[1]   Into this non-Semitic category from the north-east we should probably place the 'Hittites', Hivites, Perizzites,[2] Girgashites,[3] and possibly the Jebusites,[4] who occupied Jerusalem until the time of David.

Between the time of the Execration Texts and the Amarna Tablets the Egyptian power in Asia and even in Egypt was eclipsed by the Hyksos (c.1730–1580 B.C.), and it seems natural to suppose that this invasion introduced the above-mentioned non-Semitic elements to Palestine.   There is, however, no conclusive evidence of the racial identity of the Hyksos.   Their introduction of the horse and light war-chariot to Egypt suggests Aryan affinities.   Certain of their kings, however, had Semitic names.   Thus it may be said that the racial situation in Palestine was complicated after the Hyksos invasion, but it is not easy to particularise upon the racial elements introduced at the time of the conquest.   It has been found, for instance, that among cylinder-seals found at various archaeological stations in Palestine

---

[1] The goddess is named in the theophoric names Tadu-Ḫepa and Gilu-Ḫepa, Mitannian princesses married into the royal house of Egypt and named in the Amarna Tablets.

[2] In the Amarna Tablets a delegate of the king of the Hurrian-Aryan kingdom of Mitanni is named Perizzi (Knudtzon, op. cit., 1, 27).   The termination of the name is typically Hurrian.

[3] The sibilant termination is typically Hurrian.

[4] These may, on the other hand, be a later influx of people akin to the Philistines, perhaps mercenary troops.   Typical Philistine pottery, at any rate, is found at Jerusalem.

by far the largest number are Mitannian,[1] of a type which is common in the land of their origin in upper Mesopotamia no earlier than 1600 B.C.[2] The bearers, however, may have been officers in the Egyptian service in Palestine after the expulsion of the Hyksos in 1580 B.C., and may even have been refugees from their homeland after it was divided and made a vassal state of the Hittites under the aggressive Shubbiluliuma in the 14th century B.C. From the Amarna Tablets it is apparent that Egypt maintained control in Palestine by means of feudal barons, who held strongholds which had been fortified in the time of the Hyksos domination. Some of these officers were Aryan, others were Hurrian, and in certain cases native Semites were employed, their ancestral authority being recognised by the suzerain power. Many of these cities, with their long military tradition, long defied the Hebrew invaders, and it is probable that the Philistines and their kindred peoples later occupied the same fiefs, either on their own initiative or by the authority of Ramses III.

The Hurrians, first known through their peculiar names in cuneiform texts from Mesopotamia, where they were associated with the state of Mitanni, where an Aryan aristocracy ruled a Hurrian subject people from the 18th century to the 14th century B.C., next emerged in documents from the Hittite capital, Boghazköi, as a definite ethnic element in the Near East from the vicinity of Lake Van to Syria. Texts from Kirkuk and Nuzu, about a hundred miles north of Baghdad, enable Hurrian names in other texts to be more precisely determined. Hurrians are thus indicated in Palestine in the Amarna Texts and others from the same period from Taanach and Shechem. They are found again at Ras Shamra, where by the 15th century B.C. they were apparently an influential class and the power behind the throne. Certain of the Amarna Tablets from Qatna and Tunip in central Syria are further evidence of the distribution of the Hurrians. These may be the Biblical Horites, and it was possibly after them that the Egyptians named Palestine Ḫaru, a term which is not found before the Hyksos invasion. It should be noted that in the account of the population of Palestine before the Hebrew settlement the Greek versions read Hurrite for ' Hivite '.

There is no reliable record of the Hittites of Anatolia ever extending their influence as far south as Palestine. Even at the zenith of their power in the days of the great Shubbiluliuma

[1] B. Parker, ' Cylinder Seals from Palestine ', *Iraq* XI (1949), 1-42
[2] E. A. Speiser, *Mesopotamian Origins* (1930), 132 ff.

(*fl.*1370 B.C.) the Hittites did not advance beyond southern Syria, as the Amarna Tablets indicate. Thus the term ' Hittite ' in the Old Testament is probably applied loosely to denote a race from the north beyond the sphere of Amorite occupation in central Syria. The ' kings of the Hittites ' of 1 Kings 10:29 refers to the peoples settled in the land-bridge between Mesopotamia and Syria, who were loosely federated with the Hittites of Anatolia at the height of their power, were perhaps related to them in the remote past, and shared with them certain fundamental elements of culture. In the 10th century B.C., to which this text refers, it is possible that after the destruction of the Hittite Empire in Anatolia Hittite nobles and feudatories sought refuge in Syria, or asserted their independence in Hittite fiefs there, which, even after the settlement of Aramaeans in the Early Iron Age, became small states under Hittite rulers. The symbiosis of Hittite and Semite in north Syria is demonstrated by the number of Hittite hieroglyphic inscriptions found in the area. These, however, are so far an unsolved problem, to which, however, the bilingual inscription of Azitawwad, King of the Danuni, from Kara Tepe, north of the Plain of Adana, promises to provide the key. The inscription is in the Phoenician alphabetic script (linear) and language and in Hittite hieroglyphic. The name of the king is Hittite but the gods mentioned are the familiar Semitic deities—Baal of the Heavens ; El, Creator of the Earth ; the Eternal Sun ; and Reshef.[1] The term ' Hittite ' in the Old Testament seems, generally, a geographic rather than an ethnic one, in which sense it was used by the Assyrians in the 8th century B.C. to denote Syria and Palestine without any ethnic connotation. In so far as there may be any ethnic significance in the Old Testament usage of ' Hittite ', it may refer to the non-Semitic Hurrian element in Palestine familiar to us from the Amarna Tablets. They are found at Hebron, where Abraham bought the cave of Machpelah from Ephron the Hittite (Gen. 23), and Esau is said to have married at least one of ' the daughters of Heth ' (Gen. 36:2). The names of various chiefs in Jerusalem suggest that the ' Hittites ' of the Old Testament were really Hurrians. The chief in the Amarna Tablets is Abdi-Ḥepa, the worshipper of the Hurrian goddess Ḥepa. Araunah, the Jebusite from whom David bought the threshing-floor as the site of the

[1] The most accessible studies of this very important text are those of A. M. Honeyman, *Palestine Exploration Quarterly* (1949), 21–39 ; R. T. O'Callaghan, *Orientalia* XVIII (1949), 72–120 ; C. H. Gordon, *Journal of Near Eastern Studies* VIII (1949), 108–15, and R. Marcus and I. J. Gelb, ibid., 116–20.

Plate 5   Prisoners from the campaigns of Ramses III—Libyan, Semite, Hittite, one of 'Sea Peoples', Semite.   Relief from Medinat Habu

Temple, and Uriah the Hittite, whose wife he seduced, seem to re-echo the title *ewir* or *ewirni*,[1] known from Ras Shamra as a Hurrian title.   There is thus substance in Ezekiel's indictment of Jerusalem ' Thy father was an Amorite and thy mother a Hittite ' (Ezek. 6:3, 45).

With the Amorites the Old Testament associates the Canaanites as the inhabitants of Palestine at the Hebrew conquest and as the immediate neighbours of Israel.   The term Canaan derives from the Akkadian Kinnaḫna, by which the Phoenician coast is denoted in Mesopotamian texts.   The name is an appellative, denoting the local trade in purple dye (*kinnaḫḫu*) from the murex, for which the Syrian coast was famous.[2]   The specific application of this name to the Phoenician coast is known also in the Old Testament, e.g. Joshua 13:4 (the vicinity of Sidon), Isaiah 23:11 (Tyre), and possibly Judges 5:19 (' kings of Canaan ' in alliance with Sisera in the west of the great central plain of Palestine by Megiddo).   The last reference extends the application of the name to the inhabitants of the great cities of the plains of Palestine, which maintained contact with the cities of Phoenicia proper and shared in their culture and religion (cf. Num. 13:29, which locates the Canaanites by the seashore and the Jordan, the natural channels of culture and commerce).   Such a centre of Canaanite culture was Hazor in the plain of the upper Jordan commanding the fords south of Lake Huleh, whose king, Jabin, is termed ' the king of Canaan ' (Jg. 4:2, 23–4).   Here there can be no question of a strictly ethnic category in view of the racial admixture of Semites and non-Semites which we have already noted in Palestine.   The term denotes a culture rather than a race.   The use of the term Canaan to denote the whole of Palestine, or rather the foreland of the north Arabian desert including Syria, in the Old Testament and certain Egyptian inscriptions, for instance those of Amenhotep II and Merneptah, refers to the predominant culture mediated to that area by the Phoenician cities and those of the plains of Palestine through the Semites, the largest ethnic element in the population.   This unity of culture is demonstrated by the agreement between the Old Testament references to Canaanite culture, material remains from the various archaeological sites, and the documentary evidence from Ras Shamra.   In these texts, which we shall later cite as evidence of the religion of Canaan, we have

---

[1] First suggested by J. A. Montgomery, *Journal of the American Oriental Society* LV (1935), 94 note   [2] Hence Phoenicia, from φοινικεος, ' purple '.

recovered a considerable cross-section of the literature of ancient Canaan, for which scholars a generation ago scarcely ventured even to hope.

The political situation in Palestine in the Amarna Age was complicated by the activity of the Ḫabiru. They are mentioned in the Amarna Tablets in the letters of Abdi-Ḫepa of Jerusalem and were a menace to the peace of the vicinity, and are reported to have been put in possession of the land about the town of the chief Labaiya, probably Shechem. They appear to have been a restless people, invading probably from the direction of the desert. In Syria the Amarna Tablets mention a people of similar nature and habits named in ideographic cuneiform SA GAZ. In certain passages this ideogram is capable of translation ḫabbatu, ' robbers.' The SA GAZ, like the Ḫabiru in Palestine, are notorious plunderers and mercenaries, who turn the weakness, or inertia, of Egypt and the confusion in Syria and Palestine to account by taking service with whoever was best able to recompense them among the various intriguing chiefs in the land. In the north the SA GAZ seem to remain content with the hire of mercenaries ; in the south they seek a home. The difference was owing to the respective political situation in Syria and Palestine. In the mountains of Syria, more remote from Egyptian control, there was a fairly solid Amorite confederacy under Abdi-Ashirtu and his sons who seem to have had a definite nationalist policy. In the south there was no such political bloc to resist either the authority of Egypt or the penetration and settlement of the Ḫabiru.

The name Ḫabiru, as it is written in Akkadian cuneiform, or 'Apiriw, as it appears in Egyptian hieroglyphic and hieratic texts, is suggestive. Are the Ḫabiru the Hebrews ? It was once thought, and is still held, that the notice in the Amarna Tablets of the activity of the Ḫabiru is objective evidence of the Hebrew invasion under Joshua, whose name has in fact been found by A. T. Olmstead under the form Iashuia.[1] This, however, is merely a coincidence of name, and two quite different persons are denoted, Iashuia being cited by the Canaanite chief Mutb'alu as a corroborative witness of his statement to the Pharaoh.

There seems no longer any ground for doubt that the SA GAZ and the Ḫabiru were but different groups of the same people. The cuneiform tablets from the archives of the old Hittite capital at Boghazköi equate them, mentioning ' the gods of the Ḫabiru '

[1] A. T. Olmstead, *History of Palestine and Syria* (1931), 188, 198.

in syllabic cuneiform and ' the gods of the SA GAZ ' in ideogram. The same identification is suggested by evidence from
Ras Shamra in certain administrative texts, the ideogram SA GAZ
corresponding to ʿprm in the local alphabetic cuneiform.[1] Here
the variation between b and p is common in Semitic dialects and
gives no difficulty. The equation Ḥabiru—ʿIbhrîm (Hebrews)
is thus advanced one step nearer.

At the same time, if the Ḥabiru and the SA GAZ of the
Amarna Tablets are to be identified, it is obvious that we are
dealing with a movement far larger than the Hebrew occupation
of Palestine associated with Joshua. Actually there seems to be
more reason to associate the movements of the Ḥabiru and
SA GAZ with the penetration of Palestine by Jacob and his
people from the north-east, though Jacob and the tribes were but
certain elements among a larger group.

Not only are the Ḥabiru a larger force than Jacob and his
tribes or even than the Hebrews who settled Palestine later, but
they are mentioned in many other texts besides the Amarna
Tablets over a long period. The Babylonian records mention
them in the 21st century B.C. and the Mari Texts show them
active in the mid-Euphrates region between the 18th and the
17th centuries. They are mentioned on the statue of Idri-mi
from Alalakh, which Woolley dates not later than the first
quarter of the 14th century B.C.,[2] and Albright dates not later
than c.1450 B.C.[3] There they are located in Syria, perhaps in
the vicinity of the Homs gap.[4] A stele from Memphis recording
a campaign under Amenhotep II (1448–1420 B.C.) in his seventh
year mentions 3,600 ʿApiriw together with other classes of prisoners
of war from Palestine and more particularly from Syria.[5] ʿApiriw
are mentioned again on the stelai of Seti I from Bethshan, dated
1313 B.C.,[6] and from now until the 12th century B.C. they continue to be mentioned in Egyptian inscriptions as labourers in
Egypt.[7] Thus, even if we exclude the last references as denoting

[1] C. Virolleaud, ' Les Villes et Corporations du Royaume d'Ugarit ', *Syria*
XXI (1940), 123–51 ; *Revue des Études Sémitiques* (1940), 74 ff.
[2] S. Smith, *The Statue of Idri-mi* (1949), 2
[3] W. F. Albright, *Bulletin of the American Schools of Oriental Research 118*
(1950), 14   [4] S. Smith, op. cit., 72–3
[5] A. M. Badawi, ' Die neue historische Stele Amenophis II ', *Annales du
Service des Antiquités d'Égypte* XLII (1942), 1 ff.
[6] A. Rowe, *The Topography and History of Bethshan* (1930), 30
[7] The latest reference is to their employment in quarries in the reign of
Ramses IV (E. A. Speiser, *Ethnic Movements in the Near East in the Second
Millennium B.C.* (American Schools of Oriental Research Offprint Series, no. 1)
(1933), 38)

labour-gangs rather than a class or race, the term is widely diffused and can scarcely refer to one homogeneous race. The texts of the Hurrian community from Nuzu in north Mesopotamia *c.*1400 B.C. point to the same conclusion. They are found there as mercenaries, servants, and even slaves. In Babylonia they had special by-laws to secure their rights, and at Nuzu they had an overseer to maintain their privileges. At Nuzu and later in Egypt they were used mainly as menials. The Hittites in the 14th century B.C. used them as mercenaries. In Syria, in the Amarna period, as we have seen, they were employed by the aspiring princes of the Amorites, and in Palestine they apparently acted on their own initiative.

Thus with the Ḥabiru we are dealing with landless people of loose social structure, who infiltrate into the settled lands in search of livelihood, land, or plunder. This group, a class rather than a race, would normally be recruited from the Semitic tribes of the desert hinterland and probably included many, if not most, of the ancestors of the historical Hebrews. The inhabitants of the settled land at the time of the penetration of the Israelites and Joshua would consider them as just another wave of the Ḥabiru, who were a permanent scourge in the second half of the second millennium B.C. after the break-up of the empire of the Hyksos and the decline of the XVIIIth Egyptian Dynasty under Amenhotep III and his successors. In the Old Testament itself there is no clear case of the use of ' Hebrew ' as an ethnic term until the Book of Jonah (1:9) in the post-Exilic period, and as late as the time of Jeremiah in the beginning of the 6th century B.C. the term *'ibhri* refers to servile status (Jer. 34:9).

If we are thus to reject the view that the Ḥabiru of the Amarna Tablets and other records of the Late Bronze Age refers exclusively to the Hebrews, it may be asked what evidence archaeology has been able to provide for the settlement of Israel in Palestine. This implies the vexed question of the date of the Exodus, on which opinion is still divided between a date in the 15th century B.C. and one two centuries later. We accept the latter date, the Scriptural traditions of the Sojourn in Egypt agreeing with circumstances there in the XIXth Dynasty (1350–1205 B.C.), when the court was in the Delta, and not in the XVIIIth Dynasty, when the administrative centre was in upper Egypt at Thebes. The later date better suits the circumstances of the Israelite settlement in Palestine, since there is no hint in Joshua or Judges of conflict with Egypt in Palestine. If Israel had settled in

Palestine c.1400 B.C. there would surely have been some reflection in these narratives of the punitive raids of Seti I (1313–1292 B.C.) and Ramses II (1292–1225 B.C.) in Palestine. The bulk of the genealogical references to personalities during the Sojourn and Exodus, as against particular numbers given in late sources of the patriarchal narratives, support the late date, as has been indicated by H. H. Rowley.[1]

When we come to seek archaeological evidence from Palestine, however, it is not so simple to date the settlement of Israel in Palestine.

The key to the solution of the problem, on first sight, would seem to be the fall of Bronze Age Jericho, which plays such a prominent part in the Hebrew traditions of the conquest (Jos. 2:6). The ruin of the town in the end of the Bronze Age was dated by Garstang in the Amarna Age ' between 1400 and the accession of Akhnaten '.[2] Garstang, however, based his dating mainly upon the absence of Mycenaean pottery, which dates from c.1375 B.C. to c.1225 B.C. Such evidence from tombs, however, was cited by Père H. Vincent, the doyen of Palestinian archaeology, who contended for a date between 1250 and 1200 B.C.[3] Controversy raged on this issue until the recent excavation of Jericho by Miss K. Kenyon, which, in the light of accumulated ceramic knowledge, revealed that there is little or no evidence for a Late Bronze settlement at all from which any conclusion may be drawn for the date of the fall of the Bronze Age city. Nevertheless she does suggest a date c.1350–1325 B.C.,[4] a conclusion which agrees with the evidence of Mycenean pottery from the tombs, though, to be sure, that was very scanty. Indeed it may very well be, as M. Noth has suggested,[5] that the story of the dramatic collapse of the walls of Jericho is an explanation of the fact that the tribe of Benjamin, possibly the last element in Israel to enter the land, found the city in ruin, possibly as a result of an earthquake, or possibly through the activity of some raiders, Israelite or others, not certainly identified. Many features in the narrative suggest cultic practice rather than events of history, e.g. the mass-circumcision at Gilgal,

[1] H. H. Rowley, ' Israel's Sojourn in Egypt ', Bulletin of the John Rylands Library vol. 22, no. 1 (1953)
[2] i.e. 1400–1375 B.C. (J. Garstang and A. Rowe, Palestine Exploration Fund Quarterly Statement (1936), 170)
[3] H. Vincent, Palestine Exploration Fund Quarterly Statement (1931), 104–5
[4] K. M. Kenyon, Digging up Jericho (1957), 261–2
[5] M. Noth, Geschichte Israels (1950), 63 ff.

explained as the place where the reproach of Israel was 'rolled away', the sevenfold circumambulation and the blowing of trumpets, a feature of the Feast of Tabernacles and of the Year of Jubilee, when there was a reversion of property (Lev. 25). These lead us to suspect its historical accuracy, or at least seriously to limit the historical element.

On the basis of the sequel to the narrative of the fall of Jericho (Jos. 7–8) we might have expected evidence from Ai. Here indeed archaeology gives a clear declaration, but it is negative; the excavation of the late Mme. Marquet-Krause demonstrates that Ai lay derelict between c.2000 B.C. and c.1200 B.C.[1] If the whole Ai incident is not simply a tradition which had grown up to explain the name Ai ('the Ruin'), we may suppose that the site had been temporarily occupied by the fighting men of Bethel in order to resist the invaders advancing up the pass from Jericho. The circumstantial account of the fall of Ai and the death of the king, however, is in entire disagreement with the facts ascertained by archaeology. Perhaps the facts of the fall of Bethel were transferred to the account of the fall of Ai.

In the case of Bethel just over a mile to the north-west of Ai we seem to be on surer ground. The excavations of W. F. Albright and J. L. Kelso show that the Late Bronze Age settlement here was destroyed in the latter half of the 14th century B.C. or the first half of the 13th, and rebuilt on a much meaner scale. This evidence appears to support Judges 1:22–6, which attributes the taking of Bethel not to all Israel but to the tribe of Joseph operating independently.

The present excavation of the great fortress of Hazor (Tell el-Kedah) commanding the crossing of the Jordan between the lakes of Tiberias and Huleh proves that the place was destroyed at the end of the 13th century B.C.[2] This seems at first sight to enable us to date the destruction of Hazor attributed to the Israelites under Joshua (Jos. 11:10–15). Again, however, the case is not quite so simple. The fact that Hazor is not mentioned in the account of the settlement of the district by Naphtali in Judges 1:33 would seem to corroborate the account of the destruction of the city in Joshua 11:10–15 and to suggest that the site lay derelict. Yet in the period of the Judges it is said to

[1] J. Marquet-Krause, *Syria* XVI (1935), 325–45. This is corroborated by H. Vincent, *Revue Biblique* XLVI (1937), 231–66.

[2] Y. Yadin, 'Some Aspects of the Material Culture of Northern Israel during the Canaanite and Israelite Periods, in the light of Excavations at Hazor', *Antiquity and Survival* II (1957), 166

have been a Canaanite metropolis and the capital of Jabin, whose forces under Sisera were defeated by the Israelites under Deborah and Barak by the River Kishon (Jg. 4, 5). Archaeology does not attest the rebuilding of the city until the time of Solomon,[1] and the conclusion must be that the action by the Kishon against Sisera was wrongly associated with Jabin of Hazor, who was actually the king defeated with his Canaanite allies by the Israelite invaders when the city fell at the end of the 13th century B.C. According to Hebrew tradition a victory at the Waters of Merom preceded the fall of Hazor (Jos. 11:5-9). If, as seems probable, this site is to be located at Meirun by Safed,[2] the Hebrews would probably penetrate the area from lower Galilee by way of the Wadi el-Amud, so by-passing Hazor. In this case they may have been identical with the 'Apiriw which the stele of Seti I mentions in the hills north of Bethshan in 1313 B.C. The lapse of almost a century between the appearance of the *Ḥabiru* (probably the tribe of Naphtali) in this region and the destruction of Hazor may indicate that the Hebrew penetration was more a matter of gradual infiltration than sudden conquest, a fact which has not always been reckoned with by those who would seek one definite date for the Hebrew settlement of Palestine.

Hebrew tradition emphasises also the capture of Hebron and Kiryath Sepher (also called Debir), which Albright would identify with Tell Beit Mirsim, which he excavated. He found that the Late Bronze Age settlement was destroyed *c.*1225 B.C.,[3] which appears to give us a date for the Hebrew conquest of the south. Again, however, the matter is not quite so simple. There is nothing to disprove Albright's identification of the site, it must be admitted, but, equally true, there is no compelling reason so to identify it, so that its relevance to the narrative of the conquest in Judges 1:12-15 is somewhat hypothetical. Again, the capture of this place and of Hebron are attributed respectively to Othniel and Caleb, who, though affiliated with the Hebrews, were themselves actually Kenizzites (Jos. 15:17; Jg. 1:13). Can we, then, associate this movement of Kenizzites from the southern steppes

---

[1] ibid., 168

[2] As suggested by the occurrence of the place in the list of places conquered by Thothmes III in his inscription in the temple of Amon at Karnak. W. F. Albright attests potsherds of the Late Bronze and Early Iron Age at the site of Meirun (*Bulletin of the American Schools of Archaeology* 35 (1929), 8).

[3] W. F. Albright, *Annual of the American Schools of Oriental Research* XVII (1938), 78 ff.

with the movement of the Israelite tribes proper? The subsequent history of the Israelites in the north and of Judah and her affiliated peoples in the south, which runs so largely independently, rather indicates that we cannot. Indeed it may be questioned if this Kenizzite aggression can be closely associated even with Judah. The tradition of Judah's association with the Canaanite woman Tamar of Adullam, by whom he begot Perez (Gen. 38) suggests that Judah had been in the land long before the Exodus, when they had extended their settlement by connubium rather than by conquest. The genealogy of David from this union through Perez (Ru. 4:12, 18) and the local association with Bethlehem, the tribal centre of Judah, indicate that this is a genuine tradition.

The site of Tell ed-Duweir, probably ancient Lachish, some eight miles north-west of Tell Beit Mirsim, had a similar history at this period. In the fosse outside the city walls and glacis the last of a series of Egyptian temples was destroyed towards the end of the 13th century B.C.[1] and the city itself shows the same evidence of thorough destruction, though a scarab of Ramses III (1168–1137 B.C.) in a disturbed deposite from the city itself suggests to Miss O. Tufnell that the city may have fallen ' a decade or so after rather than before 1200 B.C.' [2] This late date might suggest that the fall of the city was due not to the Israelites nor the Kenizzites, but to the Philistines and other ' Sea-peoples ', who settled the coastal plain early in the 12th century B.C.[3] Some time apparently elapsed before settlement resumed on any considerable scale in the beginning of the Hebrew Monarchy. It is not easy to determine by whom it was occupied in the interim. None of the characteristic painted Philistine pottery occurs, though in certain tombs ornaments and implements of iron were found.[4] These few tombs do not indicate occupation in force, such as we might expect from the Hebrews, and this coupled with the iron objects rather suggests Philistine garrison troops holding Lachish as an outpost, or even families of independent, and possibly itinerant, smiths. The Israelites did, of course, eventually penetrate to Lachish, but we doubt if the city was included in the ' grand strategy ' associated with Joshua

[1] J. L. Starkey, ' Towards the close of the XIXth Dynasty ', *Palestine Exploration Fund Quarterly Statement* (1935), 239
[2] O. Tufnell, *Lachish* III, *The Iron Age* (1953), 46. This scarab may be the deposit of a Philistine garrison after the fall of the Bronze Age city.
[3] J. L. Starkey, *Palestine Exploration Fund Quarterly Statement* (1937), 239
[4] O. Tufnell, op. cit., 46

Plate 6 Stele of Merneptah, mentioning Israel for the first time
in history

(Jos. 10). It is significant that Lachish is not mentioned in the sober account of the occupation of Judah in Judges 1:16–21, and in the account of David's escapades as an outlaw from Saul it is explicitly stated that Keilah seven miles north-west of Hebron and ten miles north-east of Lachish was not in Judah (1 Sam. 23:3).

On the evidence of surface deposits of pottery in Transjordan, Nelson Glueck has demonstrated that the kingdom of Edom with clearly demarcated frontiers came into being some time about 1300 B.C.[1] Since the presence of this consolidated power played a vital part in the Ephraimite tradition of the migration of the Hebrew tribes to Palestine, it follows that this movement must be dated after 1300 B.C. Here Glueck's evidence is corroborated by the fact that there is no reference to the state of Edom in Egyptian records before the time of Ramses II (1292–1225 B.C.) [2] and by the statement in Genesis 36:31–9 that there were eight kings in Edom before there was a king in Israel. Dating Saul c.1050 B.C. and reckoning an average of thirty years for each king in Edom, we arrive at a date c.1290 B.C. for the foundation of the kingdom of Edom, so that this may serve as a *terminus post quem* for the Exodus.

A conspectus of the history of the Near East at this period reveals that the settlement and consolidation of Edom and Moab was an instance of similar movements all round the ' Fertile Crescent'. Edom, Moab, and the Hebrew tribes who acknowledged their kinship with them, were elements of a larger Aramaean group who at this time were infiltrating from the steppes of the interior and founding states. As the Aḥlamu they are mentioned in the Amarna Tablets.[3] With other desert peoples, such as the Sutu, they are mentioned regularly in Assyrian texts from the end of the 14th century B.C.,[4] and an inscription of Tiglath-Pileser I (1114-1076 B.C.) states that they had already begun to build towns in the Jebel Bishri, between Carchemish and the Lebanon.[5] The son of Tiglath-Pileser I, Ashur-bel-kalli (1073–1056 B.C.), mentions an Aramaean state Bit-Adini, on both sides of the Euphrates in the region of the

---

[1] N. Glueck, *The Other Side of the Jordan* (1940), 15 ff.
[2] R. De Vaux, *Revue Biblique* XLVI (1937), 540
[3] J. A. Knudtzon, *Die El Amarna Tafeln* (1915), 200, 7–11
[4] These are cited and discussed in R. T. O'Callaghan, *Aram Naharaim* (1948), 95 ff. A more recent treatment is A. Dupont-Sommer, *Les Araméens* (1949), esp. 15 ff.
[5] D. D. Luckenbill, *Ancient Records of Assyria* I (1927), 239

great westward bend.   The capital of this state was Til-Barsib, modern Tell Aḥmar, which was excavated by Thureau-Dangin between 1929 and 1931.   By the end of the 11th century B.C. a whole series of independent Aramaean states was established in upper Mesopotamia and even east of the Tigris, and an Aramaean usurper, Adad-apal-iddin (1070–1049 B.C.) reigned in Babylon and had his daughter married to the king of Assyria.   A group of kindred peoples, the Kaldu, the Chaldaeans, occupied the south.   By the end of the 11th century B.C. the Aramaeans had merged with the Hittite remnants in north Syria, and there emerged the states of Arpad in the vicinity of Aleppo, and Ya'udi, also called Sham'al, whose capital was at Zenjirli, where sculptured stelai with considerable inscriptions have been found.[1] Another of those states was Hamath on the Orontes, where the Danish archaeologist Ingholt attests a cultural break c.1000 B.C.[2] From the Books of Samuel it is well known that by the time of David there were several Aramaean states at Damascus, southern Syria, and the Hauran,[3] of which Damascus eventually won the hegemony and was the bitter enemy of Israel throughout most of her history.

There are striking correspondences between the settlement of these Aramaeans in Syria and the occupation of Edom, Moab, Ammon, and especially Israel in the south.   Apart from the association of Jacob with the Aramaean Laban in north Mesopotamia (Gen. 28-31) and the unanimous Hebrew tradition of the intermarriage of the patriarchs with Aramaean kinsfolk from the same locality (Gen. 24), the consolidation of the Aramaean states in Syria roughly synchronises with the foundation of the Hebrew state in Palestine.   Significant too is the fact that, just as the Hebrews made little progress beyond the mountains of the interior against the superior armament and organisation of the Canaanites and Philistines, the Aramaeans never occupied the coast.   Considering the Hebrews, at least from the time of Jacob, in the context of the Aramaean folk-movement, it is difficult to visualise their appearance as a tribal confederacy in Palestine before the Amarna Age.   During this period they probably

[1] G. A. Cooke, *A Textbook of North Semitic Inscriptions* (1903), 61, 62, 63

[2] H. Ingholt, *Rapport préliminaire sur sept campagnes de fouilles à Hama* (1940), 69 ff. (Level F)

[3] These were Aram Zobah, probably in the Beq'a north of Damascus, Beth Rehob, probably in the Litany region of south Syria, Maacah, about the upper Jordan, and Geshur in the Hauran. These probably never developed beyond a loose tribal constitution before they were absorbed in the kingdom of Aram, the capital of which was Damascus.

appeared among the class of Ḥabiru mentioned in those texts, and certain of their elements may have consolidated in an amphictyony round some local shrine, which we regard as that shared by Issachar and Zebulun (Dt. 33:18–19), probably Mount Tabor. This tribal amphictyony we suppose to have been the 'Israel' mentioned on the stele of Merneptah in 1225 B.C. In this connection it is significant that 'Israel' is named in conjunction with Yenoam, which is known to have been in the vicinity of Bethshan, hence not far from Tabor.

The consolidation of the Aramaean states of Syria, their prolonged resistance to, and final liquidation by, Assyria soon after the middle of the 8th century B.C. is documented by the Assyrian annals and, to a less extent, by about a dozen local alphabetic inscriptions in Phoenician and Aramaic from Syria. Limited as the last are, they give some clue to the culture of the Aramaeans, and this may be amplified by excavations, notably at Tell Ḥalaf (ancient Guzana) in the Ḥabur region of upper Mesopotamia, and at Ḥama on the Orontes. These indicate that the Aramaean settlers from the north Arabian steppes assimilated the culture and religion of the settled lands. This they did the more readily since they brought nothing from the desert except a virile social ethic and a fierce tribal particularism, both of which are found in almost exaggerated degree in Israel. With the consolidation of these Aramaean states each with its national deity, a new era was inaugurated in the Near East, which was marked by centuries of 'holy wars' with their attendant horrors of cities laid under the ban and captives hewn in pieces 'before the Lord', like Agag, the king of the Amalekites, at Gilgal (1 Sam. 15:33).

Since the history of Israel was so intimately bound up with that of her immediate Aramaean neighbours we may briefly consider the states of Damascus, Moab, Ammon, and Edom in more detail.

In the account of David's clashes with the Aramaeans beyond Jordan in his Ammonite wars (2 Sam. 8:3–8 ; 10:6–9) Damascus plays no role, though the city was of strategic significance for David's subsequent control of the Aramaean tribes (2 Sam. 8:6). Whatever may be the actual facts of that ill-defined phase of Hebrew history, Damascus emerged as the centre of a powerful kingdom on the death of David. David's suppression of the Aramaean tribes under the hegemony of Zobah proved to be the genesis of the new state of Damascus (1 Kg. 11:23–5), which effectively limited the northward extension of the influence of Israel, but also proved a bulwark against Assyrian aggression until Damascus finally succumbed in this age-long conflict in 732 B.C.   In 853 B.C. Israel under Ahab joined an alliance of Damascus and other Aramaean states of Syria, when the Assyrians were halted on their westward drive at the Battle of Qarqar on the Orontes.   Again in 735/4 B.C. Pekah of Israel and Rezin of Damascus united in a similar policy in the days of Isaiah of Jerusalem (Isa. 7).   Such common action, however, is exceptional in the relationships between Israel and Damascus, which were generally bitterly hostile.

Moab lay east of the Dead Sea, with her southern border along the Wadi el-Ḥeṣa (the Brook Zared), which flows into the Dead Sea at its south-eastern extremity, and her northern border generally confined to the Wadi Mojib (Arnon) during the Hebrew monarchy.   This northern border, however, fluctuated.   In the period of the early Hebrew judges Moab actually occupied Jericho west of the Jordan (Jg. 3:12–29), and in the 9th century B.C. Mesha, the King of Moab, was able to occupy territory north of the Arnon which had been held by Israel in the time of Omri and Ahab and possibly since the time of David.   Mesha's war of independence is recorded on his celebrated stele, found at Diban, in language reminiscent of Hebrew historical narrative, and this inscription attests the practice of holy war with its concomitant severities, so familiar from the history of Israel :

. . . Omri, king of Israel, afflicted Moab many years, because Kemosh was angry with his land.   And his son succeeded him ; and he too said, I will afflict Moab in my days.   He said . . . and I saw my desire upon him and upon his house, and Israel perished utterly for ever.   And Omri took possession of the land of Mehedeba, and he occupied it his days and half his sons' days, forty years ; but Kemosh restored it in my days. . . .   And the men of Gad had dwelt in the land of Ataroth from of old ; and the king of Israel built Ataroth for himself.   And I fought against the city and took it.   And I slew all the people . . . and I brought back from there Ariel the governor [1] of (the city) and I dragged him before Kemosh in Qeriyyoth. . . .   And Kemosh said to me, Go and take Nebo against Israel.   And I went by night and fought against it from the break of dawn till the noon-tide, and I took it and slew all, seven thousand men and . . .

[1] This meaning is suggested by the title *dawidum* in the Mari Texts

and women and . . . and damsels, for I had devoted it to Ashtar-Kemosh, and I took thence the (furniture) [1] of Yahweh and dragged it before Kemosh. . . .[2]

This excerpt from the inscription of Mesha is a good expression of the intense tribal particularism in politics and religion introduced to the Near East by the Aramaeans. Its crudity cannot be gainsaid ; nevertheless it was the germ of a higher faith in God, who is active, not in the forces of nature, but in the history of the community, disciplining his people and guiding them on the path of their destiny, and in all vicissitudes revealing Himself. In Israel this faith reaches its highest development.

Ammon, with her capital at Rabbath Ammon (modern Amman), occupied an undefined area north of Moab, and in the time of the Judges and Saul menaced the Israelite settlers in Jabesh-Gilead, overlooking the north part of the valley of the middle Jordan. Their power, however, was broken by David and, though they continued to harry the Israelites beyond Jordan, ' ripping up pregnant women of Gilead in order that they might increase their territory ' (Am. 1:13–15), they were no longer a serious menace to Israel. Towards the end of the monarchy of Judah they resumed their harassing operations, apparently at the instigation of the Babylonians (2 Kg. 24:2). On the collapse of Judah, however, they harboured certain of the more active refugees (Jer. 40:11), including the notorious Ishmael, the assassin of Gedaliah at Mizpah in the days of Jeremiah. In spite of the fact that the Ammonites had a king, the fact that they are generally referred to as Bene Ammon, ' the Sons of Ammon ', probably indicates that they never really developed politically beyond the tribal stage.

Edom, with her capital at Sela (' the Rock '), i.e. Petra in its impressive sandstone canyon, lay to the south of the Wadi el-Ḥeṣa and extended to the Gulf of Aqaba. Like Moab, Edom enjoyed a fair precipitation of rain on the plateau and on the western escarpment, making agriculture possible. Edom also either carried or controlled the caravan routes from the oases of Arabia to Damascus (Jer. 49:7–8 ; Ezek. 25:13), the metropolis of the north Arabian desert, and the route which diverged at the head of the Gulf of Aqaba to cross the north Sinai desert to Gaza or directly to Egypt ran through her territory. The copper beds of

[1] i.e. of a shrine
[2] G. A. Cooke, *A Textbook of North Semitic Inscriptions* (1903), 1

the Wadi Araba also lay in her territory, and probably occasioned the Hebrew subjection of Edom in the time of David (2 Sam. 8:14), after which Israel enjoyed this asset.   Profiting by the temporary weakness of Judah under Ahaz, however, the Edomites asserted their independence and recovered control of the Gulf of Aqaba (2 Kg. 16:6).   It is not clear whether the liberation was the work of a native Edomite king or of the Aramaean king Rezin (Rezon in the Septuagint and Assyrian inscriptions).   If Rezin of Aram (Damascus) is indicated, his strategy would be congruous with his policy of strengthening native opposition to Assyria in the west. By supporting Edomite independence he may have aimed at neutralising Judah, who under Ahaz had sought security in vassalage to Assyria.   This phase of history is illustrated by Glueck's excavations at Ḥirbet el-Ḥeleifeh in stratum III, where a number of seal-stamps on jar-handles bear names compounded with the name of the Edomite national god Kos.[1]   From this time Judah never occupied the shore of the Red Sea.

Unfortunately there is no monument from Edom like the Moabite Stone to elucidate local culture.   From theophoric names relating to Edom, however, in Assyrian inscriptions of the 7th century B.C.,[2] from local inscriptions[3] including the seal-stamps just cited, and from the statement of Josephus (Antiquities xv, vii, 9) it emerges that the god of Edom was Kos.   The Old Testament, however, gives no hint of the god of Edom, which, significantly perhaps, is never reproached for idolatry.   Hebrew tradition consistently accredits the Edomites with wisdom (e.g. Jer. 49:7), which indicates a certain preoccupation with moral issues, so that Edomite religion may actually have had much in common with the religion of Israel.

In taking advantage of the ruin of Judah in 586 B.C. it was considered that Edom was guilty of an unnatural outrage. Actually by that time the Edomites were themselves under pressure, first from the Arabs, who, according to Assyrian inscriptions from the middle of the 7th century B.C., were aggressive in Transjordan,[4] and then from the Nabataeans, a virile stock from the Hejaz.   The passing of the power of Edom also is marked at

---

[1] N. Glueck, 'The Topography and History of Ezion-Geber and Elath', *Bulletin of the American Schools of Oriental Research* 72 (1938), 11–13
[2] e.g. Qaushmalaka (D. D. Luckenbill, *Ancient Records of Assyria* I, § 801) and Qaushgabri (ibid., II, §§ 690, 876)
[3] From Tell es-Sandaḥannah (Marissa) in the south of Palestine from the 3rd century B.C., *v. infra*, 206
[4] In the time of Ashurbanipal (A. L. Oppenheim in J. B. Pritchard, *Ancient Near Eastern Texts relating to the Old Testament* (1950), 297–8)

Ḥirbet el-Ḥeleifeh by personal names on potsherds, which were found together with Attic sherds in the 4th- or 5th-century level.[1] These were in Aramaic and the divine elements in the compound names are known as Arab deities from inscriptions in the Hejaz and south Arabia. The dispossessed Edomites found new homes in the south of Palestine, which was consequently termed Idumaea, a name which applies as far north as Hebron in the time of the great Jewish revolt of A.D. 66–70 (Josephus, *War* IV, ix, 7). The Hasmonaean prince John Hyrcanus dealt with this problem by forcibly converting the Idumaeans, or Edomites, to Judaism, and from one of these ' converts ' Herod the Great was descended.

The Philistines, the Pulusatu of the Egyptian records, are depicted in Egyptian sculptures as a race apart from the Semites of Palestine, and they give the impression of an active warrior-race. This is borne out by Egyptian inscriptions of the 15th to the 13th century B.C., which number the Pulusatu among several peoples subsumed under the name ' Sea-peoples ', who were active around the coasts of Asia Minor and raided the Delta itself. It was probably they who destroyed the Minoan Empire in Crete, whose cities Knossos and Phaestos were destroyed c.1400 B.C. This would accord with the Hebrew tradition which derives the Philistines from Caphtor (Am. 9:7), now known from the texts from Ras Shamra to be Crete. The connection of the Philistines with Crete, however, was incidental and secondary. From excavations in the coastal plain between Jaffa and Gaza, where the Philistines during the Hebrew settlement and Monarchy occupied Ekron, Ashdod, Askalon, Gaza, and Gath, certain features emerge which are distinctive of the Philistines and their kindred peoples. In the Early Iron Age (c.1200–1000 B.C.) a striking painted pottery associates the Philistines with the Anatolian coast, the Aegean, and even the Greek mainland. The long, leaf-shaped sword depicted in Egyptian sculptures suggests a Danubian provenance. At Gezer and Bethshan the burial custom of closing the mouth of the corpse with a small gold mouth-plate is thought to be a relic of the gold mask of the royal burials at Mycenae in the 16th century B.C. This custom is found in Early Iron Age graves in Macedonia, where it is associated with pottery and ornaments of north Balkan affinities. The same association is suggested by the practice of cremation attested at Askalon in the Early Iron Age, a practice entirely strange to

---

[1] N. Glueck, ' Ostraca from Elath ', *Bulletin of the American Schools of Oriental Research* 80 (1940), 3–10

Palestine and Syria since the Mesolithic Age (*c.*10,000–6000 B.C.), except for single tombs at Jericho and Tell Beit Mirsim in Palestine from the 15th century B.C., and from Hama and Atchana in north Syria at the same period. More numerous instances of cremation at the same period at Troy indicate the provenance of the exponents from the Bosphorus and beyond. The fact that the rite, commonly attested in the area and period of Philistine occupation in Palestine, is found at the sites above-mentioned two centuries at least before the Philistines occupied Palestine in force indicates that small groups of their kinsfolk had already penetrated, probably as mercenaries of the Hittites in Anatolia and north Syria and of the Egyptians in Palestine, as the records of both would suggest. It is possible too that these ‘ Sea-peoples ’ had some connection with the peoples who fought about Troy in the celebrated Trojan War, and the names of some of them, Dardanu, Akhwash, and Danuna, familiar from the Egyptian records, suggest the Dardanoi, Achaioi, and Danaoi of the Iliad.

Halted by Ramses III on their southward trek, they were, according to the Pharaoh, ‘ settled in fortresses bound in his name ’. Their precise relationship to Egypt is not certain, but they seem to have occupied certain of the old Hyksos fiefs in the central and coastal plains of Palestine and to have been organised on a feudal basis. Significantly enough, when David took service with Achish, the Philistine ruler of Gath, he received the frontier town of Ziklag, in the Judaean foothills north-west of Beersheba, as a heritable fief (1 Sam. 27:6). Archaeology and the Old Testament both attest the Philistine occupation of Bethshan (1 Sam. 31:10). The Egyptian papyrus describing the misadventures of the envoy Wenamon in Palestine and Syria (*c.*1100 B.C.) gives clear evidence of a strong maritime settlement of a kindred people, the Tekel, at Dor (modern Tanṭura) in the north of the Plain of Sharon. The consolidation of the Hebrew tribes under David and the incorporation of the Canaanite cities of the plains of north Palestine in the territorial state of Solomon limited Philistine occupation to the coastal plain between Jaffa and Gaza, where they are found in the period of the Hebrew Judges and the Monarchy. Beyond the introduction of iron to Palestine it is questionable if the Philistines made any real contribution to the culture of the land, and it is one of the freaks of history that it was the Philistines of all people who, through the Greeks, gave their name to Palestine.

Plate 7   Tablet from Ras Shamra in alphabetic cuneiform, from the
Legend of King Keret

V The Culture of Canaan

THE correspondence between Palestinian vassals and Egyptian officials and the ' Foreign Office ' in the Egyptian capital, which comprises the Tell el-Amarna Tablets, shows Palestine as a province of Egypt at a time when the great empires of the ancient East were in amicable correspondence. Egypt and the Hittites had not yet engaged in the struggle for Syria ; the day of imperial Assyria was not yet ; lower Mesopotamia was under the rule of the relatively backward Kassites, whose king corresponded with the Pharaoh as his ' brother ' ; the royal house of Mitanni, a predominantly Hurrian kingdom under an Aryan military aristocracy in upper Mesopotamia, was affiliated with the Pharaoh by marriage. This situation is reflected in the excavations at various sites in Palestine and Syria. Several of the seats of the local vassals of Egypt have been excavated, such as Megiddo, Hazor, and Bethshan in northern Palestine, and in the south Jericho and Lachish, and Tell el-Far'ah (probably Sharuhen), Tell Jemmeh, and Tell el-Ajjul on the Wadi Ghazzeh. Evidence of Egypt is abundant in scarabs and amulets ; Mitannian cylinder-seals point possibly to professional soldiers of higher rank, local commandants of Egypt, in fact, such as the bearers of non-Semitic names in the Tell el-Amarna Tablets. The relative security in the East also encouraged trading ventures of merchants from the Aegean, and wares associated with the golden age of Mycenaean Greece have been found in abundance on Palestinian and Syrian sites between 1400 and 1200 B.C. There were, in fact, trading settlements of Aegeans at Ras Shamra (ancient Ugarit) and at Tell Abu Hawam on the bay just north-east of Haifa. The size and structure of the fortified towns throughout the land and the generally high quality of the wares and utensils entitles us to regard the culture of Canaan on the eve of the Hebrew settlement as relatively advanced. Hazor, Megiddo, Bethshan, and Lachish of this age had all well-equipped defences, residences, and temples, those of Bethshan numbering no less than five, which were patronised by the Egyptian resident and occupation forces and furnished with sculptures. Nor was education neglected, as is indicated by a cuneiform letter from Shechem, where the local schoolmaster tries to extract his fees from reluctant parents. Actual alphabets and copy-texts and pupils' copies have been found at Ras Shamra from this period, the first ABC so far known in the world's history. In the light of all the material evidence from archaeological sites in Palestine it is possible to reconstruct a most impressive picture of the Canaan into which the Hebrews settled. Though this would give a fair general impression, however, there would still be an element of conjecture, especially in details. This, however, is all but obviated by the epoch-making discoveries of literary, ritual, and administrative texts at Ras Shamra near the coast of north Syria, which were providentially inscribed, in alphabetic cuneiform for the most part, on durable clay tablets. These may safely be taken as evidence of the culture of the Phoenicians of the Late Bronze Age, which we recognise on Biblical evidence to be essentially that of the Canaanites, the native population of Palestine at the Hebrew settlement.

The religion of the Canaanites, to judge from the myths of Ras Shamra concerning the vicissitudes of Baal, the god of winter storms and secondarily the vegetation thereby promoted, was largely directed to predisposing Providence in Nature. As in Babylonian mythology related to the ritual of the spring New Year, the gods bow before the threat of Chaos. The young god Baal, whose proper name, we learn from the texts, was Hadad, the Thunderer, champions the cause of order. He is supported by the divine craftsman, the Skilful and Percipient One, who assures Baal :

> Have I not told thee, Prince Baal,
> Have I not declared, O thou who mountest the clouds ?
> Behold, thine enemies, O Baal,
> Behold, thine enemies thou shalt smite,
> Behold, thou shalt subdue thine adversaries.
> Thou wilt assume thine eternal kingdom,
> Thy sovereignty everlasting.[1]

Baal engages the waters, Prince Sea and Judge [2] River, with a pair of maces ' Driver ' and ' Expeller ',[3] made for him by the

---

[1] Text in C. H. Gordon, *Ugaritic Handbook*, 67, 7 ff. The literary form of this passage has been aptly compared by W. F. Albright to Ps. 92:9, *Catholic Biblical Quarterly* VIII (1945)

[2] The word is the same as that for the Judges of Israel.

[3] cf. the staves Beauty and Bands in Zech. 11:7

divine craftsman, and is eventually victorious, the waters being
' scattered ', i.e. distributed, so that the potential curse proves a
blessing :

> Then soars and swoops the mace in the hand of Baal,
> Even as an eagle in his fingers.
> It smites the head of Prince Sea,
> Between the eyes of Judge River.
> Sea collapses and falls to the earth ;
> His strength is impaired ;
> His dexterity fails.
> Baal drives Sea away and disperses him ;
> He annihilates Judge River.
> Exultantly Athtarat cries out :
> ' Scatter him, O Mighty Baal,
> Scatter him, O thou who mountest the clouds,
> For Prince Sea held us captive,
> He held us captive, even Judge River.'

In the fragmentary text which follows Baal is acclaimed as king,
a most significant fact, which suggests the occasion to which the
text was relevant, and also connects it with certain highly significant passages in the Old Testament.

   The many literary correspondences in form and language to
the poetic portions of the Old Testament are apparent even from
the limited fragments to which we have advisedly confined ourselves. The theme and imagery of the fragments which we have
cited was appropriated by the Hebrews with due adaptation to
the cult of Yahweh, as appears clearly from psalms celebrating
the kingship of Yahweh (e.g. Ps. 22, 47, 93, 96, 97, 98, etc.).
The Prophets too draw frequently on this source in the language
and imagery in which they speak of ' the Day of Yahweh ', i.e.
the day of his judgment and vindication (e.g. Isa. 2 ; Zeph. 3:15,
17 ; Nah. 1:12 [1] ; Hab. 3:8 ; Ezek. 32:2 ff.). It recurs also in
Wisdom poetry (e.g. Job) and in Jewish and Christian apocalyptic
(e.g. Dan. 7:7 ff. ; Jub. 23:11 ; 2 Esd. 8:63–9:6 ; Rev. 20:21,
etc.). It is in fact in the ideology of the kingship of God, we
believe, that the influence of Canaanite on Hebrew thought was
strongest. Jewish tradition associates the Enthronement Psalms
with the New Year Festival (cf. Zech. 14:16, which associates the
cult of Yahweh as king with the Feast of Tabernacles and the

---

[1] After Nah. 1:12, emended according to the suggestion of the Septuagint.

autumn rains).   We think it highly probable that the Enthronement Psalms and their Canaanite prototype were relevant to this
supreme crisis in the agricultural year.   We think that, with due
adaptation, the Hebrew settlers adopted the myth as an appropriate incantation at this most important juncture of the year
just as they perforce had to learn new techniques of agriculture.

The rest of the Ugaritic myths of epic form and proportions
relating to Baal dramatise the tension in local agriculture as a
conflict between Baal and Mot (Death, Sterility).   Here Baal is
a vegetation-god, a dying and rising god like the Mesopotamian
Tammuz and the Syrian Adonis, whose cult in Graeco-Roman
times was practised at the head of the Adonis River, Nahr
Ibrahim, a little north of Beirut, and the myth is obviously related
to various phases in the agricultural year.   A great part of it, for
instance, is concerned with the building of a ' house ' [1] for Baal,
a conspicuous feature of which is a roof-shutter, the opening of
which, as a rite of imitative magic, coincides with the opening of
the clouds and the fall of the vital autumn rains :

> Let a window be opened in the house,
> A shutter in the midst of the palace,
> And the clouds shall be opened with rain.[2]

We may note that Solomon's Temple in Jerusalem was dedicated
in the same season in the seventh month Ethanim, the month of
the ' Regular Rains ' (1 Kg. 8:2).   The ' house ' is eventually
completed, a blaze of gold and silver, and the god holds a hearty
house-warming :

> Baal prepares the menage of his house,
> Yea, Hadad orders the arrangement of his palace.
> He has slaughtered oxen and sheep,
> He has felled bulls and fatlings of rams,
> Yearling calves,
> Lambs the young of sheep.
> He has called his brothers into his house,
> His kinsmen into the midst of his palace
>
> . . . .
> They drink wine in a flagon,
> In a cup of gold the blood of trees.[3]

---

[1] The word means house or temple.
[2] Text in C. H. Gordon, op. cit., 51, vii, 14 ff.
[3] Text in Gordon, op. cit., 51, vi, 38 ff.

This gargantuan hospitality is reminiscent of Solomon's hecatombs at his dedication of the Temple :

And Solomon offered a sacrifice of communion-offerings which he offered to the Lord, two and twenty thousand oxen and a hundred and twenty thousand sheep. So the king and all the children of Israel dedicated the house of the Lord.

(1 Kg. 8:63)

Baal's sovereignty, however, is now challenged by Mot, or Death, manifest in the drought and sterility which are perpetual menaces to husbandry in the Near East. Baal apparently seeks a *modus vivendi* with Mot, who, however, is intransigeant and dismisses Baal's envoys :

Though thou didst smite Lotan the Ancient Serpent,
Yea, didst annihilate the Tortuous Serpent,[1]
The Foul-fanged with Seven Heads,[2]
The heavens will dry up, yea languish ;
I shall pound thee, consume and eat thee,
Cleft, forspent and exhausted.
Lo, thou art gone down into the throat of Mot the Son of El,
Into the gullet of the Hero, the Beloved of El.[3]

Baal eventually succumbs to Mot ; his dead body is sought by his sister, the goddess Anath, who gives his remains due burial and laments her brother :

She makes the mountain re-echo with her lamentation,
And with her clamour the forest to resound.
Cheeks and chin she rends,
The upper part of her arm she scores,
Her chest as a garden-plot,
Even as a valley-bottom her back she lacerates.
Baal is dead !
What is become of the Prince, the son of Dagon ?
What of the multitudes, the followers of Baal ?

. . . .

When at length she was sated with weeping,

---

[1] This is, of course, Leviathan of Isa. 27:1. Here and in Job 26:12–13, the epithets of the Serpent are precisely as in Ugaritic, an indication of the source of the Hebrew tradition.
[2] cf. Ps. 74:14, Thou brakest in pieces the *heads* of Leviathan.
[3] Text in Gordon, op. cit., 67, i, 1 ff.

Drinking tears like wine,[1]
Aloud she shouts to the Sun, the Light of the Gods,
' Lift upon me, I pray thee, Baal the Mighty.'

. . . .

She takes him up to the crags of Saphon [2] ;
She weeps for him and buries him,
She puts him in the niche of the divinities of the earth.[3]

The search for the god in the power of the underworld and the
mourning by a goddess is a common motive in myth and ritual
related to the fertility-cult throughout the Mediterranean world,
and here we have the local counterpart to Isis' search for Osiris,
Ishtar's search for Tammuz, Demeter's search for Kore, and that
of Aphrodite for Adonis.

Eventually the goddess Anath takes vengeance on Mot :

She seizes Mot the son of El ;
With a blade she cleaves him ;
With a shovel she winnows him ;
With fire she parches him ;
With a millstone she grinds him ;
In the field she sows him ;
His remains the birds eat,
The wild creatures consume his fragments,
Remains from remains are sundered.[4]

This suggests a close connection between the myth and the
ritual whereby the new crop, instinct with mysterious life, was
de-sacralised, or set free for common use. The rite is that noted
in Leviticus 2:14, which refers to the offering of the first sheaf,

green ears of corn, dried by the fire, even corn beaten out of
full ears.

Baal, however, shall rise again, and his resurrection is antici-

---

[1] cf. Ps. 80:6 (A.V., v. 5), Thou feedest them with the bread of tears ; and
givest them tears to drink in great measure
[2] This was the seat of Baal, whose title was Baal Saphon. The mountain,
modern Jebel el-Aqra on the northern horizon of Ras Shamra, was the
Canaanite Olympus, and was known to the Greeks as Mount Kasios. Baal
Saphon on the coast east of the Nile Delta, known to the Hebrews in the
Exodus, was so named because it was a cult-place of the Canaanite Baal and,
in the Roman imperial period, of his Greek counterpart Zeus Kasios. *Saphon*
in Hebrew means ' north ', but this is a secondary meaning.
[3] Text in Gordon, op. cit., 62, 2 ff.
[4] Text in Gordon, op. cit., 49, ii, 30 ff.

pated by a vision of fertility cast in imagery familiar to readers of the Old Testament :

> The heavens will rain oil,
> The wadis run with honey.[1]

With the revival of Baal his conflict with Mot is renewed. The latter is apparently held at bay for six years, after which ' in the seventh year ' a final battle is fought :

> They glare at each other like glowing coals,
> Mot has rallied his strength ;
> Baal has rallied his strength.
> They thrust at each other like wild oxen,
> Mot has rallied his strength ;
> Baal has rallied his strength.
> They bite each other as serpents,
> Mot has rallied his strength ;
> Baal has rallied his strength.
> They kick like stallions,
> Mot is down ;
> Baal is down on top of him.[2]

This would seem to have some relation to a seven-year cycle in agriculture, such as was, in fact, known to the Hebrews. In a land exposed to such vicissitudes as sirocco winds, drought, and locusts it was felt that after a few good years disaster was overdue. This the Hebrews sought to forestall by an artificial famine, the Sabbatical Year, when the land lay fallow ; the peasants of Ugarit seem to have staged a ritual combat, Mot, the power of sterility, being given full scope against Baal, the power of fertility, so that he might be exhausted in the conflict. The victory of Baal was at the same time an act of imitative magic to predispose the issue for the ensuing time-cycle.

This then was the mythology related to phases of the cycle of growth in Canaan. No doubt some modified form of the ritual underlying the myth was also practised by the Hebrew peasant as an important part of his agricultural operations, as the desacralisation rite in Leviticus 2:14 suggests. This myth, how-ever, made no impact on Hebrew faith and was taken up into

---

[1] Text in Gordon, op. cit., 49, iii, 6 ff.   cf. Jl 3:18 :
> The mountains shall drop down new wine,
> And the hills shall flow with milk.

[2] Text in Gordon, op. cit., 49, vi, 16 ff.

Hebrew literature only sporadically and as purely literary matter. In Egypt and Greece the counterpart of this seasonal myth depicting the vicissitudes of Osiris, Dionysus, Triptolemus, and Persephone was developed beyond the scope of the simple seasonal myth and related to the life of man and society. Thus in Athens the sympathy of the worshippers in the conflict and death of Dionysus was developed into the great Attic tragedies of human life. In Eleusis and Egypt this same sympathy with the dying and rising vegetation-deity was applied to the needs of man and society, who emerged through tragedy to triumph, through death to life, as a result of initiation into the respective mysteries. There is no evidence of a similar application of the Baal-cult in Canaan, to say nothing of Israel. So far indeed was the ancient Canaanite from aspiring after personal survival that the very possibility is rejected with scorn in one of the legends of Ugarit :

> As for mortal man what does he get as his latter end ?
> What does mortal man get as his inheritance ?
> Glaze will be poured out on my head,
> Even plaster on my pate,[1]
> And the death of all men will I die,
> Yea, I will surely die.[2]

So replied the prince Aqhat to the goddess Anath, who endeavoured to entice him by the promise of immortality.

The ancient Canaanite priests in their wisdom knew that the emotions of the community, engaged in the agony of Baal in his struggle with Mot, must not be overstrained. Accordingly they permitted comic relief, an example of which is a certain text,[3] the second half of which describes in gross terms the seduction by El, the senior god of the Canaanite pantheon, of two women. In the broad, bawdy humour of this text we see a characteristic of Attic comedy, which was developed from the myth relating to seasonal ritual. There is no obvious counterpart to this in the Old Testament, though the Song of Solomon may have taken its origin thus, and possibly also the Song of the Vineyard [4] (Isa. 5:1–7), which was adapted to quite another purpose by the prophet.

The fertility-cult of Canaan may have been quite amoral, but the mythology of its cult-dramas presented a most colourful and

---

[1] Referring possibly to baldness and grey hair of age
[2] Text in Gordon, op. cit., 2 Aqht vi, 35–8   [3] Gordon, op. cit., 52
[4] The Hebrew text suggests that this may have been entitled a love-song.

Plate 8a   A goddess of the Canaanite
fertility cult

Plate 8b   The Canaanite Baal, stele
from Ras Shamra

Plate 9a   Cuneiform dispatch from Abdi-Hepa, the ruler of Jerusalem, to the Pharaoh. (From the archives of Tell el-Amarna)

Plate 9b   The Gezer Calendar

vivacious pantheon. The senior god El, in the fertility-cult at least, is well content to enjoy *otium cum dignitate* while he leaves Baal to play a more active role ; he receives his consort Atherat (Asherah of the Old Testament) sitting comfortably on his throne twiddling his fingers ; he has amours with women. He cannot quite restrain the impulses of the younger members of the divine family, particularly Anath, who endeavours to extort his sanction to build a house for Baal by savage threats :

> I shall make thy grey hairs run with blood,
> The grey hairs of thy beard with gore.[1]

To this the wise old god returns the soft answer that turns away wrath. In epic style the protagonists consistently preserve their character. Baal is Baal the Mighty, the Thunderer, He who Mounts the Clouds; Anath is the Virgin Anath, a young virago, goddess of love and war ; El is the Kindly and Merciful ; Atherat his consort, Lady Atherat of the Sea, is not always in agreement with him, but can exploit her conjugal charm to secure her own ends. Athtar, the Venus-star, who proves such a sorry substitute for Baal when the latter is in eclipse, bears the stock epithet the Terrible, on what grounds it is not apparent from the extant mythology. Doubtless the rest of the pantheon would also be vividly particularised if we had their appropriate mythology.

The anthropomorphism of the mythology of Ras Shamra has its own peculiar value, shedding a bright light on the manners of ancient Canaan. Birth, at which professional singers, ' Skilful Ladies ', were employed, doubtless to improvise and sing incantations, was a critical phase of life, after which, as among the Hebrews, a period of ritual seclusion was observed. The two women whom El has impregnated with the deities of Dawn and Evening are bidden to withdraw with their progeny after the birth :

> Take your equipment to the awful desert.
> There shall ye sojourn amid stones and bushes
> For seven whole years,
> For eight seasons' circuit besides.[2]

Marriage in ancient Canaan is illustrated by the marriage of the Moon-god and his bride Nikkal :

[1] Text in Gordon, op. cit., 'nt, pl. vi, v, 32–3
[2] Text in Gordon, op. cit., 52, 65–7

> The Moon paid the bride-price for Nikkal,
> Her father set the beam of the balances ;
> Her mother set the pan of the balances,
> Her brothers arranged the standard weights,
> Her sisters the weights of the scales.[1]

Here, as in modern Arab society, the matter is almost a
business transaction between the families concerned, mutual
emotion between the principals being almost improper.   The
status of women in ancient Canaan is suggested by the fact that
in one of the sagas the daughter of King Dan'el rises early
and carries water from the well, and is able also to harness a
donkey :

> She straightway saddles an ass,
> Straightway she harnesses a donkey,
> Straightway she hoists her father,
> Placing him on the back of the ass,
> On the fair back of the donkey.[2]

This, however, was in the heroic past, and legal texts from
c.1400 B.C. show that women had their rights, especially in matters
of property contingent upon divorce, which was apparently uni-
lateral and as easy as it is in modern Arab society.   Death, like
birth and marriage, imposed certain prophylactic rites on the
community, or, more strictly, on the immediate relatives of the
defunct.   On the death of Baal, El comes down from his throne
to the ground :

> He lets down his turban in grief from his head ;
> On his head is the dust in which he wallows.
> He tears asunder the knot of his girdle ;
> He makes the mountain re-echo with his lamentation,
> And with his clamour the forest to resound.
> Cheeks and chin he rends,
> The upper part of his arm he scores,
> His chest as a garden-plot,
> Even as a valley-bottom his back he lacerates.[3]

Due burial is important, after which the community may resume
its suspended activity and return to normal life.   Blood revenge

---

[1] Text in Gordon, op. cit., 77, 33–7
[2] Text in Gordon, op. cit., 1 Aqht, 57–60
[3] Text in Gordon, op. cit., 67, vi, 14–22

by the next of kin was a social duty in ancient Canaan as in
modern Bedouin society, and explains the role Anath plays in
avenging Baal in the myth of the fertility-cult.

The long sagas or legends of Ugarit recounting the vicissitudes
of the kings Keret and Dan'el and their families indicate the sacral
status of the king. Keret's peculiar relationship to the gods is
indicated by his sonship to El. This probably expresses a sacramental relationship only, El being thought of as the father of, or
supreme authority in, the community, which was represented in
the person of the king. The ancient king was *ex officio* priest,
though in the administrative texts from Ras Shamra, which can
be dated in the Late Bronze Age, the office of the priesthood had
devolved upon twelve different priestly families. The ancient
king in the two sagas we have mentioned was the channel of
divine blessings to the community, and had an important role to
play in the maintenance or restoration of fertility. It would be
interesting to know to what extent the king exercised this office
in the historical period, but there is no evidence from Ras Shamra,
though we may cite evidence from Assyria in the 7th century B.C.[1]
that, in a sense, ' every king was a Messiah '.[2]

The administrative texts contain many references to priests, of
whom the chief priest is named as the authority for the version of
the Baal-myth which has come down to us. The fact that this
myth and the sagas above-mentioned were found in what was
obviously a scribal school adjacent to the temple of Baal indicates
the important function of the priesthood as the custodians of
literature. The same individual is also termed *rb nqdm*, generally
translated ' the chief of the shepherds ', and the administrative
texts list *nqdm* a class or guild in ancient Ugarit. The Semitic
word (*nqd*) is the same as that used to describe Mesha King of
Moab (2 Kg. 3:4) and Amos (Am. 1:1), which has suggested the
possibility that in both cases the term is not to be taken literally
as shepherds, but is a cultic title. Actually it may be cognate with
the Akkadian word *naqidu*, one skilled in divining by the liver of a
sacrificial victim, this practice being attested by clay models of
livers, divided and charted for the instruction of aspiring augurers,
which have been found at various archaeological sites in Palestine
and Syria. Our opinion is that the term has this significance
in the case of King Mesha, but not so in that of the prophet,

---

[1] *v. infra*, 135–6
[2] M. Canney, ' Ancient Conceptions of Kingship', *Oriental Studies in Honour
of C. E. Pavry* (1934), 74

whom the Lord took from following the flock and said : ' Go prophesy to my people Israel.' The administrative texts from Ras Shamra list also sculptors (*pslm*), who may or may not have been sculptors of images, singers (*shrm*), whom we assume to have chanted the liturgies, makers of vestments (*yshm*), and butlers (*shrm*), or cupbearers at communion feasts, consecrated persons (*qdshm*), who may have been the equivalents of the Hebrew sacred prostitutes (*qᵉdēshîm* and *qᵉdēshôth*),[1] silver-casters (*nskm*), who perhaps melted and minted the silver of temple offerings, as in the Temple at Jerusalem (2 Kg. 22:4, according to the Targum), merchants (*mkrm*), either business assessors to the priests (2 Kg. 12:7), who assessed their perquisites or invested temple funds in business, or who possibly sold animals for sacrifice in the temple-precinct, as Jesus found in the Temple at Jerusalem in his day (Mt. 21:12), and temple-servitors (*ytnm*), possibly the equivalent of the Hebrew *nᵉthînîm*. Probably many more craftsmen who are mentioned in the fiscal lists of Ugarit were organised around the temple, as in the great temples of Mesopotamia, which were centres of industry and the arts. However that may be, those texts, together with lists of offerings for various sacrifices and deities, both Semitic and non-Semitic, give a fairly full picture of religious activity in ancient Canaan on a regular and fully organised basis.

In spite of the preoccupation of the ancient Canaanites with material values there are certain indications in the Ras Shamra Texts of a social conscience. In the two sagas above-mentioned the two kings Keret and Dan'el are guarantors of the social order,

> Deciding the case of the widow,
> Judging the suit of the orphan.[2]

From the reiterated description of Dan'el's son we may form an impression of religious institutions and social conventions in ancient Canaan. The son of the king as head of the community maintains the continuity of the common cult which gives the community cohesion. He also pays the due funeral rites to his father. He is

> One who may set up the stele of his ancestral god
> In the sanctuary, the refuge of his clan ;

---

[1] Dt. 23:18 ; 1 Kg. 14:24 ; 22:46, etc.
[2] Text in Gordon, op. cit., 2 Aqht v, 6–8

Who may pour out his liquid offering to the ground,
Even to the dust wine after him.[1]

In his father's absence, or after his death, the son takes his place in the sanctuary at the communal meal whereby the community realises its solidarity as a social and religious unit,

Eating his slice in the temple of Baal,
His portion in the temple of El.[1]

He maintains his father's credit for hospitality, apparently a point of honour in ancient Canaan as it still is in the desert,

Heaping up the platters of his company,
Driving away any who would molest his night-guest.[1]

He must see that his father never falls into dishonour, as might well happen when he is drunk, either in social conviviality or in religious observance, as, for instance, at the harvest festival. Then the son must support his father,

Holding his hand when he is drunk,
Carrying him when he is sated with wine.[1]

The last duty of the son is

Washing his (father's) garment when it is dirty.

This gives us a hint, in our opinion, of the role that magic played in ancient Canaan. The garment, as being in contact with the person, could be washed safely only by the son. This task could not safely be entrusted to a woman, through whom invasive evil influences had, to the primitive mind, more easy access. Nor could it be entrusted to a menial, who might be suborned to put a *ju-ju* on the garment and so on the king.

At the time when Jacob and his Aramaean kinsmen made their first contact with Palestine there were such city-states, which, if less cosmopolitan than Ugarit, had yet evolved a fairly complex urban civilisation. The native Semitic religion was, however, rooted in the soil ; the cult was intimately related to local agriculture, the foundation of the economy of the state. Shechem, Ophrah, Mizpah, Hebron, and perhaps even Beersheba,

---

[1] Text in Gordon, op. cit., 2 Aqht i, 27–34. Philological notes in support of our translation of this passage may be found in J. Gray, *The Legacy of Canaan* (*Vetus Testamentum Supplement* v) (1957), 75–7.

might all have reflected in some degree the Canaanite fertility-cult as we know it from the Ras Shamra Texts, and the cult of Yahweh with bull-images [1] at Bethel and Dan may have borrowed much from the cult of Baal, whose cult-animal was the bull. Shiloh also had its vintage-festival, which could not have had anything in common with the cult of the desert-deity Yahweh, and Gibeon also had a long-established religious tradition. The place-names Beth Anath in Naphtali (Jos. 19:38), Beth Anoth in Judah (Jos. 15:59), and possibly also Anathoth in Benjamin, indicate the cult of Anath, the most active goddess in the fertility-cult, in Palestine, and at Bethshan in one of the five Late Bronze Age temples a basalt panel was found with a dedication in Egyptian hieroglyphics to 'Antit, Queen of Heaven and Mistress of the Gods'. Many references in the Old Testament to Asherah and Ashtaroth indicate that the Mother-goddess of the Ras Shamra Texts, Atherat, and Athtarat, a less significant goddess in the Ras Shamra Texts, were also worshipped in Palestine. Bronze figurines of Baal as a young warrior in short kilt, armed with spear and mace and helmet with bull's horns from Late Bronze Age sanctuaries at Tell ed-Duweir (Lachish) and Megiddo, which are identical with figurines from Ras Shamra and its coastal neighbour Minet el-Beida, suggest that the mythology, festivals, and institutions of the Phoenician Baal-worship were also diffused in Palestine, though perhaps not so highly elaborated as at Ras Shamra.

Such, in its various aspects, was the culture of Canaan with which Israel was brought into intimate contact with her settlement in Canaan, and it is idle to suppose, in face of archaeological and documentary evidence, that Israel was uninfluenced by the local culture. The distinctive genius of Israel, however, and the strength of her spiritual leaders is to be discerned in the selective way in which she drew on the legacy of Canaan, and in the purposeful way in which she adapted what she borrowed. The theme of Baal's conflict with the powers of Chaos, the unruly waters, was borrowed and developed. So the Hebrews found expression for their faith in Providence, not only, as the Canaanites did, over Nature, but as Lord of History and the Moral Order, whose victorious conflict with the powers of Chaos, his Kingship, and Judgment, runs like a golden thread through the Hebrew Psalms and Prophets and Jewish apocalyptic and comes to fruition in the Gospel. No less significant is what Israel

[1] These, however, were probably pedestals for the presence of God.

rejected of the Canaanite heritage. The rest of the Canaanite mythology of the fertility-cult, the conflict of Baal with Mot, in spite of its relation to seasonal agricultural festivals observed by the Hebrews with similar rites, was never incorporated into the faith of Israel, but was drawn upon only for imagery, a conscious literary borrowing. Yahweh, God of Israel, was no dying and rising god, alternately victor and vanquished in his perpetual conflict with Death, as Baal with Mot. As Baal rather in his conflict with the unruly waters He was the champion of order in heaven and earth, triumphant over the powers of Chaos ; his sovereignty is everlasting ; he is the same yesterday, today, and forever.

The fact is that Israel really belonged to a new era in the history of the ancient East. With the irruption of the Aramaean tribes into the Fertile Crescent at the end of the Bronze Age (*c.*1200 B.C.) an age of religious intolerance was inaugurated. The nature-cult of Canaan was universalistic. It was not exclusive and nationalistic ; it was a-moral and quite neutral, and, however much Hebrew prophets might condemn its licentious rites of imitative magic, they could not allege homicidal fanaticism. Now the invading tribes and tribal confederacies brought in the cults of their particular gods, who were not beneficent powers of nature like the Canaanite Baal, but were fiercely intolerant of all but their own worshippers. Now the fanatical ' holy war ', with all the brutality of death-devotion (*ḥerem*), the total destruction of goods and lives of the conquered enemy, is a feature of the history of the Near East, leaving a legacy of fierce militant nationalism for more than half a millennium until Israel and Judah, Edom, Moab, and Ammon, Damascus, and the Aramaean states of Syria were annihilated by the imperial advance of Assyria, Babylon, and Persia.

All this is familiar from the Books of Joshua, Judges, Samuel, and Kings in the Old Testament, and nothing is really added by the contemporary record in the inscription of Mesha of Moab at Diban commemorating his victorious war of liberation from the House of Omri.[1] The ideology and the actual language of the famous Moabite Stone re-echo the Old Testament. The Israelite oppression is admitted to be owing to wrath of the national god Kemosh against ' his land ', and the eventual success of the resistance movement is ascribed to Kemosh, who let Mesha ' see

[1] Text and translation in G. A. Cooke, *A Text-book of North Semitic Inscriptions* (1903), no. 1

his desire upon ' his enemies. In return he builds a sanctuary (lit. ' high place ') for Kemosh. The crowning triumph of his campaign is the capture of the fortress of Nebo, where apparently there was a shrine of Yahweh. This place and its inhabitants, men, women, and children, were put under the ban, as Joshua, according to Hebrew tradition, had treated Jericho and its inhabitants in the days of the Israelite settlement. In token of triumph the equipment of the cult of Yahweh was dragged off as a trophy before Kemosh.

This was the crude experience out of which Israel, under the inspired guidance of her great prophets and the more insistent influence of her priests, was to develop her sublime faith in the power of God in history and her sense of destiny as the chosen instrument of His grace to mankind. Of the consciousness of purpose in the history of men and nations and personal involvement therein there is no trace in the documents of Canaan, nor is there any prophet, except one solitary phrenetic at Byblos c.1100 B.C., who may declare ' Thus saith the Lord '. It is significant that this word is a simple *ad hoc* declaration ; none apparently swept the political horizon with the vision of an Amos and communicated the grand strategy of the Lord of History.

PART II

ISRAEL AMONG THE NATIONS

VI The Days of the Judges

THE emergence of Israel as a nation coincides with the first phase of the Iron Age in the Near East, which may be dated between *c.*1200 and 900 B.C., and the political situation in the Near East and the peculiar course of Israel's national history were directly conditioned by the new economic situation.

Iron had already been known for a long time,[1] though the economic working of terrestrial iron ore was a comparatively new discovery, associated with a subject people of the Hittites in the mountains of Armenia. The Hittites were using iron weapons by the 14th century B.C., though the kings of the Hittites guarded the secret as a state monopoly.[2] Ultimately, however, the secret was divulged. From the middle of the 15th century B.C. peoples of the Aegean and the European mainland penetrated Anatolia and settled in the coastlands of the west. The Hittites from their seat of Empire on the central plateau endeavoured to absorb these new elements by using them as mercenaries, both Hittite and Egyptian records of the next two centuries referring frequently to them. They it was who, through the use of iron weapons, learned the secret of the smiths. They eventually turned their weapons against their masters, probably on the occasion of a fresh influx of their kinsmen from beyond the Bosphorus, as is suggested by the Danubian affinities of the material remains of Troy in the first phase of the Iron Age.[3] The result was the collapse of the Hittite Empire *c.*1200 B.C. Among those peoples were the Philistines, who settled ultimately on the coastal plain

---

[1] Meteoric iron, ' metal of heaven ', is found in objects from pre-Dynastic Egypt and from strata of the third millennium B.C. in Mesopotamia, while iron wrought from terrestrial ores first appears in the third millennium B.C. at Khafajeh on the Diyala, twenty miles east of Baghdad (V. G. Childe, *New Light on the Most Ancient East* (1935), 189). A useful account of the sporadic occurrence of iron, both meteoric and terrestrial, in Egypt before the Iron Age proper is given by G. A. Wainwright, ' Iron in Egypt ', *Journal of Egyptian Archaeology* XVII (1932), 3–15.

[2] In the correspondence of the Hittite king, probably Hattushilish III (fl. *c.*1280 B.C.) and the Pharaoh, the Hittite tactfully refuses the Pharaoh's request for iron, but sends him the gift of a dagger in the coveted metal (F. Thureau-Dangin, *Syria* x (1929), 204–5).

[3] V. G. Childe, *The Aryans* (1926), 53–4 ; *The Dawn of European Civilization* (1947), 36

of Palestine and are noted as possessing the art of metal-working, which, however, they endeavoured to keep as a monopoly (1 Sam. 12:19–22).[1]   Archaeology and the records, however, demonstrate that they did not succeed.   The secret was out and barbarians diffused the resources of the great empires of the Bronze Age.

Of this revolution Professor Childe wrote [2] :

Cheap iron democratized agriculture and industry and war-fare too.   Any peasant could afford an iron axe to clear fresh land for himself and iron ploughshares wherewith to break stony ground.   The common artizan could own a kit of metal tools that made him independent of the households of kings, gods or nobles.   With iron weapons a commoner could meet on more equal terms the Bronze Age knight.   With them, too, poor and backward barbarians could challenge the armies of civilized states whose monopoly of bronze armaments had made them seem invulnerable.

Thus, in the ancient Near East the *entente* of the early empires, which is reflected in the Amarna Tablets and the later archives of the Hittite Empire from Boghaz-köi, was shattered beyond repair.   Now is the period when small national units assert themselves.   Now Israel and Judah, Moab, Ammon, and Edom, Damascus, Hamath, and the Aramaean states of north Syria maintain a sturdy independence against one another and resist the imperial designs of Assyria and Egypt.   No longer is imperial expansion after the approved pattern safe or easy. Through many fluctuations of fortune Assyria advanced through Syria and Palestine to Egypt only after three centuries of effort and finally found herself exhausted in the attempt.

The settlement of Israel in Palestine is depicted in the Book of Judges, in contrast with the main tenor of the Book of Joshua, as being effected by a series of local conflicts whereby the various elements of the Israelite confederacy, acting either singly or in small groups, gradually consolidated the foothold they had won in the land.   The urbane Canaanites, who had grown rich on the profits of trade which flowed along the arterial trade-routes traversing Palestine, naturally resented the rude, land-loping

---

[1] Iron is not actually mentioned, but it is well known that iron was by this time in current use.

[2] V. G. Childe, *What Happened in History* (1950), 183

tribes, who had pressed up the eastern passes and were now seeking to effect their solidarity with one another and with kindred elements already settled in Palestine. With their ' chariots of iron ' the Canaanites were generally more than a match for the Israelites. Hence we find the Hebrews and the Canaanites clashing in the days of Deborah and Barak in the great central plain ' in Taanach by the waters of Megiddo ',[1] (Jg. 5:19), where a sudden rainstorm converted the plain about the River Kishon into a quagmire, immobilising the dreaded chariots. Again, the success of the Hebrew invaders and the general confusion in Palestine, over which Egypt under the weak priest-dynasty of Thebes had abandoned all but the pretence of supervision,[2] encouraged the incursion of other desert tribes such as the Midianites in the days of Gideon. Those invaders from the east and the Amalekites from the south (Jg. 6:3) wasted the land far and wide ' till thou comest unto Gaza '. Indeed, even in the central mountains, comparatively remote from the desert, property was not safe from the marauders, and Gideon is introduced clandestinely threshing his corn to hide it from the Midianites. It is commonly accepted that Gideon was threshing his corn by the wine-press. The word *gath*, meaning ' wine-press ', is commonly found in Ras Shamra Texts referring to land-grants to feudatories, and it may be that in the Hebrew text it means ' ancestral plot ' or the like rather than wine-press. Again, in the coastal plain west and south of the mountains of the interior, the Philistines were firmly established, mainly in the five towns, Ashdod, Ekron, Gath, Askalon, and Gaza, thus keeping an effective check on permanent Hebrew expansion westward, and even compelling the migration of the tribe of Dan from the western foothills of Judah to the far north at the headwaters of Jordan (Jg. 18). The migration involved some three thousand souls from two localities, Zorah and Eshtaol.

This general situation is reflected in the excavation of strata of the Early Iron Age at various Palestinian sites. Most of the sites in the coastal plain are marked by a level of destruction

[1] Noting that the occupation of the near neighbouring towns of Megiddo and Taanach tended to be complementary rather than simultaneous, W. F. Albright stresses the fact that in the Song of Deborah Taanach is apparently the occupied site. He notes a period of recession in the occupation of Megiddo in the last quarter of the 12th century, which is a feasible date for this action. We doubt if we may take so literally the phrase ' the waters of Megiddo ' in what is, after all, a poem.

[2] A bronze statue-base of Ramses VI of this dynasty at Megiddo had probably only token significance.

which terminates the Late Bronze settlement, and the ensuing phase of occupation is on a definitely lower cultural plane. Recovery, however, was more rapid and conditions apparently more stable on the coast and in the low hill country of the south than in the mountains, though settlements both in the foothills of Judah and in the mountains reflect the unsettled conditions of the period of the Hebrew Judges with raid and counter-raid, as in the narratives of Samson, Samuel, Saul, and David.

The coastal plain was the area properly settled by the Philistines, though there is also evidence of their penetration of the interior. We have already suggested that the iron objects from a certain limited number of tombs at Lachish at this period may indicate the presence of a Philistine garrison.[1] From the first phase of the Iron Age at Bethshan anthropoid coffins of pottery were found, crudely moulded on the outside with the features of the defunct, a travesty of Egyptian sarcophagi, the corpse being buried with a gold mouth-plate, which has been associated with the Aegean.[2] It will be recollected that it was at Bethshan that the Philistines exposed the bodies of Saul and his sons after the Battle of Gilboa. The distinctive painted pottery associated with sites in the coastal plain occupied by the Philistines in the first two centuries of the Iron Age (c.1200–900 B.C.) is also found at this time as far inland as Jerusalem and Tell en-Naṣbeh (probably one of the sites named Mizpah) some nine miles north of Jerusalem, and may be evidence of Philistine expansion when they established garrisons in Gibeah and Michmash in Saul's own district (1 Sam. 13).

The settlement of the Hebrews as peasants in Palestine is illustrated by the building and modest fortification of hill-towns in an area in the centre of Palestine hitherto thinly populated. A feature of the fortifications was casemate walling, a double wall divided into chambers by cross-walling. Of strength more apparent than real, though quite efficient, this may have been conceived as a quick temporary fortification, to be strengthened by filling the intermediate space as occasion demanded. The space between the walls seems also to have served for storage. Such fortifications may be a development of the temporary laager defence of the Hebrew nomads. The fact, however, that this technique is associated with Anatolia suggests that it was introduced to Palestine by the Philistines and was borrowed from them by the Hebrews.

[1] *v. supra*, 96   [2] *v. supra*, 103

A good illustration of a hill-settlement of this time is Tell el-Ful some three miles north of Jerusalem, identified by Albright with Gibeah of Saul and excavated by him between 1923 and 1933. The first settlement, of the 12th century B.C. and apparently unfortified, was destroyed by fire, which may reflect the civil strife between the local Benjamite inhabitants and the rest of the Israelites after the incident of the Levite's concubine (Jg. 19–20). A feature of the next settlement was a considerable fortress with casemate walling. This building, with an inside measurement of 32 m. × 17 m. and an overall outside measurement including four corner towers of 50 m. × 34 m., is generally taken as Saul's palace. The dimensions, however, suggest that it was less palace than fortress, and it may have been the redoubt of the Philistine garrison which occupied Gibeah before Saul and Jonathan dislodged it (1 Sam. 13:3, after the Septuagint version). After that the fortress may have contained Saul's dwelling, and it may be safely assumed that his striking-force of professional soldiers, such as David, was quartered here.

Another site of the same period to be excavated was Ḥirbet Seilun (probably Shiloh), the centre of the Israelite amphictyony and the seat of the ark, some twelve miles south of Shechem. This was a case of 'Biblical archaeology' in the narrow sense, since the site promised no prospect of evidence of the interplay of races and cultures. No trace of the sanctuary of the ark was certainly identified, though the narrative of the dedication of Samuel indicates a built sanctuary (1 Sam. 1:9). It was established, however, that the site was occupied in the first phase of the Iron Age (c.1200–c.1000 B.C.), but was destroyed in the same period, an event to which Jeremiah (7:12) possibly alludes.

The status and function of Saul, the first king of Israel, are worthy of note. Apart from the fact that Saul had already proved himself an able and heroic leader in the relief of Jabesh Gilead (1 Sam. 11), the selection of a man of Benjamin as the first king of Israel is not without significance. Benjamin, which signifies, in fact, the 'southernmost' clan of north Israel, was strategically placed to sustain the brunt of Philistine attack from the coastal plain of southern Palestine. Benjamin, again, probably the last clan to penetrate Palestine, had little valuable land conducive to settlement, and was therefore by nature a warrior clan (Gen. 49:27, 'Benjamin shall ravin as a wolf . . .'). This clan, then, was the natural spear-head of resistance to the Philistines and admirably adapted for professional military service.

It is pre-eminently as a war-lord that we should understand Saul. He was in effect the head of a feudal system, which, however, applied not to all Israel but only to his professional troops. This system is now known from documents from the excavations at Ras Shamra and Atchana in north Syria to have been a feature of the life of Canaan from at least the 15th century B.C. In a deed from the palace archives at Ras Shamra, for instance, the king, Ammistamru, makes one Adadsheni and his family equestrian feudatories (*mrynm*),[1] and in a similar deed from Atchana the king, Niqmepa, declares that he

> has released Qabia to be a *marrianu* (equestrian feudatory) ; as the sons of equestrian feudatories of the city-state of Alalakh are, so also are Qabia and his grandsons in perpetuity. . . .[2]

Whether or not this feudal system was actually visualised by those who elevated Saul to the kingship, as according to one source it was (1 Sam. 8:10 ff.),[3] the administration of Saul did develop along feudal lines. In the campaign which culminated in David's combat with Goliath, we read that Saul offered to make the successful antagonist of the giant ' free ' (*hophshi*) in Israel [4] (1 Sam. 17:25), and on the escape of David from his entourage Saul asks of his ' servants ' (also a technical term), ' Hear now ye Benjamites, will the son of Jesse give every man of you fields and vineyards, and make you all captains of thousands and captains of hundreds ? ' (1 Sam. 22:7). This important aspect of the new office of the king must be borne in mind in view of developments in the time of David and Solomon.

---

[1] J. Nougayrol, *Mission de Ras Shamra VI. Le Palais Royal d'Ugarit. Textes accadiens et hourrites des Archives Est, Ouest, et Centrales* (ed. C. F. A. Schaeffer) (1955), 140. The term *mrynm* is Aryan.

[2] After S. Smith, *Antiquaries Journal* XIX (1939), 43

[3] This is from the antimonarchic source of Samuel, associated with the Deuteronomic view of history, so late in the Hebrew Monarchy.

[4] The precise meaning of *hophshi* is not certain. We suggest on a survey of the evidence from the Amarna Tablets and the Ras Shamra Texts that it signifies ' set free from local family ties for service to the king ' (' Feudalism in Ugarit and Early Israel ', *Zeitschrift für die Alttestamentliche Wissenschaft* LXIV (1952), 49–55). R. De Vaux suggests that it signifies exemption from state burdens, such as taxation and conscription for public works (*Les Institutions de l'Ancien Testament* (1958), 137). If the latter interpretation is correct it must reflect a more highly developed state than that of Israel in the time of Saul.

VII   The Throne of David

AFTER the fatal day of Gilboa, David, who had been winning the favour of the powerful Kenizzites, the people of Caleb in the south of Judah, by ridding them of the menace of the hostile Amalekites (1 Sam. 30:26–31) and probably by intermarriage with Ahinoam of Jezreel and Abigail of Carmel, came up to the Kenizzite tribal centre of Hebron, and there at the shrine, where relationships between the Kenizzites and men of Judah had long been solemnised, he was accepted by both and was anointed as king.

It may seem strange that the Philistines allowed David to consolidate his authority here for seven years. It must be remembered, however, that he was still, at least nominally, a Philistine vassal, retaining his fief of Ziklag, in the foothills of Judah north-west of Beersheba. The fact is that David was an example of a new class which was emerging in Israel, the feudal vassal, who was independent of all ties except his allegiance to his feudal superior. First rising in this capacity under Saul, he transferred his allegiance to Achish of Gath, and had marched with the Philistines against Israel in the Gilboa campaign, though he had been spared the embarrassment of fighting against Saul. Since they had been able to command his services in this campaign, the Philistines had no reason to doubt the loyalty of David, since he had as yet not been approached by the men of Israel. The same may be said of David's capture of Jerusalem. Though by this time he had been approached by responsible men in Israel and had been accepted as their king, there is no evidence that the capture of the city was the fruit of the new alliance of all Israel. On the contrary, it was the exploit of a small striking-force of his own retainers under his kinsman Joab (2 Sam. 5:6–8 ; 1 Chr. 11:6), and was regarded as the personal achievement of David, and for the whole period of the Hebrew Monarchy Jerusalem was literally ' the city of David ', the crown property of David and his descendants, a city-state within a state. It is of the utmost importance to appreciate this situation, made possible by feudal conditions, especially in view of the innovations in government which David and Solomon were about to institute.

Jerusalem, the political capital of the kingdom of David and the site of the Temple under Solomon, naturally attracted the attention of the Palestine Exploration Fund soon after its foundation, and in 1867 Lieutenant Charles Warren was sent out to investigate the location of the Temple, the city walls, and the site of the Holy Sepulchre. This work, conducted mainly by tunnelling, did reveal the location of various ancient walls, but produced no conclusive evidence. In fact Jerusalem has proved a most disappointing site. The city bears the scars of a long and chequered history, having suffered at the hands of foreign enemies and her own reformers. Again, the city was built of stone and not of brick. This has important consequences for archaeology, since, on the ruin of a brick settlement, debris is simply levelled to form the base of new brick building, but stones of ruined buildings are gathered and used again. In a brick site, consequently, there is a definite stratification which is not so marked in a stone site. Added to this is the fact that ancient Jerusalem was flanked by steep escarpments and deep wadis, which were the natural dumping-ground for debris when the city was rebuilt. From these valleys and the slopes of the East Hill or Ophel pottery fragments attest the various phases of the history of Jerusalem from the beginning of the third millennium B.C. We look in vain, however, for any considerable remains of the capital of David and Solomon.

Jerusalem is first named in Egyptian execration texts from the 19th century, which solemnly curse her Amorite chiefs.[1] The settlement at this time was on the south-eastern hill, called Ophel. This is actually the smallest of the three hills which Jerusalem came to occupy in the time of the Hebrew Monarchy. It is, however, a strong position naturally fortified by the valleys of the Kidron to the east and the depression between the East and West Hills called by Josephus the Tyropoean (' Cheesemakers' ') Valley. East of Ophel, moreover, in the Kidron Valley was the only accessible perennial spring in the vicinity. Here was the Jebusite fortress taken for David by his kinsman Joab, and it is very doubtful if David extended the area of occupation, though he did acquire a portion of the hill immediately north of Ophel as a sacred area and the site of the future Temple. The sacred associations of this place probably go back to a remote antiquity, centring upon the famous rock under which is a cave, over which the Moslem Dome of the Rock is built. It is generally held that

---

[1] *v. supra*, 71 ff.

here was either the Holy of Holies in Solomon's Temple or the site of his great altar of sacrifice, though on this matter it is impossible for archaeology to declare.

On the Ophel Hill certain portions of the old Jebusite wall have been discovered with revetments of really impressive strength. Behind such walls (nearly thirty feet thick) the Jebusite defiance of David's striking-force (2 Sam. 5:6) was not quite unjustified. The most satisfying feature of Warren's work in 1867 was the discovery of a vertical shaft leading down to a subterranean tunnel which connected with the spring in the Kidron Valley outside the city wall called anciently Gihon (' Gusher ') from its intermittent flow and now Ain ed-Daraj (' Spring of the Stairway '). Water being thus accessible from the shelter of the city wall, the source could be walled over and so concealed from any assailants. It is interesting to note that similar works, though on a more impressive scale, have been found at Megiddo, Gezer, and Gibeon. At Megiddo, for instance, a great shaft with a stairway was sunk over eighty feet within the city and water was brought in through a rock-cut tunnel over fifty yards long. Such works no doubt reflect the insecurity in Palestine in face of the raids of landlopers from the Ḥabiru mentioned in the Amarna Tablets to the Hebrew Settlement c.1200 B.C. The tunnel and shaft of Jerusalem, however, did not prove adequate in David's attack on the city, and may, in fact, have been the very means of Joab's success.[1]

Among the various hydraulic works which derive from the spring of Gihon there is one which almost certainly dates from the early Hebrew Monarchy. That is a channel which follows the contour on the east of the Ophel Hill. This channel sometimes travels under the rock, but more often it is open, and at various points there are traces of lateral sluices, and finally it debouches into an open pool called Birket el-Ḥamra in the depression between the Ophel Hill and the West Hill of ancient Jerusalem. There it is contained by a barrage built across the lowest point of the valley. The purpose of this channel was obviously not strategic, but agricultural, to irrigate the plots in

---

[1] In this passage the Hebrew text is somewhat uncertain, and the word for ' gutter ' or ' shaft ', ṣinnor, is not well enough attested in Hebrew to be certain. The Arabic cognate means ' baking oven '. In this connection Macalister attests a local tradition at Gezer that in the Flood the waters came up from a ' ṭannur '. Here ' baking oven ' gives no sense, and it is likely that local Arabic has preserved the Hebrew word for ' water-shaft ' (ṣinnor). One of the best examples of a watershaft and tunnel is at Gezer (R. A. S. Macalister, *The Excavation of Gezer* 1 (1912), 262 ff., fig. 134).

the Kidron Valley, where 'the King's Gardens' were. The work was only practicable at a time of unbroken peace and security. No time after the reign of Solomon until the time of Hezekiah would have permitted such a work to be made or freely used. By that time a further development of the water system was undertaken, the underground conduit to the Pool of Siloam.[1] The insecurity which necessitated the latter work would have rendered the first mere folly.

As a characteristic feature of the building of the various sites in the hill-country of the interior of Palestine and the foothills which were fortified in the period of the Hebrew settlement we have noted casemate walling. This was employed in the fortification of Bethshemesh and Tell Beit Mirsim on the Philistine frontier, which are dated in the 10th century B.C., probably under David. This technique, however, though adequate as a defence against local resistance, had its limitations. In the IVth level at Megiddo a new and more substantial, though more costly, technique of building was employed. This is the period of solid bonded masonry of stones carefully dressed in a style now recognised as a Phoenician feature. The fact, however, that the stonework of Megiddo IV shows the same technique as that of Samaria, which was not built until fifty years after Solomon in the fifth year of Omri, must make it uncertain whether the features of Megiddo IV are due to Solomon or to Omri or his son Ahab. The problem is complicated by the fact that only half a century intervenes between Solomon and Ahab and that both had intimate associations with the Phoenicians.

Now a heavily fortified double gateway with side-chambers gives access to Megiddo [2] and is found also at Gezer, Lachish, Ḥirbet el-Ḥeleifeh (probably Ezion-Geber) on the Gulf of Aqaba, and now at Hazor.[3] The defences of Lachish are generally associated with the reign of Rehoboam, the son of Solomon, after the revolt of the northern tribes and the reduction of his kingdom (2 Chr. 11:11–12), and indeed, there was need for such fortification in the time of Rehoboam rather than in the halcyon days of Solomon. Rehoboam, however, had no authority at Megiddo, so the fortifications there must be the work either of Solomon or

[1] v. infra, 155
[2] P. L. O. Guy, 'New Light from Armageddon', Oriental Institute Communications 9 (1931), 24 ff., figs. 15, 16. In its final form this gateway belongs to Level III (c.780–650 B.C.), though it is built over foundations of the Solomonic Age (R. Lamon and G. M. Shipton, Megiddo 1 (1937), 74 ff., figs. 86–8)   [3] Y. Yadin, Biblical Archaeologist XXIII (1960), 62–8

Plate 10 Aerial view of Hazor, with Israelite strata in foreground and Canaanite city in depression behind, and Middle Bronze Age ramparts of beaten earth

Plate 11   Water-tunnel at Megiddo

Omri or Ahab. The gateway of Ḥirbet el-Ḥeleifeh, however, is beyond doubt the work of Solomon, which suggests that the gateway of Megiddo is also the work of his reign. This would support the Biblical statement which ascribes to Solomon the fortification of Megiddo, Gezer, Hazor, and Jerusalem (1 Kg. 9:15). Dr Yadin in a limited, but highly significant, excavation within the wall of Megiddo just east of the main gateway determined that the great chambered gateway was originally associated not with the solid city-wall but with an earlier casemate wall,[1] as at Hazor in the Solomonic era, the imposing outer wall of solid bonded masonry at Megiddo, as at Samaria, being the work of Ahab. The association of the chambered gateway with a case-mated city-wall is a feature of the fortification of Gezer also, where Yadin on investigation recognised such a gateway in what Macalister had termed a ' Maccabaean castle '.[2] He further determined that the gateways at Gezer and Hazor were of the same plan and almost of the same dimensions, suggesting that they were from the same architect.

At his work at Megiddo in 1903–5 the German archaeologist Schumacher noted certain dressed limestone pillars standing in alignment, which he took to be cult-objects, presumably *maṣṣēbhôth*, standing-stones characteristic of Canaanite sanctuaries. Strati-fied excavation, however, by P. L. O. Guy under the Oriental Institute of the University of Chicago revealed a whole series of such pillars standing regularly in several blocks. Their true nature was indicated by the fact that each was perforated at its angle, and between each pair was a hewn limestone trough. It was obvious that these were not the standing-stones of a sanctuary but tying-posts of stables. Adjacent to these stalls the foundations and lower courses of the walls of other buildings were found which were obviously sheds for chariots and barracks for grooms, with an open parade-ground. There was, in all, accommodation for 450 horses. Recent consideration of the ceramic evidence in the light of remains from Samaria, which preclude a date before Omri, suggest that the Megiddo stables may be those of Ahab rather than, as is generally stated, of Solomon, and certainly Megiddo is not actually mentioned as one of Solomon's chariotry depots. This question too has been resolved by Yadin's limited excavation east of the main gateway at Megiddo, for he found

---

[1] Y. Yadin, op. cit., *Hazor* II (1960), 3
[2] id., ' Solomon's City Wall and Gate at Gezer ', *Israel Exploration Journal* VIII (1958), 80–6

that the casemate wall which was overbuilt by the solid city-wall
of Ahab, as well as being associated with the Solomonic gateway,
was also associated with a fort in the area excavated, which was
a counterpart to the fort on the south side of the city, attached to
which was one of the stable-complexes. Hence the southern fort
and possibly also the stables attached were Solomonic. The
north fort, however, which must be Solomonic, was actually
overbuilt by a stable-complex. Thus the north stable-complex is
definitely not the work of Solomon but of Ahab, while the south
stable may be Solomonic. Nevertheless the discovery does illustrate the conception of a great chariotry base, of which Solomon
is said to have had several throughout his realm (1 Kg. 9:19 ;
10:26). In the light of the new evidence from Megiddo, Guy
saw a similar stable-complex in the alignment of pillars which
F. Bliss attested at Tell el-Ḥesy (possibly Eglon) between Hebron
and Gaza and took to be a sanctuary.[1] At Taanach too, near
Megiddo, Guy would so identify a double alignment of pillars
which Sellin described as the standing-stones of a sanctuary.[2]
This seems to be corroborated by three pillars with perforated
corners which he found re-used in a later Iron Age stratum.[3] The
stable accommodation at Megiddo, even if not all Solomonic,
indicates that the statement that Solomon had 1,400 chariots (1 Kg.
10:26) is no exaggeration but an accurate report. Apparently
Solomon was determined to bring Israel right into line with the
powers of the day in mobile warfare, though he undertook no
major military enterprise. It is a common misapprehension that
Solomon engaged in trade in horses and chariots with Egypt.
In 1 Kings 10:29 the Greek version helps us to a clearer understanding of the doubtful Hebrew text, and the source of the horses
and chariots is stated to be Kue, known from Mesopotamian texts
as a district in the Taurus foothills in south-western Anatolia.
To be sure, the Greek text, like the Hebrew, also mentions Egypt
(Miṣraim), but the mention of Kue suggests that this is a mistake
for Muṣri, another district in the same region, which is well
known in Assyrian historical inscriptions.[4] This region is well
known also as the home of horse-breeders from almost a millennium before the time of Solomon, and the mountains of the
region would naturally supply the wood for the chariots, rather

---

[1] F. Bliss, A Mound of Many Cities (1898), 90 ff.

[2] E. Sellin, Tell Taʻannek (1904), 18, 104, fig. 10

[3] P. L. O. Guy, op. cit., 44

[4] Togarmah in the same region is noted as a place where Tyre obtained
horses (Ezek. 27:14).

than Egypt, which depended on the Lebanon for her wood supplies. Concerning Solomon's alleged traffic in horses and chariots on the grand scale, it must be noted that there are no grounds in the Hebrew text for this assumption, and still less in the Greek version. In the former it is said that the kings of the Hittites and the kings of the Aramaeans got their horses and chariots at the same price *by the agency* [1] of Solomon's dealers, who presumably drove this trade as a side-line to defray their expenses by the way, and possibly as a safe-conduct on their way through Syria to the far north. In the Greek text all that is said is that the kings of the Hittites and the Aramaeans *of the West* [1] got their horses and chariots from the same source and at the same price as Solomon. The horses and chariots which Solomon had brought to Palestine were for his own use, and the fruits of his efforts are seen in the next century when, according to the inscription of Shalmaneser III, Ahab, the King of Israel, was able to put into the field 2,000 chariots, almost twice as many as those of Damascus, the next largest chariot-force of the Syrian allies at the Battle of Qarqar in 853 B.C. [2]

The most striking extant evidence of the development of the Hebrew kingdom at this time is the mining activity in the Wadi Araba. In the deep escarpments, particularly east of this great depression between the Dead Sea and the Gulf of Aqaba, veins of copper had been exploited in open-cast mining by Egypt in the Pyramid Age (third millennium). Up to the 4th century of our era Christians were condemned with criminals to penal servitude in this torrid region, and the ores are being exploited again, after ages of inactivity, at Timnah some twenty miles north of Elath in the new state of Israel. It was probably these valuable deposits of copper and iron that induced David to subjugate Edom, in whose territory most of the mines lay (2 Sam. 8:14 ; 1 Chr. 18:11–13 ; 1 Kg. 11:15–16). This is possibly the histori-cal base of the Moslem tradition which regards David as the pioneer in metal-working. Professor Glueck, who has explored the whole region of the Araba and the country east and west of it, has discovered many of these ancient workings and the remains of the furnaces where the ore was first roughly smelted before being taken to the refinery. The pottery remains on the surface

---

[1] These two phrases in Hebrew differ by only one extra letter in the former which happens to be of the same shape as the preceding cipher.

[2] D. D. Luckenbill, *Ancient Records of Assyria* I, § 611. Damascus, however, had a contingent of mounted cavalry, which Israel had not.

indicate that the ores were worked during the early Hebrew Monarchy. Walled enclosures of the same date in the vicinity of the mines probably reveal the fact that, as in the Christian era, mining was done by slave labour, probably by the hapless Edomites and other prisoners from David's wars with his neighbours.

The most spectacular achievement of Glueck in this region was the discovery of the site where the metal of the Araba was refined, and the port from which Solomon and his Phoenician partners launched their maritime enterprises down the Red Sea (1 Kg. 9:26–7 ; 10:22). Here at Ḥirbet el-Ḥeleifeh, about half a mile from the present shore of the Gulf of Aqaba, Glueck, under the auspices of the American School of Archaeology at Jerusalem, unearthed from the low sandhills a settlement which he described as ' the Pittsburgh of Palestine '.[1] This settlement in such an unpleasant situation, some distance from fresh water and directly in the path of the prevailing wind, which blows strongly down the deep rift of the Araba, presented something of an enigma. The problem was solved when Glueck found an elaborate system of blast-furnaces with flues so placed as to exploit the prevailing wind. This town, the only settlement of comparable extent of the Early Iron Age in this vicinity, was built to refine the copper and iron mined and smelted in the Araba and probably to produce finished articles in these metals, especially in copper. The copper for the two great bronze pillars Jachin and Boaz, the ' sea ', or vast basin, on its twelve bronze bulls and other appointments of the Temple almost certainly passed through the crucibles of this very refinery, though they were actually cast in the claybeds of the Jordan Valley between Succoth and Zeredath (2 Chr. 4:17), near the mouth of the modern Wadi Faʿra on the west and the Wadi Zerqa (Jabboq) on the east.[2] Much of the copper of the Araba, however, was exported, either in finished

---

[1] N. Glueck, ' The First Campaign at Tell el-Kheleifeh ', *Bulletin of the American Schools of Oriental Research* 71 (1938), 3–18 ; ' The Second Campaign . . .', *BASOR* 75 (1939), 8–22 ; ' The Third Season . . .', *BASOR* 79 (1940), 2–18

[2] The excavations of H. J. Franken at Deir ʿAlla in this vicinity attest deposits of metal slag at every level in the Iron Age. Furnaces were sited outside the city wall and in one a pottery spout of a crucible was found with a piece of copper still in it. Surface explorations revealed that the whole region was a centre of the metal industry in the time of the Hebrew monarchy, possibly because the local clay was suitable for moulds, but also possibly because of the long experience of the local people in the craft, H. J. Franken, ' The Excavations at Deir ʿAlla in Jordan ', *Vetus Testamentum* x (1960), 386–93. We suggest that the name Sukkoth may reflect the origin of the place as a settlement of Kenites or itinerant smiths, see above, p. 15.)

articles or ingots, in the trading expeditions of Solomon and the
Phoenicians to south Arabia and east Africa. We can, however,
scarcely expect elaborate dockyards at this site, since the ships
would be of no greater draught than the coasting schooners
familiar from Egyptian tomb-paintings in antiquity and in the
Mediterranean and Red Sea ports today. There is, however,
possible evidence of ship-building in certain long spikes of iron
and of an alloy of copper and iron, together with the remains
of thick cables and lumps of pitch. The timber, no doubt, was
drawn from the well-watered western escarpment of Edom,
which was well timbered until quite recently when the Turks
made havoc with the wood for the engines of the Hejaz Railway.
The pottery, whereby the strata of the site are dated, indicates an
origin not earlier than the latter part of the 11th century B.C.
The town, in all probability Ezion-Geber (1 Kg. 9:26), was built
on a virgin site in the early Hebrew Monarchy. It was primarily
a great refinery carefully sited for that purpose, but it also
commanded an important caravan trade-route from the incense-
bearing lands of south Arabia via the oases of the Hejaz to
Egypt. The settlement was conceived and constructed as a
whole. The walls have apparently disappeared, but a great
double gateway such as those of Lachish, Megiddo, and Gezer
suggests that the place was strongly defended, possibly less against
any enemy without, since David's ruthless subjection of the
Edomites (1 Kg. 11:15–16), than against the revolt of the slave
labourers within.

The establishment of the House of David effected great
developments in the polity of the tribes of Israel. David had
come to prominence as a professional soldier under the modified
feudal system of Saul, and was the feudal vassal of the Philistine
Achish of Gath when he became King of Judah and affiliated
peoples in the south. Like Saul he was accorded the title King,
though it may well be that in the earlier part of his reign in
Hebron he adopted a title less obnoxious to the tribal suscepti-
bilities of his people. ' David ', in fact, may not have been the
name of the king at all but simply a title *dawîdum*, now known
from the political documents of Mari [1] as an Amorite word
signifying leaders of tribes or governors of districts in Mesopotamia in the 18th and 17th centuries B.C.

After his occupation of Jerusalem, however, David was to
develop the conception of the kingship in Israel as an office

[1] *v. supra*, 36

invested with all the mystery and majesty of sanctity. He was, of course, still a feudal war-lord, drawing his retainers from the whole land including Philistines, possibly promoted from among his own retainers at Ziklag, which he had received as a hereditary fief from Achish of Gath. In this as in many other respects David's kingship reflects the conception of kingship current in Canaan for more than half a millennium. With David, however, the office was to attain to a degree of sanctity which it never had in the time of Saul, even though he was ' the Lord's anointed ' after his consecration at Gilgal. The sacral aspect of the kingship might be illustrated by texts from Egypt and Mesopotamia which indicate that the Pharaoh was actually regarded as the god incarnate and the kings of Babylon and Assyria were specially called and adopted as the son of the god. The Hebrews never committed themselves to the deification of the king, though the rather fulsome and extravagant language of Egyptian royal address seems to find an echo in certain of the Hebrew royal psalms (e.g. Ps. 45:7). The Mesopotamian idea of kingship is more akin to the Hebrew conception of royalty and is consequently of great importance for a study of kingship in Israel. It is, however, more natural to regard the Davidic kingship as a development of the local Canaanite institution so well illustrated by the Ras Shamra Texts. We must, of course, do justice to the distinctively Hebrew modifications of the conception.

The ancient community was not primarily a political but a religious body. Hence in the legends of Ras Shamra the king realises in his person the sacramental union of his people and their god. He represents the people as their priest in seasonal rituals relating to agriculture, as the king in the Ras Shamra Texts, and on occasions of public disaster, experienced or apprehended, he makes confession and supplication, as the king in the Assyrian penitential psalms. The Israelite king had also priestly functions. From David's dedication of the altar on the site of the Temple (2 Sam. 24:25) and Solomon's dedication of the Temple (1 Kg. 8:12) we see a great development in the conception of kingship since the days of Saul, whose right to sacrifice, even in emergency, was considered as an infringement of the priestly rights of Samuel (1 Sam. 13:11 ff.).

In virtue of his sacral status the king is the mediator of the blessing of God to the community. In the two long texts from Ras Shamra concerning the ancient kings Keret and Dan'el both are called ' Healers ' or ' Dispensers of Fertility ', and in a time of drought the latter makes a round of his crops, kissing and embracing the plants as a rite of homoeopathic magic to stimulate fertility.[1] So in an Assyrian text the accession of Ashurbanipal (668–626 B.C.) inaugurates an era of universal fertility :

> Adad [2] let loose his showers,
> Ea [3] opened his fountains,
> The corn grew five ells high in its ear,
> The spike became five sixths of an ell,
> . . . .
> The fruit-trees brought the fruit to luxuriant issue,
> The cattle were prosperous in parturition.
> In my reign exuberance superabounds,
> In my years superfluity is heaped up.[4]

Thus in the Hebrew royal psalm, 72, the king is the channel of all kinds of natural blessings :

> He will descend like rain upon the crop,
> Like showers that water the earth (v. 6).

It is to be observed, however, that in Israel these blessings through the king were conditional upon his standing in a right moral relationship to God.

The king, standing in intimate relationship to God, discerns the true and the false, and is a medium of justice. David and Solomon occasionally dispensed justice in person, just as Keret and Dan'el in the Ras Shamra Texts

> . . . decide the case of the widow,
> . . . judge the suit of the orphan.

The royal psalms in the Old Testament are eloquent of the social blessings mediated by the king, and the prophet Isaiah saw in the birth of a prince of the Davidic house the dawn of a new age of preternatural peace and well-being :

There shall come forth a shoot from the stock of Jesse,
And out of his roots a branch sprout forth.
Jehovah's own spirit shall rest upon him—
The spirit of wisdom and insight,

---

[1] In *Midrash Rabba* on the Song of Solomon vii, 3 there is a reference to the custom of passers-by kissing heaps of grain lying on threshing-floors.
[2] The god of winter rain, storm, thunder, and lightning
[3] The god of the earth and subterranean waters
[4] *Annals of Ashurbanipal*, ed. R. J. Lau and S. Langdon 1 (1903), 45 ff.

The spirit of counsel and might,
Of the knowledge and fear of Jehovah.
He will not judge after the sight of his eyes,
Nor decide by what he hears with his ears ;
But with justice shall he deal with the cause of the helpless,
The case of the poor he will settle with equity.
With the rod of his mouth he will smite the tyrant,
And slay the unjust with the breath of his lips.
His loins shall be girt with the girdle of justice,
His waist shall be bound with the circlet of faithfulness.
The wolf shall lodge with the lamb,
And the leopard lie down with the kid ;
And the calf and the lion together shall graze,
And a little child shall lead them.
And the cow and the bear shall be friends,
And their young ones shall lie down together.
The lion shall eat straw like the ox.
The suckling shall play over the hole of the asp,
And the weaned child put forth his hand upon the hole of the viper.
None shall do hurt or havoc
On all my holy mountain :
For then the earth shall be filled
With the knowledge of Jehovah
As the waters cover the sea.[1]

This ideology of kingship may be further paralleled from Egypt. Thus the accession of Merneptah is heralded :

> Be glad of heart, the entire land ! The goodly times are come ! A lord—life, prosperity, health !—is given in all

---

[1] Isa. 11:1–9 ; after J. E. McFadyen, *Isaiah in Modern Speech* (1918), 43–4, 201. The imagery of Isaiah here is reminiscent of the ancient Sumerian conception of the delectable land of Dilmun, thought by some to be the island of Bahrein, where

> the raven croaks not,
> The bird of ill omen utters not its ominous cry,
> The lion kills not,
> The wolf snatches not the lamb,
> Unknown is the kid-devouring wild dog.
> . . . .
> The sick-eyed says not ' I am sick-eyed ',
> The sick-headed says not ' I am sick-headed ',
> Its old woman says not ' I am an old woman ',
> Its old man says not ' I am an old man ' . . .

(adapted from S. N. Kramer in J. B. Pritchard, *Ancient Near Eastern Texts relating to the Old Testament* (1950), 38, from a Sumerian tablet from Nippur)

lands, and normality has come down (again) into its place. The King of Upper and Lower Egypt, the lord of millions of years, great of kingship like Horus . . . he who crushes Egypt with festivity, the son of Re (most serviceable of any king, Mer-ne-ptah Hotep-her-maat—life, prosperity, health ! All ye righteous, come that ye may see. Right has banished wrong. Evil-doers have fallen upon their faces. All the rapacious are ignored. The water stands and is not dried up. The Nile lifts high. Days are long, nights have hours, and the moon comes normally. The gods are satisfied and content of heart. (One) lives in laughter and wonder. Mayest thou know it.[1]

One might suppose from the close proximity of Egypt and from the affiance of Solomon with a daughter of the Pharaoh that the ideology of kingship in Israel would owe something to Egyptian influence, at least after the time of Solomon. A pertinent analogy is the case of the royal family at Ugarit, sculptures of whom [2] recall the family portraits of Akhnaten from Tell el-Amarna. In Israel the affinity with Egypt is particularly close in the accession ritual. To be sure there are but two passages which note this formality explicitly, 1 Kings 1:33 ff., describing the anointing of Solomon, and 2 Kings 11, which describes the investiture of the young king Joash. It is the latter which suggests affinity with Egyptian practice. Here the young king is presented to the people at a certain spot in the Temple precinct, either by a certain pillar or a special platform associated with this ritual (2 Kg. 11:14). This recalls the Egyptian custom explicitly noted in the XVIIIth Dynasty when the Pharaoh on a similar occasion stood in the temple of Amon on a special platform. Joash was then invested with the crown (nēzer) and what was apparently also a palpable object, ' the testimony ' (ha-ʿēdūth). This word, for which an emendation ha-ṣeʿādōth (' the bracelets ') has been suggested, is elucidated from Egyptian royal texts, from which it appears that on his accession the king was handed a protocol which contained the honorific throne-name and the divine authority to rule. G. von Rad, who has admirably elucidated this whole matter,[3] cites an inscription from the mortuary

---

[1] Cited from J. B. Pritchard, *Ancient Near Eastern Texts* . . ., p. 378
[2] *Syria* XXXI, 19   , Pl. IX
[3] G. von Rad, ' Die judäische Königsritual ', *Theologische Litteraturzeitung* LXXXII (1947), cols. 211–16

temple of Seti I in Karnak (ancient Thebes), where Thoth, the god of wisdom, declares to the Pharaoh :

> I have written thy protocol with my own fingers . . . I prescribed for thee 100,000 years.

This protocol contained, among other things, the definition of the Pharaoh's relation to the gods, as is apparent from an inscription relating to the coronation of the Queen Hatshepsut, where the god declares :

> My dear daughter . . . I am thy dear father. I established thy significance as ruler of both lands. I write thy protocol.

Such a text as this elucidates the royal psalm, Psalm 2 in the Hebrew psalter, which is to be understood as a reassuring oracle to the king on his accession or on the anniversary of it. There is reference to a formal decree (ḥōq) which is declared, and the content is :

> Thou art my son, this day have I begotten thee.

This is now known as the formula of adoption, and this conception appears very early in the history of the Hebrew monarchy, being expressed in the oracle of the seer Nathan to David (2 Sam. 7:12 ff.), which recurs throughout the history of the monarchy. In Hebrew usage, however, the identification of the king with God was in purpose only and not in nature.

Nathan's oracle makes it clear that the divine favour to the king was not unconditional. He would be identical in purpose with God and would abide in the divine favour only in so far as he kept the covenant of God. Now in Psalm 105:10 the term 'formal decree' (ḥōq) is found as a synonym with covenant (bᵉrīth), so that it is very probable that the testimony ('ēdūth) which was handed to Joash, and probably to all the kings who ascended the throne of David, contained the covenant and the law in nucleus, as it appears in the ten commandments (Exod. 20:3–17) or in the form to which the sacral assembly of Israel gave its assent in the sacrament of the Covenant in Deuteronomy 27:15 ff. Corroboration of this view that on his accession there was handed to the king with the crown (nēzer) a copy of the law and covenant is supplied by the reference in the royal psalm, Psalm 132:12, to crown (nēzer) and covenant (bᵉrīth). Thus, if indeed Israel borrowed in this particular from the Egyptian coronation-ritual, this is but another instance of the spiritual vitality of Israel in that she stamped with her own spiritual ethos that which she adopted from the higher material culture of her neighbours.

With David, who was acclaimed 'the lamp of Israel' (2 Sam. 21:17), a new factor had been created in Israel, the king, who concentrated in himself, as none of the old judges or Saul had done, the life of the people, and whom they came to regard as 'the breath of their nostrils' (Lam. 4:20).[1] The unique status of the king was expressed in Egypt by the worship of the Pharaoh as the god incarnate ; in Mesopotamia he was regarded as the representative of the god, specially marked out or 'elect', suckled by goddesses, and adopted as the son of the god. The conception of the king as the son of El, the senior god of the Canaanite pantheon, is found in the Keret legend and is used in Israel to express the intimate relationship between king and god. This, however, in Israel is a social and not a natural relation. The king is the adopted son of God (Ps. 2:7), whose will is the king's will. This relationship is explicitly stated and is the subject of a covenant in God's pledge to maintain the House of David (2 Sam. 7:12–16). The concentration of the hope of the community in one particular and unique family is a new element in the social life of Israel, which is only intelligible against the background of the contemporary Near East as that is revealed by archaeology through the cuneiform documents of Mesopotamia and Ras Shamra. The regular ritual at Jerusalem by which the conception was propagated was made possible by the fact that the city was the personal possession of David and his family. David's supreme master-stroke of policy was to bring the ark, the symbol of the common faith of all Israel, to Jerusalem and to associate the covenant of Yahweh with Israel with His covenant with the House of David.

In administration too a new order was inaugurated under the House of David and here again the administrative texts from Ras Shamra show that a Canaanite pattern was followed. From conscription lists and deeds of conveyance from the palace at Ras Shamra we find that the realm was organised for fiscal purposes not by families but by districts and by classes, which at once suggests the fiscal division of the kingdom under Solomon, where

---

[1] These two passages are felicitously cited by A. R. Johnson in the beginning of his study *Sacral Kingship in Ancient Israel* (1955), 1–2.

old tribal divisions, though partially observed, were often sup-
planted by territorial divisions (1 Kg. 4:7–19). The deeds of
conveyance from Ras Shamra indicate that a large part of the
land, if not all of it, was at the disposal of the king, carrying
burdens to the palace, such as tax in money and produce, cattle,
corn, olives, and fermented drink. Here is the prototype of
Solomon's fiscal system :

> And Solomon had twelve officers over all Israel, which pro-
> vided victuals for his household . . . (1 Kg. 4:7 ff.).

Other crown burdens in ancient Ugarit were the labour of
serfs and beasts of burden. We do not know whether these
burdens were incumbent on the whole realm or only on crown
estates. In Israel, however, in spite of the fact that after the
incorporation of Canaanite towns in the kingdom of Solomon
there were probably extensive crown estates, there is good evidence that the system of forced labour under Solomon extended
to the Israelites as well as to the Canaanites, this being, in fact,
the cause of the defection of the northern tribes from Solomon
(1 Kg. 11:26 ff., 12:1–19 ; cf. 1 Sam. 8:16).

The political development under the Monarchy on the
Canaanite model shook the old tribal polity and its social ethic
to the core, and created a tension to which the prophets of Israel
bear eloquent witness. According to one tradition, which probably reflects a later date than the events it describes, and which
is generally accepted as reflecting the teaching of the prophets,
such complications had been visualised when the question of the
kingship had been raised in the time of Saul :

> This shall be the manner of the king that shall reign over
> you : He will take your sons, and appoint them for himself,
> for his chariots, and to be his horsemen ; and some shall run
> before his chariots.[1] And he will appoint him captains over
> thousands, and captains over fifties ; and will set them to
> plough his ground, and to reap his harvest, and to make his
> instruments of war, and instruments of his chariots. And he
> will take your daughters to be confectionaries, and to be
> cooks, and to be bakers. And he will take your fields, and
> your vineyards, and your oliveyards, even the best of them,
> and give them to his servants. And he will take the tenth of
> your crops and of your vineyards, and give to his officers, and

[1] *v. supra*, 128

to his servants. And he will take your menservants, and your maidservants, and your goodliest young men, and your asses, and put them to his work. He will take the tenth of your sheep : and ye shall be his servants. And ye shall cry out in that day because of your king which ye have chosen you . . . (1 Sam. 8:11–18).

This is just the situation indicated in the administrative and legal texts from Ras Shamra, where the king arranges conveyance of property, promotes overseas trade, makes grants of land in return for capital or for services rendered, as, for instance, to officials, feudatories, or concubines. From such a society we can well understand how lightly Ahab's Phoenician queen, Jezebel, regarded the matter of Naboth's vineyard (1 Kg. 21).

VIII The House of Joseph

THE achievements of Solomon were bought with a price, and from the abortive revolt of Jeroboam stimulated by Ahijah, the prophet of Shiloh, we see that Israel at least, as apart from Judah, was not in sympathy with the ' Grand Monarque '. Now on the death of Solomon the tribes of the north with the exception of Benjamin revolted from the House of David, and a leader was found in Jeroboam, who had meanwhile been a political refugee in Egypt, then under the Libyan usurper Sheshonk I (935–914 B.C.). An inscription of this Pharaoh on the pylon of the temple of Amon at Karnak (ancient Thebes) [1] agrees with the statement in 1 Kings 14:25–6, where an Egyptian expedition against Judah is dated in the fifth year of Rehoboam, the son of Solomon (926 B.C.). In the Karnak inscription, however, the Pharaoh claims to have taken certain north Israelite localities too, including towns along the trunk highways in the plains, such as Megiddo, Taanach, Shechem, and Bethshan. The fragment of a stele of Sheshonk at Megiddo bears out this statement, and the Egyptian evidence suggests that Sheshonk saw in this crisis in Israel an opportunity to secure Egyptian influence in Palestine through a vassal king, while taking the towns of the plains directly under Egyptian control. Similar evidence pointing to the same conclusion are scarabs and other material evidence of Egyptian types at this period at Gezer and Bethshemesh, and at Tell Ajjul, Tell Jemmeh, and Tell el-Far'a in the Wadi Ghazzeh.

The first capital of the Northern Kingdom was Shechem, a tribal centre and probably once the amphictyonic shrine of the tribes of north Israel early in the settlement, and traditionally associated with Jacob. The sacred significance of Shechem as the amphictyonic centre of all Israel is clearly indicated by the fact that it was here that Rehoboam, the son of Solomon, was to be made king of all Israel before a solemn assembly (1 Kg. 12:1) until his intransigeance occasioned the disruption of the kingdom. The refortification of Shechem at this time is probably associated with the assertion of Israelite independence under Jeroboam. The king's residence, however, and the seat of government until

---

[1] J. H. Breasted, *Ancient Records of Egypt* IV, §§ 709 ff.

the foundation of Samaria, was apparently Tirzah, some seven miles north-east of Shechem.

The location of this site at Tell el-Far'a, first proposed by W. F. Albright, now commands general agreement in the light of the excavations of the Dominican fathers, De Vaux and Stève, which have demonstrated the significant status of the city from the beginning of the third millennium B.C. to the Israelite period. The phases of the city's history in the latter period can be fairly accurately determined by reference to those of the not far distant Samaria, where, of course, pottery dating is much more accurate, since the site was not occupied till the time of Omri (880 B.C.) and was destroyed by the Assyrians in 723 B.C.

The tension between Israel and Judah after the disruption of Solomon's kingdom is reflected in the fortification of certain towns immediately north of Jerusalem, which was now a frontier area. Bethel was fortified at this time as the southernmost town of the North Kingdom and Tell en-Nasbeh (probably Mizpah of 1 Kg. 15:16–22) as the most northerly town of Judah, an imposing fortress with walls twenty feet thick.

The Dominican excavations at Tirzah prove that the first stratum of the Iron Age occupation of Tell el-Far'a terminates in a burnt level, which may be the remains of the fire started in despair by Zimri when confronted with the victorious troops of Omri (1 Kg. 16:18). There follows a phase of reconstruction, which, however, was somewhat abruptly broken off. Though the ramparts and fortifications were subsequently neglected, the place was still occupied, though on a much reduced scale and more in the nature of an open town than a fortified city.[1] The affinities between the pottery of this phase and that of the first two levels at Samaria [2] suggest that this is the time when Omri transferred his capital to the virtually virgin site of Samaria. By all tokens he transferred also all the influential men of Tirzah and probably also most of the artisans.[3]

There have been few men of ruling genius among the Hebrews. Perhaps owing to the inveterate tribal instinct, local feuds and neighbours' quarrels always tended to pre-occupy the kings of Israel to the exclusion of larger issues beyond the immediate horizon. Exceptions to this rule, such as Omri, are the more remarkable. We know little of Omri from the Old Testament, save that he came to the throne as the victor in a civil war,

---

[1] R. De Vaux and A. M. Stève, *Revue Biblique* LVIII (1951), 423
[2] R. De Vaux, *Revue Biblique* LXII (1955), 587   [3] ibid., 588

reigned six years in Tirzah, then shifted his capital to a virtually virgin site a dozen miles west of that town. The new town, Samaria, remained the capital of the kingdom until the end of the Monarchy of north Israel in 723/2 B.C. Omri and his son Ahab are summarily dismissed in the Old Testament with the familiar damning formula as those who ' did evil in the sight of the Lord more than any that were before them . . .'. For information of the material achievements of Omri we are referred to the royal annals. ' Now the rest of the acts of Omri and his might that he showed, are they not written in the Book of the Chronicles of the kings of Israel ? ' These royal annals have survived only as they are incorporated in the Books of Kings, and for the greatness of Omri, who lifted Israel out of the ruck of petty intrigue, civil strife, and border bickering with Judah into the community of nations, we have to rely on other sources of information.

The building of the new capital of Samaria was significant not only as a strategic measure. The town was a crown possession, Omri having actually bought the site. It was the first step taken by him to found a dynasty. In north Israel men had not yet accustomed themselves to hereditary authority, but thought of their kings as fundamentally the same as the old judges who were called *ad hoc* to meet a particular emergency and accepted by popular acclaim. By his acquisition of Samaria as a personal possession Omri hoped to make his heirs independent of the popular favour, as David had done in Jerusalem. In the north, however, the democratic spirit was too strong and the dynastic principle was apparently never freely admitted.[1]

Omri, however, did not succeed in perpetuating the authority of his house for more than half a century. Nevertheless, in his lifetime he reduced Moab to subjection to Israel, as is recorded in the inscription of Mesha from Diban in his account of his war of liberation,[2] with which we may compare the statement in 2 Kings 1:1 that Moab rebelled after the death of Ahab. Again, though Omri is never personally named in the Assyrian records, it is significant that in inscriptions of Adadnirari III (810–783 B.C.) and Tiglath-Pileser III (743–726 B.C.) and until the last days of the kingdom Israel is called ' The House of Omri ' (*Bit Ḥumria*). That the name of Omri should have been so used long after the extinction of his house is surely eloquent testimony to the real

[1] A. Alt, *Vetus Testamentum* I (1951), 9 ff.
[2] G. A. Cooke, *A Textbook of North Semitic Inscriptions* (1903), no. I

Plate 12   Stable-complex at Megiddo.

Plate 13*a*   A Canaanite rendering of the Egyptian goddesses Isis and Nephthys ; ivory plaque from Samaria of Ahab's time

Plate 13*b*   Sargon II, the conqueror of Samaria

greatness of the man, and may indicate that the policy of Omri brought Israel into harmonious trade-relations with Assyria, which had a commercial as well as a strategic interest in the west. This is suggested by the fact that Tyre and Sidon are mentioned among tributary states in Syria in the records of Ashurnasirpal II (883–859 B.C.), the contemporary of Omri and Ahab.[1]

Under Omri an alliance was effected with the Phoenicians of Tyre (1 Kg. 16:31), and Samaria shows many traces of the material culture of Tyre. In spite of the destruction which Samaria suffered, first by the Assyrians on the fall of the city in 723 B.C. and later by the Jewish prince John Hyrcanus in 134 B.C., fragments of the palace begun by Omri and finished by Ahab remain to suggest the strength and splendour of the city. The summit of the isolated hill was dominated by the palace-complex, built of fine bonded masonry. The palace of Ahab was indeed a palace of ivory (1 Kg. 22:39), since ivory plaques carved in low relief with Phoenician renderings of Egyptian motives have been found here. The fact that these are marked on the back with letters of the Phoenician, or proto-Hebraic, alphabet indicate that they were pieces for inlay of panelling and furniture (Am. 6:4), instances of which are found from roughly the same period in north Syria and Nineveh, e.g. an ivory plaque from an Assyrian palace at Arslan Tash in north Syria, probably Assyrian loot from Damascus, as the inscription ' Belonging to our lord Hazael ' indicates. The plaque probably came from a couch on which slept Hazael whom Elisha hailed as God's instrument of wrath on Israel (2 Kg. 8:12–13) (A. G. Barrois, *Manuel d'Archéologie Biblique* I (1939), 501–7, figs. 196–7). The palace-complex of Samaria was enclosed by a strong wall of fine Phoenician bonded masonry, founded on the rock and, indeed, laid in places in rock-cut foundation trenches. Two other walls and a fortified gateway lower down the hill enclosed the city, which, for its situation as well as for its fortifications, must have been most impressive.

The most significant political event in western Asia in the time of Ahab was the Battle of Qarqar on the Orontes in 853 B.C.,[2]

---

[1] So J. W. Jack, *Samaria in Ahab's Time* (1929), 120 ff., after E. Schrader

[2] This is the cardinal date in Hebrew chronology. Jehu's payment of tribute to Shalmaneser III is recorded in 841, and twelve years intervened between Ahab and Jehu, fourteen years according to the statement of the intervening reigns of Ahaziah and Joram (1 Kg. 22:51 ; 2 Kg. 3:1). But the Judaean scribe allowed one year for each reign, according to the local custom in Judah, where the accession-year did not count officially (see E. R. Thiele,

11

when a coalition of the kingdoms of the west confronted the
Assyrians and for the moment checked their westward expansion.
From the time of Tiglath-Pileser I the Assyrian kings were
attracted to the west, where the forests of the Amanus and
Lebanon offered the timber for building which they lacked in
the homeland, and the trade-routes offered opportunities to their
merchants.   Between the Assyrian homeland and the Lebanon
and Palestine, however, there were a number of small states
controlled by the Aramaeans, who had long exploited their
position as middlemen in the commerce of the Near East.   These
were the objects of Assyrian pressure, subjects and tributaries of
Assyria in her periods of strength and rebels when the opportunity
offered.   The annals of the successors of Tiglath-Pileser I attest
repeated punitive expeditions to Syria with cities reduced, mounds
of skulls piled up, populations enslaved, and heavy tribute levied
in bullion and in kind, including chariot-horses, cattle, sheep,
costly furniture, textiles, and trained slaves, such as female singers
and dancing-girls.   Eventually in the time of Ahab an effective
alliance of Aramaean states halted for the moment the drive of
Assyria to the west under Shalmaneser III (858–824 B.C.) at
Qarqar in the sixth year of his reign (853 B.C.).   In his account
of the campaign on a great monolith the Assyrian king gives a
list of his antagonists in this battle, in which we find that ' Ahab
the Israelite ' was present with a force of 10,000 infantry and
2,000 chariots.   Only Damascus contributed more infantry, while
Ahab contributed by far the largest number of chariots, the next
largest being 1,200 from Damascus.[1]   It is a significant sidelight
on the nature and limited value of the Old Testament as a
historical source that but for the Assyrian annals of Shalmaneser
nothing would have been known about this very important battle
in which so many Israelites were committed.   The Books of Kings
are part of the Israelite ' history of salvation ', and the Battle of

---

[1] The relative strength of the chief allies was as follows :

Hadadidri of Damascus .	.	1,200 chariots, 1,200 mounted cavalry, 20,000 foot
Irhuleni of Hamath .	. .	700 chariots, 700 mounted cavalry, 10,000 foot
Ahab of Israel .	. . . .	2,000 chariots, 10,000 foot

The Mysterious Numbers of the Hebrew Kings (1951)).   The date 853 must have
been the year of Ahab's death and 841 that of Jehu's succession.   From these
two points we may reckon back and forward on the basis of Biblical statements
and synchronisms.

Qarqar is one of those events of secular history which were recorded in 'the books of the chronicles of the kings of Israel', to which we are referred for 'the rest of the acts of Ahab and all that he did'.

On the fall of the House of Omri, Israel rapidly sank back into the obscurity of domestic rivalries and bitter border warfare with Judah and her Aramaean neighbours. The splendour of Ahab's Samaria was defaced by poor native building such as had always characterised the provincial towns of Israel and Judah, which were no more than large market villages, the most impressive feature of which was their fortification.

From Samaria about a century after the time of Ahab, in a building level associated with the revival of Israelite power under Jeroboam II, the contemporary of Amos,[1] a large number of inscribed potsherds were found. These are receipts from the royal treasury for corn, wine, and oil from certain districts in the vicinity of Samaria. The limitation of the localities to the vicinity of Samaria suggests that these are not fiscal dockets implying a fiscal system such as is attributed to Solomon (1 Kg. 4:7 ff.), but probably relate to crown property. The names of the local consigners and the palace officials are most interesting, being theophoric compounds of Baal as well as Yahweh. This is no doubt due to the fact that the local con-signers were Canaanite, for the most part, but in any case the situation is a vivid commentary on the prevalence of Baal worship in Israel and on the tendency stigmatised by Hosea to limit the power of Providence to the provision of the fruits of the earth.

From the middle of the 8th century B.C. the dark shadow of Assyria was never lifted from Israel, Judah, and the rest of western Asia. A dozen years after the great stand at Qarqar, Shalmaneser III records the homage of various princes of the west, among them *Yahua mar Ḥumria*, 'Jehu, the son of (the land of?) Omri'. Jehu is depicted in a very humble posture on his hands and knees before the Assyrian king, a very different figure from the man who was anointed by prophet's hand in the camp at Ramoth Gilead (2 Kg. 9:4-10), and drove 'furiously' to annihilate the House of Ahab and Jezebel and seize the throne of Israel. Hosea sees the man as an opportunist without con-science, who built his house on the 'blood of Jezreel'. Israel and Judah too had sunk to the status of vassal states to Assyria before Assyria, after the suppression of the revolt of Pekah

---

[1] J. W. Crowfoot, *Samaria-Sebaste I* (1942), 8

(2 Kg. 15:29) between 734 and 732 B.C., stripped Israel of Galilee and Transjordan. From Assyrian records we know that the latter became the Assyrian province of Gilzau (Gilead) and the former the province of Megiddo, so-called after the provincial capital. The country west of Carmel was organised as the province of Duru (Dor), and the Assyrian road was paved towards Egypt.

This phase of history is attested by the destruction of the great frontier fortress of Hazor in upper Galilee, recently excavated by Y. Yadin, where a layer of carbon has sealed off the furniture of the houses of the Israelite city (cf. 2 Kg. 15:29, and possibly Isa. 9:1). The third level at Megiddo was destroyed by Tiglath-Pileser III and the second level of the city was built, the most conspicuous feature being a large fort or watchtower. Samaria, the capital of all that remained of Israel, fell in 723 B.C., a layer of carbon indicating the destruction of the city. Samaria was rebuilt by the Assyrians as the capital of the province Samerina, and here and at the site of Tirzah and at Tell el-Farʿa in the Wadi Ghazzeh in the highway to Egypt the presence of the suzerain power is indicated by a type of pottery strange to Palestine, but common in the excavations of the palace at Nineveh just before this time. Two cuneiform deeds of convey-ance from Gezer dated in 649 B.C. are further evidence of the Assyrian domination, especially of districts along the highway to Egypt, in the time of Manasseh of Judah, who is known from Assyrian records as an Assyrian vassal.

This decisive phase of the Assyrian advance on Egypt is marked by a brutal policy of which Israel was yet to have full experience. As local risings were suppressed whole populations were deported and the country resettled with military colonists from various parts of the Assyrian Empire. The Old Testament records that Tiglath-Pileser III took Iyon, Abel-beth-Maacah, Yanoah, Kadesh, Hazor, Gilead, and Galilee, all the land of Naphtali, and carried them captive to Assyria (2 Kg. 15:29). The records of Tiglath-Pileser do not indicate the precise date here, but the event is certainly to be dated between 734 and 732 B.C. The relevant inscriptions suggest that the inhabitants of Samaria had just saved themselves by revolting from the national-ist champion Pekah. Tiglath-Pileser does not expatiate upon his treatment of the truncated remnant of Israel left under Hoshea in Samaria and the immediate environment, but we may well imagine what vassalage to Assyria implied from the statement that in the expulsion of the native ruler Hanno of Gaza at this time his personal property and his images were removed and images of Assyrian deities and of the king himself set up in their place. Sargon II, the brother of Shalmaneser V, records the final reduction of Samaria and the depopulation of all that was left of Israel in 723 B.C. to the extent of 27,290 souls, the military men, no doubt, and the influential, and the records of Sargon refer to a similar transference of population in the Philistine plain in preparation for the eventual invasion of Egypt, which materialised fifty years later.

IX The Decline of the House
of David

THE status of Judah after the death of Solomon and the disruption of the kingdom accords ill with the pretensions of the
House of David.   Year by year in the liturgy of the autumnal
New Year Festival God's covenant with Israel through the House
of David was reiterated ; Yahweh had chosen Jerusalem as the
seat of the Ark ; Zion was the new amphictyonic shrine of Israel,
'whither the tribes go up, even the tribes of the Lord' (Ps. 122:4),
and always a united Israel was visualised (Isa. 9:1 ff. ; Mic. 5:1 ff.).
Nevertheless the state of Judah was generally on the defensive,
as the fortifications of Rehoboam on the frontiers clearly demonstrate, and was even for a period a vassal state of Israel in the
days of Ahab and his family (1 Kg. 22 ; 2 Kg. 3 ; 11).   There
was, indeed, a revival of the power of Judah under Amaziah
(796–767 B.C.) and Uzziah (767–739 B.C.) and Jotham (739–
732 B.C.), which is attested by the fortification of sites in the
Negeb on the way to the Araba and the port of Ezion-geber
(2 Kg. 14:22 ; 2 Chr. 26:10 ; 27:4) [1] and of certain localiites in
the region now so well known through the discoveries at Qumran,
possibly 'the City of Salt' in its earliest stratum, which dates to
the second phase of the Iron Age (c.9th or 8th century B.C.).[2]
Uzziah's concentration on these semi-desert regions, however,
suggests a limitation of the potential of Judah.   It is rather
significant that though Amaziah, the father of Uzziah, was successful in his campaign against Edom (2 Kg. 14:7), his challenge
to Israel proved a fiasco and he had to suffer the indignity of
having the fortifications of Jerusalem dismantled by his more
powerful northern neighbour after defeat in battle at Bethshemesh
(2 Kg. 14:8–14).   The weakness of Judah was plainly revealed
by the politics of Ahaz, under whom Judah became a vassal of

[1] N. Glueck, 'The Fifth Season of Exploration in the Negeb', *Bulletin of
the American Schools of Oriental Research* 145 (1957), 11–25
[2] J. T. Milik and F. M. Cross have explored various sites in the Buqeia
in the vicinity of Qumran, which took their origin in the second phase of the
Iron Age.   They suggest that they were fortified by Jehoshaphat (cf. 2 Chr.
17:12) ('Explorations in the Judaean Buqeiah', *Bulletin of the American
Schools of Oriental Research* 142 (1956), 5–17).

Assyria. That Judah had so long escaped the embarrassing attention of imperialist Assyria was owing solely to the fact that she lay off the beaten track of world affairs. With the fall of Israel and the Aramaean states of Syria Judah came under the immediate purview of Assyria, though it is open to question if she would have suffered as she did at the hands of Assyria had Hezekiah preserved a prudent neutrality as he was counselled by the prophet Isaiah (Isa. 18 ; 19 ; 20). Nevertheless under Ahaz and Hezekiah Judah was tributary to Assyria,[1] a situation which lasted, with periodic revolts by Hezekiah, until in the days of Josiah Assyria was no longer able to make her dominion effective in the west.

Apart from the exaction of tribute from Judah, the Assyrians had practically by-passed the little hill-state in their advance through the coastal plain with Egypt as the ultimate objective. Sargon's planting of military colonies as far south as Rafah stimulated reaction from Egypt, whose agents became more active in Palestine in organising resistance in Judah, Moab, Ammon, and among the Philistines. The last seem to have been regarded as the instruments of the policy both of Egypt and of Assyria. In the revolt which eventually broke out Hezekiah of Judah played a conspicuous part, which is noted both in the Old Testament and in contemporary Assyrian records. According to the former Hezekiah ' smote the Philistines even unto Gaza ' (2 Kg. 18:8). The Assyrian records do not quite confirm this, but certainly suggest that Hezekiah had been the main instrument in substituting anti-Assyrian partisans for Assyrian agents in Askalon and Ekron, whence the Assyrian puppet Padi was removed for confinement to Jerusalem.

The insecurity of the period in face of the increasing domination of the west by Assyria is probably reflected in the Siloam tunnel in Jerusalem, the last of a series of hydraulic works from the spring of Gihon in the Kidron Valley, modern Ain ed-Daraj, ' the Spring of the Steps '. This conduit, totally underground, brought the water from east to west of the Ophel Hill to the Pool of Siloam. The script and idiom in which this work is recorded

---

[1] 2 Kg. 16 records the submission of Ahaz and the introduction of Assyrian elements in religion to the Temple precinct in the time of Tiglath-Pileser. Sargon also imposed Assyrian domination on Judah, the Philistines, Edom, and Moab, as he records in a fragmentary inscription on a prism from Ashur (E. F. Weidner, *Archiv für Orientforshung* xiv (1941), 40 ff. ; A. L. Oppenheim in Pritchard, *Ancient Near Eastern Texts relating to the Old Testament* (1950), 286–7).

on the wall of the tunnel at its egress indicates the period of Hezekiah, to whom such works are attributed (2 Kg. 20:20 and more precisely 2 Chr. 32:30). This work is described as follows :

> . . . the tunnelling. And this was the manner of the tunnelling, while yet . . . the pick towards each other, and while there were yet three cubits to be cut out one might hear them calling to one another for there was an overlap in the rock on the right. . . . And on the day when the tunnel was cut through, the miners struck out to meet each other, pick against pick, and the waters flowed from the spring to the pool 1,200 cubits, and 100 cubits was the height of the rock above the heads of the miners.

Here we have an example of the script and idiom in which the prophecies of Isaiah would be recorded if, indeed, they were written down during the prophet's lifetime.

The political situation, with its many points of contact with the Biblical account, is presented in the inscriptions of Sennacherib, supported by inscribed reliefs from his palace at Nineveh depicting the siege and capitulation of Lachish, the headquarters of the Assyrians when the memorable mission was sent to Jerusalem in the time of Isaiah. It is rather characteristic of the Old Testament that almost nothing is said about the Assyrian campaigns in Palestine at this time except concerning the episode of the Assyrian deputation to Jerusalem, in which Isaiah played so prominent a role. As an indication of the value of Assyrian inscriptions in supplementing the selective history of the Old Testament we may cite the inscription of Sennacherib describing the campaign of 702-701 B.C.[1] :

> In my third expedition I went down to the country of the Hittites. Luli, king of Sidon, was cast down by my royal brilliance and fled afar into the midst of the sea and died. The Greater Sidon, the Lesser Sidon, Bit-Zitti, Zarephath, Mahaliba, Usha, Aksib, Akko, his strongly fortified cities, where were also pasture and water, his fortified towns, the terror of the arms of Ashur overthrew and he cast himself at my feet. Tub'alu I placed on his royal throne, and tribute, yearly tribute, gifts to my majesty, I imposed upon him for the fourth time. All the kings of the Amorites brought rich presents, great gifts, before me and kissed my feet. And

[1] This is the celebrated Taylor Prism (D. D. Luckenbill, *Ancient Records of Assyria* II (1926–7), §§ 240 ff.)

Plate 14*a*   Tell Qudeirat, a Jewish fortress in the oasis of Kadesh-Barnea

Plate 14*b*   Reconstruction of Lachish of the Hebrew Monarchy

Plate 15 The siege of Lachish, from Sennacherib's palace at Ninev
torches from ramparts. Men and women leave with goods from a poste

yrian archers provide cover for a battering-ram, while defenders hurl
e the impalement of captives within sight of defenders

Plate 16   Fragments of the Lachish Letters

Zidqah, king of Askalon, who had not submitted to my yoke, the gods of his fathers' house, his sons, his daughters, his brothers I carried away and brought to the country of Ashur. Sarru-Ludarri, son of Rukibti, its former king, I set over the men of Askalon and gifts of tribute, my royal presents, I laid upon him, and he bare my yoke. In the course of my expedition Beth-Dagon, Jaffa, Beni-Barka, Azuru, Zidqah's cities, which did not hasten to fall at my feet, I besieged, took, and utterly despoiled. The governors, princes, and men of Ekron, who had thrown Padi their king and the sworn ally of the land of Ashur into chains of iron and handed him over to Hezekiah king of Judah . . . [lacuna] . . . their heart was afraid. They called on the kings of Egypt, the bowmen, chariots and horses of the country of Ethiopia, forces without number, and they went to their help. In the district of Eltekeh they set themselves in array against the charioteers, and the sons of the king of Egypt and the charioteers of the king of Ethiopia my hands captured alive in the battle. Eltekeh, Jamnia I took and utterly destroyed. To Ekron I drew near and the governors and princes who had revolted I slew and their corpses I lifted up and bound upon stakes. The children of the place, who had committed iniquity, I counted as spoil. The rest of them, who had not committed sin and wrong [i.e. revolted], whose guilt was not proved, I ordered to be released. Padi, their king, I took from the midst of Jerusalem and set him on his royal throne, and my royal tribute I imposed upon him. And Hezekiah of Judah, who had not bowed beneath my yoke, forty of his cities and numberless small towns in their neighbourhood I besieged and took ; 200,150 people, young and old, male and female, horses, beasts of burden, sheep, camels, cattle, and flocks without number I took from them and accounted as spoil.

This last statement, so graphically illustrated by reliefs from Sennacherib's palace at Nineveh, helps us to understand the personal predicament of the prophet Micah, whose home was at Marissa, some four miles from Lachish, Sennacherib's head-quarters during his campaign in Judah. In the significant expansion of the eschatological oracle (Mic. 4:3), where the prophet visualises every man secure ' under his vine and under his fig tree ', we have the fervent personal hope of the ruined peasant.

Sennacherib goes on to describe his reduction of Hezekiah to allegiance :

> Himself I shut up in Jerusalem, his royal city, like a bird in a cage ; strong forts against him I built. His towns which I had spoiled I took from him and gave them to Mitinti, king of Ashdod, Padi, king of Ekron, and Sili-Bel, king of Gaza, and made his country small. To the former gifts, my royal presents, I added tribute and laid it upon him. As for Hezekiah himself, the fear of my royal brilliance cast him down. . . .

In the light of this evidence it is probable that Hezekiah was left with little more than Jerusalem and the immediate environs in the hill-country of Judah, including his family possessions. At the utmost the reduced kingdom of Judah was limited to the mountains and remained so until Josiah recovered the lost lands and apparently extended his territory into the coastal plain in the decline of the power of Assyria after 621 B.C.[1]

It has been suspected that in the reign of Hezekiah there were two Assyrian expeditions associated with Sennacherib. The Old Testament is not clear on this matter, and it has been considered possible that accounts of two expeditions may be telescoped. Archaeology has now confirmed the theory of two expeditions of Sennacherib to the west. In 2 Kings 19:9 and Isaiah 37:9 Tirhaka is mentioned as creating a diversion against Sennacherib. Now inscriptions discovered by Laming Macadam in the Sudan [2] show that Tirhaka was too young to have taken part in the campaign mentioned in the Assyrian records in 701 B.C., hence there must have been two expeditions of Sennacherib in Judah, the second before the death of Sennacherib in 681 B.C., and of Hezekiah in 686 B.C.

Concerning the death of Sennacherib the Old Testament makes clear what is cryptic, though unmistakable, in the Assyrian records, the assassination of Sennacherib in a palace intrigue and the family feud which attended the accession of Esarhaddon, the son of Sennacherib, who ' reigned in his stead ' (2 Kg. 19:37).

---

[1] This situation is reflected in the description of the territory of Judah in Jos. 15, according to A. Alt (' Judas Gaue unter Josia ', *Palästina Jahrbuch* xxi (1925), 100–16). Recent exploration of sites in the vicinity of Qumran, itself the City of Salt, probably, indicates that the mention of settlements in the vicinity of Engedi in Jos. 15:61–2 is an anachronism, since they were not settled till the end of the 9th or possibly the 8th century B.C.

[2] M. F. L. Macadam, *The Temples of Kawa. I, The Inscriptions* (1940)

His succession once established, Esarhaddon carried the policy of his predecessors to its logical conclusion, and mounted an attack upon Egypt. Judah was now firmly under Assyrian control under Manasseh, who is named in Assyrian inscriptions of the period together with the kings of Edom and Moab and others from Syria as present in Nineveh as supervisors, or perhaps as hostages, while their subjects worked as labour gangs on Esarhaddon's public works.[1] The fact that Ashurbanipal mentions Manasseh as a vassal in his campaign against Egypt in 668 B.C.[2] suggests that in view of the situation in Egypt a very tight control was exercised on Judah. It is not remarkable that in this period the astral cults of Assyria were practised in Jerusalem (2 Kg. 21) and the reign of Manasseh was a blank period in Hebrew prophecy, so frequently associated with nationalism.

His flank thus secure, Esarhaddon invaded the Delta. In 670 B.C. the Egyptian forces were driven back on Memphis some fifteen miles upstream from Cairo. The Pharaoh Tirhaka was forced to withdraw to his native Sudan, and Egyptian resistance was, for the meantime, broken. An attempt at revolt was suppressed in 668 B.C. by Ashurbanipal, the successor of Esarhaddon, under whom Egypt was organised into twenty provinces, each under a governor directly responsible to the Assyrian king in person. In this remote western province of the Assyrian Empire, however, the local governors intrigued against one another and sought the support of Tirhaka, the native ruler of the Sudan. Taking advantage of this situation, Tirhaka actually established himself for a time in Thebes, the old capital of Egypt. The Assyrians, however, stormed and spoiled Thebes. The glory of the Pharaohs in their secluded garden-land was departed. The downfall of Egypt before the power of Assyria is a recurrent theme in the works of the Hebrew prophets, notably Nahum, who paints the ruin of Thebes, No-Amon ('the City of Amon') in striking colours (Nah. 3:8-10). The ruin of Thebes, however, suggests to the same prophet the circumstances of the fall of Nineveh herself. Assyria had apparently over-reached herself, and half a century after her ultimate triumph in Egypt her empire rapidly disintegrated.

[1] A. L. Oppenheim, *Ancient Near Eastern Texts relating to the Old Testament* (ed. J. B. Pritchard) (1950), 291. This is probably the source of the tradition of the deportation of Manasseh to ' Babylon ' (2 Chr. 33:11).
[2] Oppenheim, op. cit., 294

The Babylonian Chronicle, the decipherment of which is one of the significant achievements of recent archaeology,[1] makes it possible to trace this process and to date events accurately from 626 B.C. In that year in south Mesopotamia, which had always been uneasy under Assyrian domination, the Assyrian army was repulsed before Babylon, and Nabopolassar was proclaimed king. The next decade saw Assyria forced back on the defensive, and the situation brought the Medes from the eastern highlands under their king Cyaxares into the field, apparently independently of the Babylonians. It was apparent that Assyria could no longer take an active interest in Palestine, and accordingly in 621 B.C. Josiah introduced his famous reformation in Judah and then in the Assyrian provinces of north Israel. As well as being a reformation of religion this was a political gesture, an assertion of national independence in defiance of Assyria. In 614 the Medes captured and plundered Ashur, the old capital of Assyria, and effected an alliance with Nabopolassar, which conditioned the policy of Babylon until her fall to Cyrus of Persia in 539 B.C. Nineveh fell in 612 B.C. to the combined forces of Medes and Babylonians, who claimed respectively the Assyrian homeland in the north and her former provinces in the south of Mesopotamia as the fruits of victory.

Now Egypt, herself under Necho, who had been a vassal king of Assyria, entered the arena in an attempt to retrieve the situation, ostensibly for Assyria, but actually to anticipate Babylonian control of Syria and Palestine and a possible advance on Egypt herself. Supported by Egypt, an Assyrian king, Ashur-uballit, maintained at least token state in Harran, the ancient cult-centre of the moon-god in north Mesopotamia. Harran fell to the Medes and Babylonians, however, in 610 B.C. Still the Egyptians maintained their support, based apparently on the fortress of Carchemish commanding an important crossing of the Euphrates. Here the Babylonian Chronicle bears directly on the Old Testament. In the summer of the seventeenth year of Nabopolassar's reign (609 B.C.) an Egyptian army advanced over the Euphrates and made a great, though unsuccessful, effort to retake Harran. Josiah of Judah saw in Egyptian policy a menace

---

[1] The parts of the Babylonian Chronicle, extant on cuneiform tablets in the British Museum, which refer to the Neo-Babylonian period have been published with translations by C. J. Gadd (*The Fall of Nineveh* (1923)), Sidney Smith (*Babylonian Historical Texts* (1924)), and D. J. Wiseman (*Chronicles of Chaldaean Kings (626–56 B.C.) in the British Museum* (1956)).

to his designs for Hebrew independence and a revival of the united Monarchy, and, with a fine sense of opportunism, though obviously with insufficient strength, he opposed the Egyptians under Necho at Megiddo, the fortress commanding one of the vital passes from the plain of Sharon to the great central plain. In this encounter, now to be certainly dated in the early summer of 609 B.C., Josiah lost his life (2 Kg. 23:29–30 ; 2 Chr. 35:20–5). When Necho returned from Mesopotamia three months later he deposed Jehoahaz, the son of Josiah, whom his subjects had raised to the throne (2 Kg. 23:31),[1] and replaced him by his half-brother Eliakim. Now it is known that in the ancient Near East when a king acceded to the throne he was given a new 'throne-name', which was in fact an oracular assurance of the favour and support of God. The fact that Necho presumed himself to give the new king his throne-name, Jehoiakim, clearly emphasised the vassal status of Judah.

The power of Egypt in Palestine, however, was of short duration. According to Jeremiah 46:2 Necho again marched north in the fourth year of Jehoiakim (605/4), but was defeated by Nebuchadrezzar, the son of Nabopolassar at Carchemish, the Babylonian Chronicle again bearing out the accuracy of the statement in Jeremiah.[2] Once he had succeeded to the throne of his father in 604 B.C. Nebuchadrezzar apparently followed up this victory by making the authority of Babylon more effective in Syria and Palestine as far as the border of Egypt (2 Kg. 24:7). The Babylonian Chronicle dates this expedition in 604 B.C., explicitly mentioning the destruction of a city, probably Askalon.[3] Josephus, on the authority of the Babylonian chronicler, Berossus (3rd century B.C.), is more explicit, dating this in the regnal year of Nebuchadrezzar in the fourth year of Jehoiakim, i.e. 604 B.C.[4] Judah remained free from Babylonian invasion, though it is obvious that the kingdom became a vassal state of Babylon, since Jehoiakim paid tribute for three years (2 Kg. 24:1). The Book of Kings does not make it clear from what date Jehoiakim paid tribute, but in Josephus it is stated that the tribute was withheld in Nebuchadrezzar's fourth year, or the eighth of Jehoiakim,[5] when a punitive expedition was sent against Judah. This would

---

[1] This agrees with the statement in the Babylonian Chronicle that Necho's campaign in north Mesopotamia lasted from Tammuz (June–July) to Elul (August–September) (Wiseman, op. cit., 62–3).
[2] Wiseman, op. cit., 66–9   [3] ibid., 68–9
[4] Josephus, *Antiquities* x, vi, § 1   [5] ibid.

be in 601 B.C., when in fact the Babylonian Chronicle records an encounter with Egypt somewhere in Palestine. Egyptian resistance was now much stiffer, and the Babylonians withdrew after a bitter and indecisive battle.[1] This obviously was taken by Jehoiakim as a hopeful sign, and he witheld his tribute from Babylon. Eventually submitting to Babylon for three more years, Jehoiakim ventured again to withold tribute, in reliance, according to Josephus, on Egyptian support. This, however, did not materialise. The Babylonians advanced ; Jerusalem was laid under siege, and what remained of Judah outside the city was harried by troops of Aramaeans from the east and north-east, possibly at the instigation of the Babylonians (2 Kg. 24:2). The Babylonian Chronicle gives the precise date of the siege of Jerusalem, from December (Chislew), 598 B.C. to March (Adar), 597 B.C., when the city fell and Jehoiachin, the son of Jehoiakim, was captured with his family [2] after a reign of three months (2 Kg. 24:8). With the king all potential men of influence and nationalist sympathies in Judah were deported to Babylon. So thorough was the Babylonian repression that the land was denuded of all skilled craftsmen (2 Kg. 24:12 ff.). The king, who was but eighteen when he was deported (2 Kg. 24:8), spent the rest of his life in custody in Babylon until, at least, 561 B.C. in the accession-year of Awil-Marduk, the son of Nebuchadrezzar, which is the last date to which the final editor of the Books of Kings refers (2 Kg. 25:27 ff.).

Though the family of Jehoiachin was deported, Nebuchadrezzar retained Judah as a vassal kingdom under the uncle of Jehoiachin, Mattaniah, whose throne-name, Zedekiah, significantly, was given by the Babylonian war-lord. Zedekiah was a weakling, and, though he was a willing vassal of Babylon, he was not able to withstand forces in Judah and Jerusalem who still cherished hopes of national revival and even of the restoration of the deported king Jehoiachin (Jer. 28:1–4). The spirit of resistance was apparently fostered by Egypt, and when finally Zedekiah had been forced into open revolt in his ninth year (587 B.C.) a contingent from Egypt actually did take the field and succeeded in diverting the Babylonians from the siege of Jerusalem (Jer. 37:5, 7–9). Jewish resistance, however, was in vain and Egyptian help inadequate. The Babylonians invested Jerusalem, containing the city while they overran the provinces, reducing such fortresses as Lachish and Azekah (Jer. 34:7). Eventually after a

---

[1] Wiseman, op. cit., 70–1   [2] ibid., 72–3

year and a half Jerusalem fell, reduced by starvation and the concentrated attacks of the Babylonians in the eleventh year of Zedekiah in the summer of 586 B.C. (2 Kg. 25:8).

This last phase in the history of the kingdom of Judah is graphically illustrated by the excavation of Lachish, notably by the famous Lachish Letters. These documents, brief and to all but contemporaries cryptic, are inscribed potsherds, eighteen of which were recovered from the ashes of a guard-room flanking the city gate and three from inside the city. Significant as they are, it must be frankly stated that not only are they cryptic but they are also fragmentary, and certainly do not substantiate the Old Testament narrative to the particular degree which has been occasionally claimed. No less than sixteen sherds contain only a few disjointed lines, or even letters, or are mere lists of personal names. Notwithstanding, a reference has been found in one of these (Letter XVI) [1] to 'the prophet', either Jeremiah or his contemporary Uriah, the pacifist prophet who fled to Egypt in the time of Jehoiakim, but was brought back and put to death (Jer. 26:20–3). The actual text, in the middle of a large lacuna, reads '. . . yahu the prophet . . .'. While it is possible that the full name might be Jirmiyahu (Jeremiah) or Uriyahu (Uriah), the termination of the name was the common one at that time and the Book of Jeremiah testifies to many 'prophets' in his day attached to both court and cult, and as numerous as dervishes in Islam. Of the remaining five letters more is legible and intelligible, but none is complete. In two (Letters IV and V) the correspondents are not named ; the remaining three are addressed to a superior officer Ya'ush, probably the military commandant of Lachish ; one of these is from Hosha'yahu, possibly a political agent or an officer in charge of a military post, possibly between the main fortresses of Lachish and Azekah, twelve miles to the north-east. It is from the larger fragments of these five letters (Letters III, IV, V, and VI) that we are able to glean information on the local situation in the last unhappy years of the kingdom of Judah, and these we now quote [2] and annotate to indicate the precise extent and limitation of their value for the history of the period of Jeremiah.

[1] Numbered according to the enumeration in *Lachish III* (ed. O. Tufnell) (1953), 331–9
[2] We have advisedly refrained from textual and philological controversy, and, with slight modifications, cite the translation of D. Diringer in *Lachish III* (O.U.P.), 331–9.

Letter VI

(1) To my lord Ya'ush. May Yahweh let (2) my lord see (this season in good health). Who (3) is thy servant (but) a dog that my lord has sent the (letter) (4) of the king and (the letter) of the princes, saying (5) Read, I pray thee, And behold, the words of the (?) (6) are not good, weakening the hands. (7) . . . the hands of . . . . . . (8) My lord, wilt thou not write . . . . (9) . . . Why (?) should ye do (10) thus . . . . Jerusalem (?) . . . . . (11) king (?) . . . . (12) . . . . . . As Yahweh liveth, thy God (13) . . . . . . thy servant (14) . . . . has read the letter . . . . . (15) to . . . .

Lines 5 and 6 seem to refer to pacifism which weakened native resistance. This charge had been brought against Jeremiah, and it is interesting to note that the idiom ' weakening the hands ' (Jer. 38:4) is probably also used in the ostracon.

Letter V

(1) May Yahweh let my lord hear (2) a report of peace and good, this very (3) day, this very day. Who is thy servant (4) but a dog, that (thou hast sent) to thy (5) servant the letters . . . . . ? (6) Now thy servant has returned the letters (7) to my lord. May Yahweh (8) let see . . . (9) What has thy servant that he might (10) benefit or harm the king ?

Lines 9 and 10 seem to imply that the loyalty of the correspondent, a subordinate officer, had been impugned.

Letter III

(1) Thy servant Hosha'yahu has sent to (2) tell my lord Ya'ush : May (3) Yahweh let my lord hear a report of peace ! (4) And . . . . the open-eyed (5) . . . . thy servant to the letter which (6) my lord sent to thy servant yesterday to the effect that the heart (7) of thy servant . . . . since thou didst send to thy servant, (8) and that my lord has said : Thou dost not know it ; (9) read a letter. As Yahweh

liveth, no one has ever tried (10) to read me a letter, moreover (11) whatever letter may have come to me I have not (12) read it . . . . (13) . . . . anything, and to thy servant it has been told (14) saying : Down went the commander of the army (15) Koniyahu, the son of Elnathan, to go (16) to Egypt, and (17) Hodayahu, the son of Ahiyahu, and (18) his men he sent to take . . . . (19) and as for the letter of Tobyahu, the servant of the king, which came (20) to Shallum, the son of Yaddua͑ from the prophet saying : (21) Beware !   Thy servant has sent it to my lord.

The reference in lines 14–18 to the visit of the general Koniyahu, son of Elnathan, to Egypt is interesting in view of the mission of Elnathan, son of Achbor, to Egypt to bring back the prophet Uriah in the reign of Jehoiakim (Jer. 26:20–3).   It may well be that Koniyahu of the Lachish letter was the son of that Elnathan. The occasion of Koniyah's mission was possibly to enlist the help of Egypt, either before or after the diversion created by the Pharaoh during the final siege of Jerusalem (Jer. 37:5, 7–9). The reference to the prophet as the medium of a warning or cautionary message is also interesting.   Was this a counsel of moderation which Tobyahu sought to reinforce by prophetic authority ?   Or was a prophet such as Jeremiah, or even Jeremiah himself, acting through Tobyahu on his own initiative ? Or does the message Beware ! indicate some sinister intrigue, the prophet being party to a plot, like the ' son of the prophets ' who anointed Jehu at Ramoth Gilead (2 Kg. 9) ?   And was the letter transmitted by Hosha͑yahu to his master Ya͑ush as intended, or was it handed on as a piece of incriminating evidence ?   The truth of the matter will never be known in the state of the evidence, and any attempt to particularise must be a matter of pure conjecture.

Letter IV

(1) May Yahweh let my lord hear this very day (2) a good report.   And now according to everything my lord has sent (3) thus has thy servant done.   I have written on the tablet (?) [1] according to all (4) that my lord has sent to me.   And con-

---

[1] The word *deleth*, meaning usually ' folding-door ', may mean a folding tablet of wood covered with wax (the Latin *diploma*), a meaning, however, not otherwise attested in Hebrew.

cerning what my lord has sent (5) about Beth Ha-Rpd (?) there is no- (6) body there. And as for Semachyahu, Shema'yahu has taken him and (7) brought him up to the city, and thy servant . . . . . (8) . . . . has sent there . . . . . (9) but (with each recurring morning) [?] (10) and let it be known that for the signals of Lachish we (11) are watching, according to all the signals which my lord is giving (12) for we do not see (the signals of) [?] Aze (13) kah.

The reference in lines 10–13 is particularly interesting in view of the mention of Lachish and Azekah as key fortresses in the final Babylonian campaign against Judah, which we may now date in the light of the Babylonian Chronicle of the reign of Nebuchad-rezzar from 587 to 586 B.C., a year and a half. The statement that the writer cannot see the signals of Azekah some twelve miles north-east of Lachish, may signify that Azekah had already fallen, though that does not necessarily follow. This would certainly be a dramatic document if it could be dated. Only one of the letters, however, is possibly dated (Letter XX) ' on the 9th '. This has been taken to refer to the ninth year of Zedekiah's reign, which would be 587 B.C., when the siege of Jerusalem began (Jer. 39), but there is no explicit reference in the letter to a year, and we think it more likely that the reference is to the day of the month. In any case the text contains only one complete word ' on the 9th ' and a dozen more single letters which do not permit of reconstruction.

Our citation of these texts will indicate, no doubt, the tenuous nature of the materials on which so much has often been too confidently built. Nevertheless the documents from the ashes of the destruction of Lachish in 586 B.C. attest divided counsels of resistance and non-resistance (cf. Jer. 38:4), with suspicion and state espionage, where men of doubtful loyalty or pacifist leanings were closely observed and taken into custody like Semachyahu (Letter IV, 6), whose fate recalls that of Jeremiah himself (Jer. 38:13–21). The letters are thus an excellent commentary on the Book of Jeremiah. The idiom is also that of the period, and the script—almost a cursive—enables us to visualise the appearance of Jeremiah's oracles written by his friend Baruch on the roll which Jehoiakim slit up and burned as he sat by his winter brazier (Jer. 36).

X Daily Life in Ancient Israel

EXCAVATIONS in Palestine in the Israelite period, unlike those in Egypt and Mesopotamia, have discovered few spectacular monuments or long detailed inscriptions, and the life and history of the people, apart from the record of the Old Testament, must be painstakingly reconstructed from many fragmentary relics of their daily activities. Since, however, the normal life of a people, its many tasks and problems, are also of the stuff of history as well as the spectacular achievements of culture and the conquests and calamities of war, the archaeology of Palestine has its own peculiar value. Let us, then, attempt to reconstruct the daily scene in ancient Israel in the middle of the Hebrew Monarchy, as seen from the standpoint of the prophet Amos.

In the middle of the 8th century Amos left his home at Tekoa on the desert edge just east of the watershed of the hills of Judah between Bethlehem and Hebron on his mission to 'drop his word' against the Northern Kingdom at the national shrine of Bethel. Passing Bethlehem above its steep olive-clad hillsides he came after an hour within sight of Jerusalem, by that time sprawling across three hills between the deep ravines of the Kidron Valley and the Valley of the Sons of Hinnom. The South-eastern Hill, the Ophel, was heavily fortified and contained the palace at its northern part. Over the depression to the west of the Temple on the northern hill, or Mount Zion, which is called in Josephus the Tyropoean Valley, a Second Quarter (ha-Mishneh) had developed with the expansion of the new class associated with the cult and the administration of the kingdom. Here Huldah the prophetess lived in the time of Josiah (2 Kg. 22:14, 2 Chr. 34:22), and the upper slopes of the western hill may have been the residential quarter of the ruling class, extending southwards along the slopes, where tradition, probably correctly, locates the house of Caiaphas, the high-priest before whom our Lord was tried. The lower slopes both east and west of the Tyropoean Valley just west of the Temple, locally termed 'the Mortar' (ha-maktesh), was apparently the business quarter of the city, where Zephaniah (1:11) mentions merchants and silver-smiths, and Josephus (*War* v, viii, 1) merchants of

wool and cloth.   Immediately north of the palace-complex on
the Ophel Hill, bearing the double aspect of a fortress and a royal
chapel, the Temple of Solomon and its spacious courts occupied
the high open site where David had housed the Ark in a tent.
There in the inmost shrine, or Holy of Holies, in secret sublimity
dwelt Yahweh, the God of Israel, and there year by year the
great public festivals and processions were celebrated.   Year by
year God's choice of Jerusalem as his abode and his covenant
with Israel through the House of David were solemnly proclaimed
(e.g. Ps. 78:68 ff., 132 ; cf. 2 Sam. 7:12–16), and the devotees
were assured that Yahweh was enthroned and that to the menace
of the powers of Chaos in Nature and in History there was a limit
which they could not pass (e.g. Ps. 47, 93, 96, 97, 98, 99, etc.).
Here, a decade or so after Amos, Isaiah was to realise the deeper
and more personal implications of the fact that Yahweh was
King (Isa. 6).   Though Jerusalem was the political and religious
capital of Judah, the seat of the king and his entourage, the
government officials and the most influential priests, the cultural
and economic centre of the kingdom, where foreign merchants
and ambassadors were familiar, it was nevertheless a city in the
country.   The steep slopes of the Mount of Olives and the hillsides over the Valley of Hinnom were green with vine, fig, almond,
pomegranate, and olive, and in the lower parts of the Valleys of
Hinnom and the Kidron were irrigated gardens of apricot,
pomegranate, quince, and fig, and of vegetables.   To the eastward, just over the summit of the Mount of Olives, the desert
reaches almost to the city, and the shepherd from the east and
the south was a familiar figure.   Amos had doubtless many a
time brought his flock to Jerusalem on the occasion of the great
feasts, and was no doubt familiar with the significance of the
official cult of Yahweh enthroned on His holy mountain.   There
is no doubt at least that the conception of the power of
Providence in nature, history, and in the moral order expressed in
the liturgy of the great New Year festival inspires Amos' message
of judgment to Israel.

Leaving Jerusalem behind him the prophet travelled northwards on the spine of the hills of Palestine, which run north and
south.   He passed the small hill-town of Gibeah (Tell el-Ful), the
home of Saul, with its small fortified watchtower, and, to the
westward, he passed the town of Gibeon (El-Jib), the scene of
Joshua's defeat of the Amorites after his night march when he
prayed that the moon should not go down nor the sun rise until

Plate 17*a*   Wall and Gateway of Tell en-Nasbeh (from the 9th century)

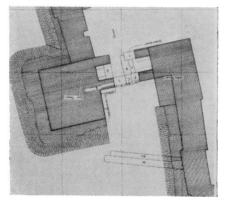

Plate 17*b*   Plan of the Gate of
Tell en-Nasbeh

The Seal of Shema   The Seal of Jaazaniah

The Seal Impression of Gedaliah . (*left*) Obverse (*right*) Reverse, showing
marks of the papyrus to which the seal was affixed

The Seal of Jotham and Seal Impression

Plate 18   Early Hebrew Seals

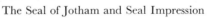

he had struck his blow (Jos. 10:12–13).[1] A conspicuous feature of Gibeon was a large rock-cut pool some thirty-five feet in diameter, with a spiral stairway in the public place within the strong city-wall (2 Sam. 2:13 ?). In another hour or less Amos would reach Mizpah, the fortress of Judah at her northern frontier, which was probably the ancient name of the modern site Tell en-Naṣbeh.

The significance of this place, standing between two ravines just three miles south of Bethel, was purely strategic. The area of the walled settlement was some eight acres, but the town by its situation and its great walls (twelve feet thick), revetments, towers, and fortified gateway, was an impressive feature in the landscape. The excavation of this place by the Pacific School of Religion under W. F. Badé in five campaigns between 1926 and 1935 provides materials for a reconstruction of daily life in Israel during the Hebrew Monarchy.

One going to Bethel would be obliged by the configuration of the land to pass very near to Mizpah, and Amos might well have paused in the open space without or within the double-silled gate with its flanking chambers to buy a cake of bread, a bunch of grapes, or some cheese from the basket of a peasant woman, and to take a meal. Country people would be gathered there with their wares for sale, vegetables and fruit, brought in ass-panniers, and shepherds might have sheep and goats for sale, with cheese and buttermilk (Arab. *libn*) in skins. With the last Amos might have washed down his frugal meal. On a long stone bench along the wall outside the city-gate the local elders would be sitting discussing affairs of the day, settling local disputes, attesting business transactions, or merely gossiping. A man's credit was established or destroyed in ancient Israel ' within the gate '.

Inside the houses and even public buildings contrasted strikingly with the outside fortifications. The dwelling-houses were small constructions of rubble-masonry poorer than in the poorest Arab villages at the present day, and by no means comparable with the houses even of peasants and small tradesmen at Ramallah, the modern Christian Arab village adjoining Tell en-Naṣbeh, to say nothing of the fine mansions of hewn stone of

---

[1] The poetic version of this incident suggests that Joshua desired a prolongation of darkness and not daylight. In the later prose expansion of this passage the point is misunderstood and a miraculous lengthening of the day postulated.

landowners and professional people of the provincial towns of
Bethlehem, Hebron, and Nablus. In certain cases, however,
there were houses of two stories, of which the upper story was
the dwelling and the lower the storehouse. The roofs were flat,
of beaten mud on timber beams and brushwood rolled after the
rains with a small limestone roller, many of which are found in
excavations and which may be seen in use among the Arabs at
the present day. In one of the legends in the Ras Shamra Texts
the industrious, provident son is described as one ' who plasters
his roof when it is muddy '. To judge from modern Arab
custom, the roof was the place of entertainment, and in view of
possible conviviality it was a wise provision which prescribed a
parapet on the roof (Dt. 22:8). In the excavation of Tell
en-Naṣbeh buildings of four rooms were sufficiently exceptional
to raise the question of sanctuaries, though it is more likely that
these were store-rooms for produce from crown-estates. The
streets were, except in the vicinity of the gate, unpaved and
undrained, narrow and crooked, and there was no town plan.
There is a spring in the wadi below the town, but the inhabitants
relied largely on cisterns hewn in the rock and lined with water-
proof lime-plaster, of which fifty-three were discovered, both
inside and outside the walls. Water was gathered in the rainy
season (October to March) by natural drainage from the ground
surface and from the roofs. In one of these cisterns, which range
from six to twenty-four feet deep and are in the shape of a bottle,
the bodies of the victims of the fierce nationalist Ishmael were
deposited (Jer. 41:7 ff.), though it is, of course, impossible to
determine the actual cistern. It will be recollected that it was
in just such a ' bottle-dungeon ' that Jeremiah was confined in
Jerusalem (Jer. 38:6), the mud in the bottom being the result
of the surface drainage from the courtyard.

The economy of all towns in Palestine was based on agriculture, and we have already noted the sequence of the peasant's
seasonal work in the Gezer calendar,[1] which, though dating to
the period of the Hebrew Monarchy, doubtless reflects the custom
of the Canaanites for the preceding ages. The valley-bottom just
south of Mizpah at the confluence of its two wadis, near ancient
Ataroth (Jos. 16:5, 7 ; 18:13),[2] would be cultivated for grain-

---

[1] v. supra, 18–19
[2] Here there is an antiquities site Ḥirbet 'Aṭṭarah. The late remains,
however, indicate that it was not the Biblical Ataroth, though the name
suggests that the old town must be sought in the neighbourhood, and is
possibly to be found at Rafat or at Kefr 'Aqab.

crops. There, when the 'early rains' in October–November softened the hard crust of earth, the ploughmen would lay the wooden yoke on their oxen and so harness them to the rude wooden plough, fashioned for the most part out of undressed branches, the wooden sock being shod with a point of iron. There was no deep ploughing and turning of the sod as in our northern lands. In Palestine the chemicals in the soil are drawn to the surface by the heavy evaporation in the summer heat, and deep ploughing, in burying these, does more harm than good. So the top-soil was simply loosened to prepare a seed-bed. After sowing the seed was ploughed in or, if the soil was not stony, harrowed by dragging thorn-branches over the field. Often, especially after a previous corn-crop or if the soil were sufficiently loose, sowing was done actually before ploughing. The seed was sown not mechanically, but broadcast by hand, being carried in the fold of the ploughman's long tunic. The light plough was held, somewhat unsteadily, with one hand (Lk. 9:62), the other wielding the pole shod at the tip with an ox-goad and at the butt with an iron scraper (Scottice *pattle*). Such light equipment is well adapted to the hill-land of Palestine, the plough being easily lifted over rocks and thorn-bushes. When the corn had swelled in the ear after the 'latter rains' of March harvest began with the reaping of the barley in mid-April, and the wheat harvest, about a month later, was completed in some seven weeks. Ceremonially the harvest began with the offering of the first sheaf at the Feast of Unleavened Bread on the morrow of Passover and it was completed with the offering of the last sheaf at the Feast of Weeks (NT Pentecost). The grain was reaped with iron sickles or with sickles of wood or bone set with serrated fragments of flint, which persisted even into the Iron Age. The reaping was the work usually of the women, and the sheaves were carried in to the threshing-floor by the men on backs of animals. Spelt was also cultivated, and millet, beans, and lentils (Ezek. 4:9) were sown in spring to be grown as summer crops.

The grain was threshed on the threshing-floor of hard-beaten earth swept bare and clean, sited so as to have the advantage of the wind. Sledges studded with sharp flints or iron (Am. 1:3) or on toothed rollers (Am. 2:13 ; Isa. 28:27) were driven round the edge of the pile of loosened sheaves. Winnowing was done by tossing grain and chopped straw and chaff to the wind with a flat-pronged wooden fork. The chaff was blown clean away where it might be gathered for fodder or bedding on wicker hurdles set up at some distance to the leeward ; the chopped straw (*tebhen*) was not carried so far away, and it was the staple of fodder (Gen. 24:25 ; Jg. 19:19, etc.) ; the grain fell where it was thrown up and was finally cleaned in a sieve (Am. 9:9).

On the hillsides, as apart from the valley-bottoms, cereals might also be cultivated where there was sufficient soil, but normally the small plots between the limestone ridges and boulders were planted with vines and olives, or with fruit-trees, fig, pomegranate, or almond.   These small, narrow plots were cultivated mainly with mattocks or hoes (Isa. 5:6), the stones being cleared on to the edges and built into drystone terrace-walls (Isa. 5:2), which prevented the erosion of soil in the torrential winter-rains, since there is no protecting turf in Palestine.   The conservation of soil and the increased growth on the hillsides of ancient Palestine was an effective means of conserving moisture also.   The vines were diligently cultivated, being pruned with a large knife like a small open sickle in early spring ' when the bud is perfect and the sour grape is swelling in the flower ' (Isa. 18:5). The Gezer Tablet mentions pruning after harvest, so that a second pruning must be visualised.   The juice of the grape was extracted by the most primitive methods in rock presses.   The grapes were trodden out in a rock-hewn vat, the juice running through a small drain into a deeper vat.   The juice of the grape was used as wine, freshly fermented (*tîrôsh*) or matured (*yayin yāshân*, ' old wine ', mentioned in the fiscal dockets of Samaria),[1] and was freely drunk for meals both common and ceremonial, profane and sacred (Am. 2:8 ; Hos. 7:5).   The new must might be rendered by boiling into a substance known in modern Palestine as *dibs,* and used for sweetening in cooking.   In Hebrew *d*ᵉ*bhash* means ' honey ', though it probably also signifies what the Arabs call *dibs.*   The grapes, like figs, might also be dried in the sun as raisins (1 Sam. 25:18 ; 2 Sam. 16:1).   Olive oil of prime quality, in which, together with wine, Judah really excelled (Gen. 49:12), was extracted from the olive-berries, the last crop to be gathered, by bruising with pestle and mortar or, when treated in bulk, by crushing by stones under a wooden lever fixed to a hole in the rock at one end and heavily weighted by great stones at the other.   The oil was used for cooking, baking, toilet, and medicine (Isa. 1:6 ; Lk. 10:34).

The bulk of the grain was stored in silos or pits sunk in the

[1] J. W. Jack, *Samaria in Ahab's Time* (1929), 37 ff.

ground within or without the town, lined with marl or small stones. Large earthenware jars of almost three feet high, recalling those in the tale of Ali Baba and the Forty Thieves, were used for the storage of grain, oil, and perhaps also wine. At various sites in Judah handles of smaller jars were found stamped with a winged beetle, winged solar disc (the ' flying roll ' of Zech. 5), and sometimes inscribed ' Belonging to the King ' and with one of four place-names, Hebron, Ziph, Socoh, Memshath. The precise significance of these, however, is not certain. If, as is generally thought, they contained wine or oil for the royal treasury of Judah, it is odd that only one place named in them, Hebron, should have any significance in the records of the history of Judah, and that they should not be more widely distributed, unless the places were official potteries. In this case the stamp in the name of the king and the note of the potteries might be a guarantee of capacity, as is certainly so in the case of a jar-handle from Lachish just before the fall of the city in 597 B.C. which was stamped *bath lammelech*, ' royal *bath* '.[1] It has been suggested, on the other hand, that the king was not the King of Judah but the Assyrian king, who had subjected all Judah except the personal estates of the family of David in the time of Hezekiah. The places mentioned might, then, have been depots in the fiscal administration of Assyria.

Bread was baked, as in the modern Arab village, on hot pebbles within an open clay cylinder (*tannur*) or dome enclosed by a lid (*tabun*) heated from without by a fire of brushwood or dried animal dung (*jellah*, cf. Ezek. 4:12). These ovens might be enclosed in a small dome-shaped house of stone or clay and timber, which are a feature of Arab villages. Remains of baking ovens in clay reinforced by potsherds were found at the excavations at Tell en-Naṣbeh.

Much of the hill-country of Judah and indeed the whole region in the rain-shadow east of the watershed was pastoral country, and most provincial sites excavated have produced evidence of textile work. Whorls and perforated loom-weights in stone and clay indicate spinning and weaving, and rock-cut vats with shallow and deep basins and communicating drains served the purpose of dyeing. Four or five dyers apparently worked at Mizpah, though at Tell Beit Mirsim Albright estimates that in the whole town there might be between twenty and forty plants. Here the proximity of the Negeb, or steppeland of the south

---

[1] Approximately ten gallons

accounts no doubt for the rather intensive textile industry. These plants were probably worked by artisans, like the pottery-kilns (Jer. 18), though no doubt much ordinary domestic pottery was made by the women in the home and only fired in the kiln. In this case the pottery would probably be hand-made. The professional potter, however, used a wheel connected by a spindle with a lower wheel which he turned with his foot. Such wheels, in limestone, are commonly found in excavations, recalling Jeremiah's reference to the potter's work ' upon the two stones ' (Jer. 18:3).

In the towns the commodities of life were bought or bartered by merchants in the open space without or within the gate, and doubtless also in the open cubicles which serve as shops in the East. Nothing was found at Tell en-Naṣbeh which might certainly indicate such shops, but weights were found here and in other Judaean sites in polished stone and in metal. The stone weights recall the Hebrew idiom ' stone ' with the specific meaning ' weight ' (2 Sam. 14:26 ; Prov. 11:1). Certain of these are inscribed with the words *nṣp*, *pym*, and *bqʿ*, and larger weights are marked with one or two characters, the precise significance of which has so far eluded scholars. The first of these words is known from its Arabic cognate to signify a half. The second is smaller. It is suggested that this was two-thirds of a shekel, which was called by the Sumerians in Mesopotamia *shanabu*. The first part of this word *shan* was taken by the Semites to indicate ' two ' and the second part was taken as a noun. Hence the word, so misunderstood, was written as a dual *payim*. The relative weight of the two pieces *nṣp* and *pym* indicates that both cannot be fractions of the same unit, so that among the Hebrews there were at least two standards of weight. The discovery of the weight *pym* is of importance as giving the clue to an obscure passage in Samuel (1 Sam. 13:21), which is now known to refer to the price for the sharpening of tools. The weight *bqʿ*, used in weighing gold (Gen. 24:22), is definitely known as a half-shekel from the passage in Exodus 38:26, concerning the poll-tax incumbent on Israelites. It is interesting to find that some of these stone weights were hollowed out on their flat base and others had blobs of metal inserted. This might be for the honest purpose of adjusting the weights, but might substantiate the charge of Amos and other prophets that certain merchants kept one set of weights and measures for selling and another for buying, ' making the shekel great and the ephah small '. In view of the holes we have mentioned in the weights we may see the point of the dictum :

Deceitful balances are an abomination to Yahweh,
But a whole weight [lit. stone] is his delight (Prov. 11:1).

The furniture of the homes of Mizpah was apparently as simple as among the Arab peasants at the present day, and the 'houses of ivory' and the 'houses of ebony'[1] against which Amos inveighs were the property of the nobles in the capital, Samaria. The houses of the common folk of Mizpah were much more poorly furnished. A rough carpet of goat-hair and mattresses on the ground served as couch by day and bed by night ; a mat of leather or straw-plait served as a table, and perhaps a large wooden platter or tray on special occasions, as among the Bedouin, when meat was eaten at a communal meal. None of this, of course, would survive in the humid soil of western Palestine. The cooking-pots, jars, and juglets for wine, oil, and water, and other pieces of domestic pottery are found in profusion at all sites, and according to their varying shapes and decoration are a most important medium of dating. The housewife ground her own corn with stone pestle and mortar or with an ovoid rubbing-stone on a flat base, which through wear suggests the shape of a saddle, hence the name ' saddle-quern ', or with a cylindrical millstone (Hebrew *pelah ha-rekhebh*, lit. ' the riding millstone ') turned on a spindle on an immobile stone, usually by two women (Mt. 24:41). The hard black basalt of Galilee was preferred to the smooth limestone of southern Palestine, its coarse, open grain being admirable for grinding. The houses were heated in winter by braziers of clay or basalt burning charcoal, and were lit when required by pottery lamps in the form of small open saucers with a pinched nozzle in which a wick floated in olive oil. These too, in their evolution from almost round open saucers with a very slightly impressed nozzle to a closed vessel with a spout, supply a most important clue to the chronology of the strata of sites in Palestine.

Articles of clothing have, of course, disappeared beyond trace, though impressions of the fabrics occasionally survive, and in Assyrian sculptures, especially of the Judaean campaigns of Sennacherib, the loose robes of the civilians and the tight-girt kilt and vest of the Israelite soldiers are illustrated. Eyelet pins or primitive safety-pins were used to fasten garments in place of

[1] A plausible conjectural emendation for ' great houses ' in Am. 3:15

buttons, and belts were also used. The women wore anklets, bracelets, ear-rings, and nose-rings of bronze and more precious metals, like the modern Arab peasant women, and beads were popular. Certain of these, on which eyes were painted in blue and white suggest that the dread of the evil eye is nothing new in Palestine. These were worn on the person and were put on children and possibly also on animals, as at the present time. Imitations of Egyptian scarabs and ornaments with geometric design, like small figures of minor Egyptian deities at Lachish at this time, were doubtless used as amulets. The women were addicted to cosmetics, and cosmetic-palettes in stone indicate that in their own degree the ladies of the provincial towns emulated the arts of Jezebel (2 Kg. 9:30) and the ladies of the town in Jerusalem (Isa. 3:16–24). Like Jezebel (2 Kg. 9:30) and the modern Arab women they touched their eyelashes with *kuhl*, which they kept in small pots and applied with little rods, and treated their eyelids with greenish copper ore, or antimony, which, incidentally, is an admirable disinfectant, of no small value where sanitation is primitive and flies abound.

Clay figurines of domestic animals may have been used as toys, and such evidence of consideration for children would be a pleasant discovery. It is generally held, however, and the view is probably correct, that these were used in apotropaic magic, as we know images were used in primitive Mesopotamian medicine, where the demon of sickness was exorcised into such concrete objects. The clay figurines of nude females with sexual organs exaggerated and holding the breasts may have been made and used in accordance with the principles of imitative magic, for the purpose of stimulating pregnancy—an obsession among the Semitic peasants—rather than as representations of the mother-goddess as an object of veneration. In pre-Israelite Canaan such figurines often exhibit features of one or other of the goddesses of the fertility-cult, but this does not demonstrate that they were objects of veneration, and the use of such objects is notably diminished by the time of the prophet Amos.

The extent to which the Israelites of the time of Amos were literate is uncertain. The books which bear the names of the pre-Exilic prophets are obviously compilations edited later, not so much for individual reading as for record, as in the case of the work of Isaiah of Jerusalem (8:16) and Jeremiah (36). The prophets themselves did not produce books or even sermons of any length, but under the stimulus of inspiration uttered oracles,

Plate 19   Bath-measure and weights from Lachish

usually quite short, and always striking and colourful and in verse form, such as we find most notably in the first chapter of Amos. Such 'lively oracles' were well calculated to arrest the imagination and hold the memory of Orientals, even though that had been less powerful than it is, and to visualise the extent of literacy among the Israelite contemporaries of Amos as no greater than among the modern Arab peasants is not necessarily to disparage the reliability of the tradition of Scripture.

It may, however, be argued that the well-developed memory of the Oriental would easily surmount the first obstacle to literacy, the alphabet, which consisted of but twenty-two signs, and those the more easily learnt since in most cases, if not in all, they were stylised pictures of familiar objects, such as an oxhead (*aleph*), a house (*beth*), and a camel (*gimel*), etc. It wants but resolution and concentration to possess oneself once and for all time of this valuable instrument in the course of a couple of hours. It would be precarious to argue from the considerable number of seal-inscriptions on the actual seals or in impressions on clay or pottery which have been found in Palestinian sites to the general knowledge and use of writing. These are in most cases seals of fiscal officials or stewards of nobles, probably literate men. On the other hand they may have been made for the latter in certain cases in order to be used simply as stamps indicating the con-signer of a jar and its contents. The name of a female on a seal from Tell en-Naṣbeh, for instance, may indicate a female slave who served her master as a potter, the stamp being a guarantee of measure on the jar on which it was impressed. Nevertheless, there are certain indications of a fair degree of familiarity with letters among the Israelites of the period of the Hebrew Monarchy. Earlier, in the account of Gideon's pursuit of the defeated Midianites, he finds a youth of the town of Succoth who, on his demand, writes down the names of seventy-seven men of the town (Jg. 8:14). The agricultural calendar from Gezer (prob-ably 10th century B.C.), by its content as well as by its characters, has all the appearance of the exemplar, or copy-text, of a country schoolmaster, and at the end of the Jewish Monarchy the mili-tary dispatches found in the gate-chamber of Lachish suggest by their almost cursive nature that writing was a familiar art. Here, it must be admitted, the writers are not definitely known. Certain of these, if not all, came from an officer, Hoshea, who possibly commanded a hill-post between the fortresses of Lachish and Azekah. The content of the letters, however, indicates that the status of this man was probably higher than his comparatively junior command would suggest, since he was as much a political agent as a military commander. Moreover, he might have had a professional scribe with him for the sake of dispatches. On the other hand, the first letters of the Hebrew alphabet scored on the side of the steps of the Jewish palace-fort of Lachish suggest that some sentry or a comrade off duty, or perhaps some callow boy, had been eager to parade his incipient prowess.

A regular feature of an Israelite settlement in the Hebrew Monarchy was the cemetery, which was in caves, which honeycomb the limestone hills of Palestine, natural or artificially adapted, or in artificial chambers hewn in the soft white limestone, usually in the hillside near the settlement. At Mizpah such tombs were in the hillside beyond the wadi west of the settlement. At most settlements such caves are available and served as tombs from the end of the third millennium B.C. In the Canaanite period in the Middle and Late Bronze Age the dead had been buried with ample grave furniture, such as weapons and pottery, for use in the hereafter, whatever that existence should be. In the Israelite period the grave furniture is less abundant, since they regarded the present life as man's great opportunity of responding to his God and of living with his neighbours. The Israelite of the Monarchic period did not preoccupy himself with the hereafter, which was thought of as an insubstantial existence beyond contact with God Himself. Hence there was no elaborate preparation for burial, beyond the provision of a decent interment in a cave, the family vault where the Israelite was 'gathered to his fathers'. Anything else apparently seemed to the Israelite to smack of personal ostentation and an impious attempt to appropriate a portion beyond the grave which did not pertain to one. Here we recall Isaiah's stigmatisation of the royal chamberlain Shebna for presuming to hew himself out a rock-tomb, which was less of a grave than a personal monument (Isa. 22:15 ff.). It is interesting to note that such a tomb in the village of Silwan (Siloam) beyond the Kidron whose defaced inscription intimates that it was the tomb of a royal chamberlain (. . . . .)iah, possibly Shebaniah, a variant of Shebna, the royal chamberlain (' who is over the house '), may have been this very tomb. In any case the rank of the person is clearly shown by his office and by the fact that it is unique among tombs of the Hebrew Monarchy in bearing an inscription. Mention of the slave-wife to be buried with him sheds an interesting light on Hebrew sociology. The earliest code of law in the Old Testament, the Book of the Covenant (Exod. 20:22–23:33), in a section which reflects the Hebrew adaptation of Canaanite law, recognises marriage with a slave-girl, whose rights are defined and safeguarded (Exod. 21:9–10). From the rather naïve announcement that the tomb contains no silver or gold we wonder if tomb-robbing was as rife as it was in ancient Egypt. Or perhaps the apprehended robbers were soldiers of invading armies !

The impression we gain from the material remains of Israelite life in the time of Amos is that the Israelites made little contribution to the progress of man in arts and in technical science. Their art as exemplified in sculpture on ivory or on semi-precious seal-stones was derivative, though, notably in the seals, occasionally well executed. They built too for strength rather than grace. The interest of most Israelites was in agriculture, utilitarian crafts, or in the defence of the realm. Their poetry too is derived in form and also to a large extent in imagery from their Canaanite predecessors, as the literature from Ras Shamra demonstrates. Nevertheless, here they were often carried, by the sheer sublimity of the religious content, far beyond the Canaanite prototype. Moreover, the Israelite, even the townsman, was too near to nature not to experience the stimulus to poetic imagery, of which Psalm 23 is a fine expression. Like Amos, the shepherd of Tekoa, he was too near to the core of life's fundamentals not to be moved to great enthusiasm. His zeal for the God of Israel not seldom made the Hebrew peasant both poet and prophet, like Amos, with aesthetic appeal and with a gripping challenge for men of susceptibility in all ages.

XI Dispersion and Restoration

THE Book of Jeremiah introduces us to the first phase in the history of Israel after the Exile. Jeremiah, whose unhappy fate it was to witness the final collapse of the nation Judah, was actively concerned about his fellow-countrymen who had been deported to Mesopotamia in 597 B.C. (Jer. 24:1, 29:1–2); after the destruction of Jerusalem and the Temple and the second deportation in 586 B.C. he was left in Palestine and was one of those who rallied round the moderate Jewish notable Gedaliah, the son of Ahikam the son of Shaphan at Mizpah (Jer. 40:5–6); he was forced against his will to accompany this community down to Egypt in the general panic in the disorders after the murder of Gedaliah. The interest of the prophet in affairs in Babylon, Palestine, and Egypt foreshadows the future of the Jewish people for the remainder of the period of the Old Testament, and archaeology has elucidated the local background in each of these three regions.

Doubtless the Jews deported to Mesopotamia were settled in various districts, of which Ezekiel mentions several, namely the region of the Ḥebar canal between Babylon and Nippur (Ezek. 1:1, 3), where Tel Abib was situated (Ezek. 3:15), Tel Harsa and Tel Melaḥ (Ezr. 2:59), and Kasiphia (Ezr. 8:17). Most of the notable exiles, however, were probably settled in Babylon itself, being detained as political prisoners in the vicinity of the palace.

The city of Babylon in this period was revealed in its ruins by the excavations of the German archaeologist Koldewey. The most conspicuous features are the gate known as the Ishtar Gate, with its lions, bulls, and dragons in low relief, once faced with coloured glazed tiles, the foundations of the *ziggurat*, or staged tower, on which the temple of the city-god Marduk was built, and the Processional Way connecting these two features. Throughout the whole city, in spite of the age-long use of the site by the natives as a brick-quarry, one may still pick up fragments of brick stamped in cuneiform with the name of Nebuchadrezzar, an ironic comment on his reputed boast, ' Is this not great Babylon which I have built ? ' (Dan. 4:30). From this context, from one of a complex of small rooms below the floor level of the citadel of Nebuchadrezzar, Koldewey discovered a number of cuneiform tablets which record rations served out to various foreigners from Egypt and western Asia including Philistines and Jews,[1] many of whom were artisans, who had been deported from Palestine with the notables and influential Jews. Of the Jews Jehoiachin is also named as receiving a certain ration in dry and liquid measure :

½ PI [2] for Yakukinu, the son of the king of Yakudu,
and
½ SILA [3] for the five sons of Yakudu at the hands of Qana'ma.

These dockets bear out the Biblical statement that Jehoiachin was provided for in his captivity,

> And his allowance was a continual allowance given him of the king, a daily rate for every day, all the days of his life (2 Kg. 25:30).

It is even suggested that the small rooms in which these tablets were found were the actual apartments where Jehoiachin and his notables were confined.[4] This, however, we think less likely than the suggestion of Koldewey himself that they are store-rooms.[5]

We should like to know how Palestine was administered as a Babylonian province after the liquidation of the state of Judah, but here both the documents and field archaeology present almost a complete blank. In his account of the events affecting the community at Mizpah, Jeremiah does not indicate the official capacity in which Gedaliah served the Babylonians, and from the explicit mention of husbandmen and vinedressers left by the Babylonians in the depopulated land (2 Kg. 25:12) we suspect that Gedaliah was a fiscal officer, a steward rather than a governor. It may well be that a certain seal-impression from the last phase of Jewish occupation at Tell ed-Duweir,

Belonging to Gedaliah who is over the house,[6]

---

[1] E. F. Weidner, ' Jojachin, König von Juda, in babylonischen Keilschrift-texten ', *Mélanges syriens offerts à M. René Dussaud* II (1939), 923–35
[2] A liquid measure, probably of oil or wine
[3] A dry measure, of corn or dates   [4] Weidner, op. cit.
[5] R. Koldewey, *Das wieder erstehende Babylon*, 4th ed. (1925), 99
[6] S. H. Hooke, ' A Scarab and Sealing from Tell Duweir ', *Palestine Exploration Fund Quarterly Statement* (1935), 195–6, pl. xi

belonged to this very individual. The title 'who is over the house' is reserved in the Old Testament for high-ranking officers, especially for royal chamberlains. Whatever the humbler origins of this office may have been, the fact that the term is used to denote the regency of Jotham, the son of King Uzziah (2 Kg. 15:5) indicates the dignity of the office which Gedaliah filled.[1] The role that his father played in support of the moderate counsels of Jeremiah (Jer. 26:24) certainly suggests that by his family tradition as well as by his personal status Gedaliah was well qualified to represent the Babylonians and to salvage something of the heritage of his people from the wreckage of the state.

The site of Mizpah is in dispute, some scholars contending for its location at the modern Arab village of Nebi Samwil, commanding access to Jerusalem by the upper part of the Wadi Ṣurar and some five miles north-west of the city, and others for its location at Tell en-Naṣbeh, some nine miles due north of Jerusalem. From a superficial examination of the potsherds from the former site, it might be said to be a feasible location. The same might also be said about Tell en-Naṣbeh. Incidents in the Philistine wars located at Mizpah (1 Sam. 7 and possibly 10:17 ff.) might perhaps better be located at Nebi Samwil, but the fortification of Mizpah by Asa of Judah after Baasha of Israel had been diverted from the fortification of Rama is is certainly better located at Tell en-Naṣbeh (1 Kg. 15:21–2). The fortifications of this place, out of all proportions to its size, clearly indicate its significance as a frontier fortress of Judah. In the account of the fortunes of the community at Mizpah under Gedaliah the fact that the place lay directly on the road from Shechem to Jerusalem (Jer. 41:5) suggests Tell en-Naṣbeh rather than Nebi Samwil on its isolated hilltop. We believe that both places were anciently named Mizpah (Watchtower),[2] but that Gedaliah's Mizpah was Tell en-Naṣbeh. This is confirmed by archaeology. It is significant that, though almost every archaeological site in Judah shows traces of destruction at this period, Tell en-Naṣbeh was undisturbed. Here then we may visualise the events so graphically described in the Book of Jeremiah (chs. 40–1). One of the many rock-hewn cisterns discovered both within and without the walls

---

[1] For a study of the development of this office, with the analogy of the office of vizier in Egypt, see R. De Vaux, *Les institutions de l'Ancien Testament* 1 (1958), 199–201

[2] Similarly there were places Geba', Gibe'ah, and Gibe'on (Hill) within a radius of two miles

is probably that into which the extremist Ishmael threw the bodies of his victims (Jer. 41:7), but what particular cistern it is not possible to determine.

The late blossoming of the power and splendour of Babylon was short-lived, lasting barely a century. The end is described in the Book of Daniel as being somewhat luridly heralded at the feast of Belshazzar (Dan. 5) by a supernatural hand which wrote on the wall of the banqueting-hall the mystic words,

MENE MENE TEKEL UPHARSIN [1]

The message of the writer of the Book of Daniel, who flourished some four centuries after the events depicted, is cast in a mould which, except in the Greek period, in which it was compiled, is only loosely historical. It is nevertheless interesting to note how faithfully, in certain details, local circumstances in Babylon are reproduced. The building of Babylon, as it remains, is indeed mainly the work of Nebuchadrezzar, as we have indicated. So in the case of Belshazzar, he was not actually king, as Scripture suggests, but did act as viceroy or regent in the frequent absences of his father, the King Nabona'id, the royal antiquary, who spent most of his latter days at the oasis Tema in north Arabia. Belshazzar is actually named in a certain incantation to Nannar, the moon-god of Ur, whose favour Nabona'id invokes for his son. But before Belshazzar could ascend the throne of Babylon ' God had numbered his kingdom and finished it . . . the kingdom was divided and given to the Medes and Persians '. Here, however, the Book of Daniel lapses ; it was not Darius (Dan. 5:31) but Cyrus who ' took the kingdom '.

The story of the Persian Conquest is told in the Babylonian Chronicle, which dates from the twenty-second year of Darius I, i.e. 500 B.C., but is given more graphically in the foundation cylinder of Cyrus the Great from the temple of the moon-god at Ur, which Cyrus repaired. The conqueror claims that he was called to punish Nabona'id's insults to Marduk, the city-god of Babylon, who

scanned and looked through all the countries, searching for a righteous ruler. . . . He pronounced the name of Cyrus

[1] An alternative to the conventional interpretation, ' Numbered, num-bered, weighed, divided ', is suggested, namely that the reference is to the relative significance of Babylonian kings, Nabopolassar and Nebuchadrezzar being regarded as of the weight of a *mina*, Nabona'id, or perhaps Awil-Marduk, as of the weight of a *shekel*, and Belshazzar, or perhaps Nabona'id, as of the weight of a half-shekel.

King of Anshan, pronounced his name to be ruler of all the
world.[1]

Cyrus claims, moreover, that Marduk

made him set out upon the road to Babylon, going at his side
like a real friend. . . .[1]

Having captured Babylon without a blow and, in fact, by
the collaboration of its inhabitants, Cyrus ' took the hands of
Marduk ' and became formally King of Babylon. He claims
that he

resettled upon the command of Marduk, the great Lord, all
the gods of Sumer and Akkad whom Nabona'id had brought
into Babylon . . . in their former chapels, the places which
made them happy.

The restoration of captive peoples also was part of the regular
policy of Cyrus, of which such Jews as wished to return to
Jerusalem took advantage.   The restoration of gods to their
ancient seats, however, was not part of a general policy of Cyrus
but applied only to Mesopotamia, where the antiquarian zeal of
Nabona'id had upset the religious practices of the various cult-
centres throughout the land.   It was, however, of great significance in the administration of the new empire that the faith of
the ruling power should be ethical and universalistic rather than
nationalist and particularist.   It is definitely known from his
inscriptions that Darius I (522–486 B.C.) was a Zoroastrian.   The
date of Zoroaster, the founder of this ethical faith, is not definitely
known, but it seems likely that even before the time of Darius,
in the days of Cyrus and Cambyses, the influence of the new
faith was felt.   The natural consequence was toleration in the
treatment of subject peoples such as the East had never known
for well-nigh a millennium, and it is significant that almost
simultaneously with the resettlement of Judah after the edict of
Cyrus the Temple was rebuilt on a modest scale.

[1] A. L. Oppenheim in Pritchard, *Ancient Near Eastern Texts* . . ., 315 ;
cf. Isa. 45:1, 2, 4. Thus saith the Lord to his anointed, Cyrus, whose right
hand I have holden, to subdue nations before him. . . . I will go before
thee. . . . For Jacob my servant's sake and Israel mine elect, I have even
called thee thy name ; I have surnamed thee, though thou hast not known
me. cf. also Isa. 41:2.   [2] ibid.

Plate 20   Reconstruction of Ishtar Gate at Babylon, rebuilt by Nebuchadrezzar

The place and volume which the restoration of the Jewish community occupies in the Old Testament tends to distort the picture of actual conditions in Palestine under the Persian régime. In fact a limited number of Jews availed themselves of the permission to return. There is no evidence of a general resettlement, and the returned exiles were apparently content to settle in Jerusalem and the immediate vicinity. The organisation of Palestine, now part of the fifth Persian satrapy 'Beyond the River', did not encourage Jewish settlement elsewhere. Judah was but one district of this province along with Samaria, Ammon, Ashdod, and Arabia, and other districts in Syria and Cyprus. In the other districts in Palestine non-Jewish races were in the majority.

Galilee and Samaria, it will be remembered, had been incorporated in the Assyrian empire as the provinces of Megiddo and Samerina, and the latter at least had been settled with military colonists from Mesopotamia and Syria. In the general destruction which marks the Babylonian reduction of Judah in 586 B.C. Megiddo and Samaria in the north were untouched, and it is likely that they continued to serve as administrative centres in the Babylonian period, together with their administrative personnel. It is probable that the *status quo* was preserved under the Persians. In the account of the phase of the restoration of Jerusalem under Nehemiah, at any rate, Samaria was certainly an administrative centre, and the fact that Sanballat (Sin-uballit) bears a good Mesopotamian name suggests the predominance of the foreign elements introduced to the district by the Assyrians. The fact, however, that the sons of Sanballat have the theophoric names Delaiah and Shelemiah indicates that the native faith of the Israelite subjects had prevailed over the foreign faiths and such syncretism as is noted in 2 Kings 17:27 ff., and this is corroborated by the eventual building of a temple to the God of Israel on Mount Gerizzim, probably about 400 B.C.

The district of Arabia in the south of Palestine extended as far north as Hebron and included Lachish, which was reoccupied and had its fortifications repaired at this time. Lachish, in fact, may have been the administrative centre of the district of 'Arabia', and in that case would be the seat of 'Geshem the Arabian', who joined Sanballat of Samaria and Tobiah of Ammon in opposing the fortification of Jerusalem (Neh. 2:19). The old palace-fort, the acropolis of Lachish, was now occupied by a small, though still ample, residence, which has all the appearance of the residence and offices of a district governor,[1] and in the vicinity a notable feature is a small shrine.[2] An open courtyard backed by several apartments was the largest part of this complex. Six steps led up to an antechamber, and three more steps to an inner shrine, or holy of holies. A drain in the doorsill of the inner shrine probably indicates that libations were made there. A small limestone incense-altar was found with the relief of a man with arms raised, presumably in appeal to the god, who is probably represented as blessing his devotee on the opposite side of the altar by the symbol of a large hand upraised.[3] The entrances to the antechamber and inner shrine were in line from the east, so that the rays of the rising sun could shine into the inmost shrine. The excavator, the late J. L. Starkey, recalled the passage in Ezekiel 8:16, where the prophet animadverts on a company in the Temple standing with their backs to the Temple and their faces to the east, worshipping the sun. There are other traces of occupation in the Persian period at Tell Jemmeh and Tell el-Far'a in the Wadi Ghazzeh. These were important fortresses on the limit of the settled land before the ten grim desert marches to the Delta, and it is natural that the Persians, with designs on Egypt, should garrison these. A number of grain-silos at Tell Jemmeh, the filling debris of which include Greek potsherds, probably indicate the significance of these places as Persian bases for provisioning expeditions against Egypt.

The reason for the official name of 'Arabia' is uncertain. Already in the first half of the 7th century B.C. large tribal confederacies under their kings, and more often queens, contested the control of the north Arabian steppes with the Assyrians. Esarhaddon mentions his defeat of them, but this was merely temporary, since they are found active again in the time of Ashurbanipal. The Assyrian policy was to insist on rulers amenable to imperial control, and Ashurbanipal records how he removed a usurper and kept him pilloried together with a dog and a bear at the gate of his palace at Nineveh.[4] The same inscription records the defeat and capture of Ammuladi the king of the Arab kingdom of Kedar. This Arab power, which suffered a further check at the hands of Nebuchadrezzar (Jer. 49:28), presumed to attack the Assyrian vassal kings in the west. The extent of the influence, if not the actual occupation, of the

---

[1] O. Tufnell, Lachish III, The Iron Age (1953), 131–41, pl. 22
[2] ibid., 141–5, pl. 24   [3] ibid., 141, pl. 42, 8 and 9
[4] A. L. Oppenheim in Pritchard, Ancient Near Eastern Texts relating to the Old Testament (1950), 298

King of Kedar is suggested by an inscribed votive silver vessel in a temple to the north Arabian goddess han-Allat at Tell el-Maskhuteh in the Wadi Tumilat which runs from the Nile Delta eastwards.[1] This inscription runs :

Qainu (Cain) the son of Geshem King of Kedar.

However far west the occupation of Kedar extended, the south of Palestine was largely populated by Edomites, this influx having been encouraged partly by Jewish depopulation after the Babylonian conquest and partly being the result of pressure in the Edomite homeland by Arab elements, whose personal names replace Edomite names on inscribed ostraca from Ḥirbet el-Ḥeleifeh (Ezion Geber) by the 5th century B.C. Edom was eventually occupied by the Nabataeans, a virile mercantile people from the oases of the Hejaz. In this folk-movement of Edomites westwards over the Araba the family of Herod the Great came to Palestine, where they emerge in the Hellenistic period as the hereditary priests of Apollo, the Greek counterpart of the Semitic god Reshef, and possibly also of Kos, the national god of Edom, at Askalon.

In the coastal plain, in the administrative district of Ashdod, there was a great admixture of races. In addition to native Semites and non-Semitic Philistines, there were military colonists from Mesopotamia planted by the Assyrians, Edomites, who had settled in the Babylonian period, and, more recently, Phoenicians. The last settled in considerable numbers in the Persian period at Tell Abu Hawam just north-east of Haifa,[2] Athlit,[3] and Dor south of the Carmel headland,[4] Straton's Tower, the site of later Caesarea, and in the vicinity of Jaffa.[5] The Greek geographer

---

[1] F. M. Cross, ' Geshem the Arab, Enemy of Nehemiah ', *Biblical Archaeologist* (1955), 47. Some such Arab power seems to have occupied Edom east of the Araba during the Persian period, when Glueck has noted traces of a cultural and political recession at various sites in Edom.

[2] H. Vincent, ' Tell Abou Hawam. Origines de Haifa ', *Revue Biblique* XLIV (1935), 435 ff.

[3] C. N. Johns, ' Excavations at Pilgrim's Castle, Athlit ', *Quarterly Statement of the Department of Antiquities of Palestine* VI (1938), 121–52

[4] Eshmunazzar, King of Sidon, mentions Dor and Jaffa as being conceded to the Sidonians by the ' King of kings ', i.e. the Persian king (G. A. Cooke, *A Textbook of North Semitic Inscriptions* (1903), nos. 5, 11, 19, pp. 31, 32, 38.

[5] In his inscription (G. A. Cooke, op. cit., no. 5) Eshmunazzar mentions these places in the Plain of Sharon as excellent cornland, suggesting that the district relieved the strain on the limited resources of the Phoenician homeland. The district seems to have played the same role in Phoenician economy in the days of Herod Agrippa, when the Phoenicians were probably appealing to their rights conceded in Persian times (Ac. 12:20).

Scylax in the 5th century B.C. terms Askalon ' a Tyrian city ',[1] and it is possible that the Sidonian colonies at Gaza and Marissa, known to us from the Greek period,[2] go back to this time.

The Jewish settlement in the Persian period was limited to Jerusalem and the vicinity, which we know from the legend on coins and from official stamps on jar-handles to have been called Yehud, as it is in the Book of Ezra. The limited extent of the district is clearly indicated in the note of the settlements in Judah which helped in the rebuilding of the walls of Jerusalem under Nehemiah, namely Jericho, Tekoa, Bethsur, Keilah, Zanoah, Jerusalem, Gibeon, Mizpah, and Beth-haccerem. The distribution of stamped jar-handles with the impression YHD in Hebrew or Aramaic characters in excavations at Gezer, Jerusalem, Jericho, and mostly at Tell en-Naṣbeh confirms this delimitation of the district of Judah. The comparative abundance of official pottery stamps at Tell en-Naṣbeh suggests that this was the site of Mizpah, which is mentioned in Nehemiah 3:7 apparently as the capital of the district of Judah (' which pertained to the throne of the governor of ' Over the River ').[3]

From a papyrus letter from the elders of a Jewish military colony by Assouan it is clear that at the end of the 5th century B.C. the district of Judah was under a Persian governor Bigvai (Bagoas of Josephus). It is not clear what precisely is implied in the heading to the Book of Haggai (1:1) that Zerubbabel, the head of the Jewish community in the first decade of the restoration, was the governor (pahath) of Judah, but it is natural that such notables as this scion of the House of David should have been made a liaison between administration and subjects, especially in affairs of religion. Nehemiah also claims to have been appointed governor (Neh. 5:7) and dispatched with a military escort (Neh. 2:9). The high priest was eventually admitted as an assessor to the government, and his name actually appears on provincial coins of the period, as we know from a piece from Bethsur. This coin, stamped with the Attic owl and the legend YHD, bears also the personal name Hezekiah, who may have been the high priest mentioned by Josephus as an able statesman at the end of the Persian period and the beginning of the

---

[1] Scylax 104, ed. C. Müller, Geographi Graeci Minores I, 79
[2] v. infra, 206
[3] ' Over the River ' was the designation of the satrapy, of which Judah was one district. The statement probably indicates that Mizpah and district was a royal estate or even the personal perquisite of the satrap rather than that it was the administrative centre of the whole satrapy.

Hellenistic era.[1] The district was apparently subdivided into smaller regions, each with a native officer (Neh. 3), whose precise functions escape us.

From Nehemiah 5 it appears that the expenses of administration were met by local levy in money and produce, and the stamped handles of storage jars are almost certainly evidence of this fiscal administration. These are of various design, some with the stamp YHD in Semitic characters, some having the place-name Jerusalem and some MṢH, probably an abbreviation for Mizpah. A further stamp of a small cross in a circle suggests similarly impressed jar-handles from Egypt, where the addition of LMLK ('for the King') indicates the use of such vessels for collecting royal revenues.

It is in the Persian period that coins make their appearance in Palestine, making it possible from this time to date archaeological strata with a precision hitherto seldom possible. Coined money was a Lydian invention adopted by the Greek communities of the Anatolian seaboard and the Greek islands and mainland, the stamps of individual merchants, communities, or city-states guaranteeing the weight and purity of the specie. So the coins now current in Palestine bear the stamps of the Greek city-states most active in the Levant, such as the owl of Athens. Such coins as that said to be of the 5th century B.C. from the neighbourhood of Gaza with the bearded fertility-deity Triptolemus and the Attic owl, but stamped with the legend YHD, anticipate the story of the penetration of Greek influences to the mountain fastness of Judah.

The Books of Haggai and Zechariah indicate that the rebuilding of the Temple and the revival of the life of Judah was not the result of the immediate and spontaneous enthusiasm of such Jews as remained in Palestine or even the first exiles who returned and settled about Jerusalem. The impulse came from the Jews in Mesopotamia, and until well into the Christian era the influence of Babylonian Jewry was felt in the spiritual, as against the political development of Judaism. With this community of Eastern Jews we are brought into touch in the archives of the business house of Murashu Sons, great bankers and estate brokers in the reign of Artaxerxes I (464–424 B.C.) and Darius II (423–404 B.C.), found by Hilprecht in 1898 at Nippur. In these

---

[1] Josephus, *Contra Apionem* I, §§ 187–9 ; O. R. Sellers, *The Citadel of Beth-Sur* (1933), 73 ; A. Reifenberg, ' Ancient Jewish Coins ', *Journal of the Palestine Exploration Society* XIX (1939), 59–60, pl. IV, 2

documents various individuals are mentioned bearing such obviously Jewish names as Pedaiah, Benjamin, Hananiah, and Gedaliah. These, however, are but isolated individuals ; the fact that Ezra spent four months in his journey from Babylon to Jerusalem (Ezr. 7:7–9) indicates that the Jewish communities which he visited to stir up enthusiasm for a return to Zion must have been both numerous and widely distributed.

The conclusion of the Book of Jeremiah directs us to Egypt as the future home of the remnants of the community which the good Gedaliah had rallied at Mizpah after the ruin of Jerusalem. Jeremiah refers more specifically to settlements of Jews at Migdol just east of the Delta, Tahpanhes in the Delta,[1] Noph, or ancient Memphis near modern Cairo, and Pathros [2] in upper Egypt. In Isaiah 19:18–19, either as a reflection of existing conditions or as a forecast of what should come to pass, there is a reference to ' five cities in Egypt speaking the language of Canaan ' and ' an altar to Yahweh in the midst of the land of Egypt and a pillar at the border thereof to the Lord '.

Actually there are direct references to two such cult-localities of Yahweh in Egypt. That there were more may be inferred from Josephus' reference to the letter of the priest Onias to Ptolemy Philometor (181–145 B.C.), where it is stated ' In various places inhabited by our people I have found almost everywhere sanctuaries (*hiera*) after an improper manner so as to set one another at variance '.[3] On one of those places Onias concentrated and asked permission from Ptolemy to build a temple after the pattern of that in Jerusalem and of the same dimensions. The temple and the altar which he actually built were said by Josephus to be like that in Jerusalem but smaller and poorer.[4] This building Sir W. Flinders Petrie claimed to have found at Tell el-Yehudieh about twenty miles north of Cairo, its dimensions corresponding to those of Solomon's Temple on the reduced scale of a span to a cubit.[5] A feature of this site was the number of pottery ovens which conform to the regulations in the Mishnah regarding the ovens in which the Passover lambs should be roasted. Petrie maintained that at Tell el-Yehudieh, apparently ancient Leontopolis, he had found in the ovens a relic of the

---

[1] Modern Tell Defenneh, about nine miles west of El-Qantara
[2] Egyptian Pe-te-res, ' the Southland '
[3] Josephus, *Antiquities* XIII, iii, 1, trans. Whiston
[4] ibid., XIII, iii 3,
[5] W. F. Petrie, *Egypt and Israel* (1911), 102 ff.

ritual of the consecration of the new Jerusalem,[1] but the Passover ceremony was by no means a foundation sacrifice and Petrie's conjecture seems very wide of the mark.

Long before this, however, there was another Israelite colony with a temple and cult of Yahweh in Egypt. That was on the island of Elephantine, ancient Yeb, at the first cataract of the Nile opposite Assouan. Here a garrison of mercenaries was posted, of which we have the first intimation in their private and public papyrus documents, which were acquired by purchase just before and after the beginning of the century and published in various stages in 1906, 1908, 1911, and 1958.[2] These records, which are accurately dated in the year of the reigning Persian king and according to the Babylonian and Egyptian systems, come from the 5th and the beginning of the 4th centuries B.C. and introduce us to a Semitic community. This was primarily a military colony stationed on the island and at Assouan, and they also practised agriculture, building, commerce, and the crafts. Nor were they racially exclusive, since they had business dealings with the natives and even intermarried with Egyptians,[3] and in one case an oath was taken by one of their number in the name of a local Egyptian goddess.[4] The names are mainly Hebrew in form, recalling those of the last period of the Jewish Monarchy, but there are also such names as Bethel-nathan and Herem-nathan, which do not occur in the Old Testament, and such as Ashem-Kudurri, which is Babylonian, and others which indicate Aramaean affinities with north Syria and upper Mesopotamia. There are certain legal features too which suggest a Babylonian origin. Such evidence seems to support the contention of W. O. E. Oesterley [5] that the colony was not one of Jews from Judah, but of Israelites from the Northern Kingdom of Israel who had been deported to Assyria on the fall of Samaria and had later been drafted by the Persians to serve as a garrison at Elephantine on their southern frontier. Our own view is that Aramaean elements were certainly there, the documents referring repeatedly to ' Aramaean of Syene ' (Assouan), but the dominant

---

[1] ibid., 105–7

[2] The most accessible publications of text, translation, and commentary are A. C. Cowley, *Aramaic Papyri of the Fifth Century B.C.* (1923), and, for those recently deciphered, E. G. Kraeling, *The Brooklyn Museum Aramaic Papyri* (1953).

[3] Cowley, op. cit., 15. A Jewess Mibtahiah is married to one Ashor, an Egyptian.

[4] Mibtahiah and an Egyptian Pii take an oath by the Egyptian goddess Sati in a marriage contract.

[5] W. O. E. Oesterley, *A History of Israel* ii (1939), 161 ff.

element in the community were Jews, possibly descendants of those who found refuge in Egypt after the catastrophe of 586 B.C.

The domestic archives of the colony, which comprise the bulk of the documents, are full of interest, giving us valuable insight into actual social practices in a Semitic community in antiquity.

As in ancient Canaan and in modern Arab society, marriage was primarily a contract not between man and wife but between a man and the bride's father. There was apparently a minimum of ceremony, a verbal declaration to the father ' She is my wife and I her husband from this day and for ever ' being legally binding. A bride-price, in one case five shekels,[1] was paid to the bride's father by the bridegroom, who paid a further sum to the bride to acquire furniture and a trousseau. She in turn, presumably out of her dowry, made him a payment to defray the cost of furniture. A contract was drawn up to this effect, presumably in duplicate, and was attested by several witnesses.

From such documents it is apparent that where there were no children the relict of the dead party inherited. Divorce was also visualised, this, like marriage, being valid by verbal declaration, in this case before the ' congregation '. If the wife divorced the husband she returned the portion of the bride-price which she received. If the husband divorced the wife, he forfeited the bride-price, both what he paid to the bride and to her father, but gifts he subsequently made to his wife were returned. In case of the forcible ejection of the wife without divorce compensation was made and no further marriage was possible.

The status of women, therefore, in this Jewish and Aramaean settlement was considerable. They might own property and engage in loans. One document,[2] an agreement between two sons over the share of their mother's property at her death, indicates that the widow retained usufruct of her husband's property even when there were sons. This document is of further interest as evidence for slavery in the Elephantine community. A family of a mother and three lads, who, incidentally, all bear Egyptian names, are apportioned, somewhat callously, we feel, between two brothers, the mother and the youngest boy being meanwhile unallocated, presumably because the child was still dependent on the mother. The slaves, we learn, were branded on the arm with a mark and the name of the owner, an inhuman indignity which many Jews suffered recently in the slave-camps of Europe.

[1] Cowley, op. cit., 15   [2] ibid., 28

Yehūd Coin : *(left)* Obverse *(right)* Reverse

Hezekiah Coin

John Hyrcanus Coin
(left) Obverse *(right)* Reverse

Alexander Jannaeus Coin
(left) Obverse *(right)* Reverse

Plate 21   Jewish Coins of the Persian and Greek periods

Money-lending is the subject of many of the contracts and women lend and borrow on the same terms as men. Loans were given on security of property, goods, slaves, and even food. In a small community of the Jewish faith isolated in a strange land we might have expected some accommodation in the matter of loans. The prohibition against usury, which is common to Hebrew law from the Book of the Covenant (Exod. 22:25) to the Priestly Code (Lev. 25:35-8),[1] is so far ignored that interest amounted to 60 per cent and, when it could not be paid regularly month by month, was even added to the principal and charged at the same rate. In the Deuteronomic law in the Old Testament (Dt. 23:19-22) usury, while forbidden between Israelites, was permitted where the borrower was a stranger. But in Elephantine the parties were both Jews. It must, however, be admitted that even in Palestine there were means of evading the law against usury, and as late as the time of Nehemiah, though men might not lend on usury, they did so on the security of the lands and persons of the debtors. Nor was there any reversion of mortgaged property at the year of release, as in Palestine, but debts, together with the accumulated interest, were heritable.

None of these documents give any certain indication of the actual origin of the community. Correspondence between the local elders and the Persian governor in Judah makes it clear by a certain reference that the community was established certainly by 525 B.C., when their temple was spared in spite of the general desecration of local sanctuaries by Cambyses.

The most interesting feature in the life of this community at Yeb was the temple and cult of Yahweh. The temple, which had certainly been standing in 525 B.C., had been destroyed in a pogrom in the fourteenth year of Darius (II) in 410 B.C., when the native Egyptians, incited by the priests of the neighbouring temple of Khnub, had suborned the local Persian governor Widarnag to turn a blind eye to their activity, if not actually to aid and abet them. It has been suggested that the motive for this was religious, the priests of the ram-god Khnub objecting to the slaughter of lambs at Passover. This is an interesting conjecture, but the reason for the outbreak was probably political. A certain papyrus mentions the fact that in rebellion against the Persians, probably on the accession of Darius II (423 B.C.), the Yeb garrison remained loyal. It is then suggested that the

[1] The practice is condemned in Ps. 15:5 and Ezek. 18:8, 13.

Egyptians took reprisals for the part the Jews had played.[1] The copies are extant of a certain letter dated in the seventeenth year of Darius II in 407 B.C., wherein the local high priest Jedoniah and his colleagues appeal to Bagoas, the Persian governor of Judah, lodging their complaint and claiming permission to rebuild the ruined temple. This letter gives fuller information about local conditions, the temple, and the cult, and mentions the fact that the people of Yeb had sent a similar appeal to Delaiah and Shelemiah, the sons of Sanballat the governor of Samaria, who is known from the Old Testament as the opponent of Nehemiah. They mention also their appeal ' at the time when this evil was done ' to Johanan the high priest and influential men in the Jewish community, who, however, had hitherto ignored it.

This most important letter, in Aramaic like the rest of the Elephantine papyri and other documents of the period in the Persian provinces, may be cited in full :

> To our lord Bigvai, governor of Judah, your servants Jedoniah and his colleagues, the priests who are in Yeb the fortress. The health of our lord may the God of heaven seek after exceedingly at all times and give you favour before King Darius and the princes of the palace a thousand times more than at present, and may he grant you long life and may you be happy and prosperous at all times. Now your servant Jedoniah and his colleagues state that in the month of Tammuz in the fourteenth year of King Darius, when Arsham departed and went to the King, the priests of the god Khnub, who is in the fortress of Yeb, were in collusion with Widarnag, who was governor here, saying, ' The temple of the God Yahu which is in the fortress of Yeb let them remove from there.' Then that reprobate Widarnag sent a letter to his son Nephayan, who was commander in the fortress of Syene, saying, ' The temple which is in Yeb the fortress let them destroy.' Then Nephayan led out the Egyptians with the other forces. They came to the fortress of Yeb with their weapons ; they entered that temple ; they destroyed it to the ground, and the pillars of stone which were there they broke. Five gateways of stone built with hewn blocks of stone, which were in that temple, they destroyed and their doors they lifted off, and the hinges of these doors were bronze, and the

---

[1] E. G. Kraeling, *The Brooklyn Aramaic Papyri* (1953), 102–4. See also G. R. Driver, ' New Aramaic Documents ', *Zeitschrift für die Alttestamentliche Wissenschaft* LXVII (1949–50), 232)

roof of cedar wood, all of it, with the rest of the furniture and
other things which were there, all of it they burned with fire ;
and the basins of gold and silver, and everything which was
in that temple, all of it they took and appropriated. Already
in the days of the kings of Egypt our fathers had built that
temple in the fortress of Yeb, and when Cambyses came to
Egypt he found that temple built, and the temples of the gods
of Egypt, all of them, they destroyed, but no one did any
harm to that temple. When this was done we with our wives
and our children put on sack-cloth and fasted and prayed to
Yahu the Lord of Heaven, who let us see our desire upon that
Widarnag, that son of a dog ; they removed the anklet from
his legs and all the riches he had gained were lost, and all
his men who had sought to do harm to that temple were
killed and we saw our desire upon them. Also before this, at
the time when this evil was done to us, we sent a letter to our
lord and to Johanan the high priest [1] and his colleagues the
priests who are in Jerusalem, and to Ostanes the brother of
Anani, and the nobles of the Jews. They have not sent any
letter to us. Also since the month of Tammuz in the fourteenth
year of King Darius till this day we wear sackcloth and
fast. Our wives are made widow-like, we do not anoint
ourselves with oil, and we drink no wine. Also from that
time to the present day in the seventeenth year of King Darius
neither meal-offering, incense, nor sacrifice do they offer in
that temple. Now your servants Jedoniah and his colleagues
and the Jews, all of them inhabitants of Yeb, say : If it seem
good to our lord, take thought for that temple to build it,
since we are not allowed to build it. Look to your well-
wishers and friends who are here in Egypt, and let a letter
be sent from you to them concerning the temple of the God
Yahu, to build it in the fortress of Yeb as it was built before ;
and the meal-offering, incense, and sacrifice will be offered
in your name, and we shall pray for you at all times, we, our
wives, our children, and the Jews who are here, all of them,
if it is brought about that the temple is rebuilt. And you

[1] Probably Jehohanan, the contemporary of Ezra (Ezr. 10:6) and the
grandson of Eliashib (Neh. 12:22), the contemporary of Nehemiah (Neh. 3:1).
If, as the internal evidence of the Books of Nehemiah and Ezra suggest, we
should date Ezra after Nehemiah, Nehemiah's mission would date from 444 B.C.
and the arrival of Ezra in Jerusalem in 397 B.C. From the Elephantine
evidence Johanan would have been high priest at least nine years before Ezra
arrived.

shall have merit before Yahu the God of heaven more than one who offers to him burnt offerings and sacrifices worth a thousand talents of silver. And as to gold, about this we have written to inform you. We have also set the whole matter forth in a letter in our name to Delaiah and Shelemiah, the sons of Sanballat the governor of Samaria. Also Arsham knew nothing of what was done to us. On the 20th of Marheshwan, the seventeenth year of King Darius.

Characteristically of the East, this official petition to Bagoas was backed up by an offer of *bakhshish* of a substantial, but unknown, amount made in the name of Jedoniah and four colleagues, who are named in a separate letter written to ' your lordship ', the name, probably of Bagoas, being discreetly omitted.[1] The appeal to the Persian governor in Judah was effective. Permission was given, apparently orally,[2] by Bagoas and Delaiah. The emissary from Yeb, however, was careful to record the favourable reply [3] :

Memorandum of what Bigvai and Delaiah said to me : Let this be an instruction to you in Egypt to say to Arsham about the house of offering of the God of Heaven, which had been in existence in Yeb the fortress since ancient times, before Cambyses, and was destroyed by that reprobate Widarnag in the fourteenth year of King Darius, to rebuild it on its site as it was before, and the meal-offering and incense-offering to be made on that altar as it used to be.

In this permit bloody sacrifices are significantly omitted, not improbably out of respect to the Deuteronomic principle, which admitted such sacrifices only at the Temple in Jerusalem. Kraeling makes the feasible suggestion that Bagoas and Delaiah had previously conferred with religious authorities in Jerusalem, whose influence is seen here.[4] From the mention of an official of the cult of Yahu in Yeb in a letter recently published by Kraeling [5] and dated in the fourth year of Artaxerxes (II), in 402/401 B.C., it is obvious that the cult of Yahu was still practised and that the temple was probably restored.

---

[1] Cowley, op. cit., no. 33 (undated)
[2] This was probably a matter of official etiquette, since the Yeb community had appealed not to the local governor Arsham, but to Bagoas, the Persian governor in Judah.   [3] Cowley, op. cit., no. 32
[4] Kraeling, op. cit., 107   [5] Kraeling, op. cit., no. 12

Among the documents from Yeb one has a peculiar significance. That is the communication of a mandate from Darius II in 419 B.C. by one Hananiah to the local Persian governor in Egypt, Arsham, concerning the keeping of the seven days' festival of Unleavened Bread from the 14th to the 21st of Nisan (cf. Exod. 12:14–20).[1] In the papyrus there is no mention of the Passover, which was associated with the festival of Unleavened Bread, but that does not exclude the possibility that the Passover was mentioned, since the document is very fragmentary. The general situation indicated in this papyrus is interesting. The situation of Hananiah suggests that of an official commissioner for Jewish affairs in the Persian government, and enables to understand the official character of the office of Nehemiah and the mission of Ezra. Moreover, the issue of such a mandate concerning the festival of Unleavened Bread in the community of Yeb makes feasible the royal directives in Ezra, especially those given in Aramaic, and particularly the letter of Artaxerxes authorising the mission of Ezra (Ezr. 7:12 ff.). That such a document should have been transmitted from the Persian court to the remote garrison at Yeb is striking evidence of the determination of the Jews, through such commissioners, to survive political extinction.

Those times were avowedly ' the day of small things ', as the prophet Zechariah hints (Zech. 4:10), but must not be despised. We have emphasised the limitations of the restored community about Jerusalem, but, out of proportion to the small community in Judah, there was the Temple. Those who recollected the first ' house ' may indeed have wept as they compared the new with the old, but the Temple was symbolic of the tenacity of a people who refused to admit defeat. In the last calamity of 586 B.C., their state liquidated and their Temple in ruins, broken in their homeland, dispersed in alien lands, and their rulers confined in Babylon, the elders and spiritual heads of the exiles had still sobriety and faith to see in their calamities the discipline of a righteous God. In Babylonia and Palestine the religious and historical traditions of the race were searched, studied, and edited. In Egypt, for the benefit primarily of a large and influential Jewish population already cosmopolitan in outlook, the Scriptures were translated into Greek, and by the beginning of the 2nd century B.C. the word of God in the Law and the Prophets at least was open to the inquiring gentile. Men searched their

---

[1] Cowley, op. cit., no. 21

hearts earnestly before God in prayer and the confessional of the penitential psalm ; they submitted to the wholesome discipline of the fast ; and always from the rivers of Babylon, from caravan towns in the oases of Arabia, from the ' isles of the sea ', and from remote Assouan they looked to Jerusalem as their spiritual metropolis. The despised ' latter house ', where the meaningful ritual of Israel was practised and her great psalms sung, was the pulsing heart of a far-flung spiritual realm which was to survive all the empires of the ancient East.

XII   The Defence of the Faith

THE period which witnessed the restoration of the Jewish community about Jerusalem saw also the full bloom of culture on the mainland of Greece, and with both movements Persia was intimately concerned. It was the repulse of Persian invasion, first at Marathon in 490 B.C. and then at Plataea and Salamis in 480 B.C., which inspired the efflorescence of Greek culture and political independence. The struggle between the Greeks and the Persians, however, was not yet over so long as there were Greek colonies on the coast of Asia Minor, and eventually Alexander the Great united the Greeks in a crusade against Persia and in 334 B.C. took the momentous step over the Hellespont. Three years sufficed to reduce the Persian Empire, but with the victory of Issus in 333 B.C. and his reduction of Tyre and the Phoenician coastland, his capture of Gaza after a siege of two months, and his triumphal progress to Egypt, the Hellenistic period of the history of Palestine and western Asia really began two years before the final defeat of Persia at Gaugamela near ancient Nineveh.

The Hellenisation of the ancient East was part of the deliberate policy of Alexander and was accomplished through intermarriage with native women and through the settlement of cities with characteristic Greek institutions, such as the gymnasium, theatre, philosophic school, and municipal government. The most illustrious of these was Alexandria in Egypt, where both Judaism and Christianity were soon interpreted in terms of Greek philosophy. In Palestine itself there is a tradition that Alexander planted a colony of veterans at Samaria on his return from Egypt in 331 B.C. after his punishment of the local inhabitants, who had burnt his representative alive, but no new city was founded in Palestine in the time of Alexander, though in Transjordan Dion may well have been a settlement of Macedonian veterans, since there was a place of that name in Macedonia.[1]

Actually Greek influence may be detected in Palestine before the time of Alexander, when black-figured glazed Greek pottery

[1] So E. Schürer, *The Jewish People in the Time of Christ*, ET II, i (1885–90), 114–15, after Stephen Byzantius

characteristic of the 6th century B.C. is found, and later red-figured black-glazed ware. Already by the 6th century B.C. the Greeks had established a trading colony which had grown to a city at Naucratis in the Delta, and to the activities of the merchants and slave-traders of this place the prophet Joel (3:6) may refer.

After the death of Alexander, his various commanders and governors sought to emulate the great king or at least to carve out kingdoms for themselves from his empire. By 315 B.C. the struggle had resolved itself into a concerted effort of Ptolemy, the son of Lagos, in Egypt, Antipater in Macedonia, and Seleucus, the great commander of the Macedonian heavy infantry, against Antigonus, who pretended to the position of Alexander. Matters reached a crisis in 312 B.C., when Ptolemy and Seleucus defeated the forces of Antigonus under his son Demetrius at the ancient site of Gaza. In consequence Ptolemy occupied the country as far north as Sidon, though Antigonus still maintained control over the north of Syria and was able to repel Ptolemy in course of time from Syria, though not from Palestine. Seleucus claimed as his reward for his share in the victory of Gaza the rule over Babylonia, and by 311 he was able to make his claim good. Antigonus was able to curb the ambitions of Ptolemy and Seleucus until in 302 B.C the alliance between Ptolemy, Seleucus, and the rulers of Thrace and Macedonia was effectively revived. At the Battle of Ipsus Antigonus was slain and his power for the most part liquidated. His son, Demetrius, was able to retain the Syrian coast, but no longer could he hold Ptolemy and Seleucus in check, and soon Seleucus advanced into north Syria and Ptolemy occupied Palestine and the Syrian coast.

The Hellenisation of the more accessible regions on the coast and in the plains of Palestine, which had begun even before the time of Alexander, now continued under his successors. Besides Samaria and Gaza, which had been occupied by Greek garrisons in 332 B.C., there flourished such places as Raphia, Askalon, Ashdod, Joppa, Dor, and Ptolemais, anciently known as Akko, Philoteria (Ḥirbet Kerak) on the south-west shore of the Lake of Galilee and Bethshan, now named Scythopolis and also Nysa in recognition of the local worship of Dionysus. East of the Lake of Galilee was Hippos, while in Transjordan Gerasa (Jerash), Gadara (Umm Qeis), and Philadelphia (Amman) took their rise as Greek towns, together with Paneion (Banias) at the springs of the Jordan, with its shrine of the rustic Pan. Under the fostering influence of the Greek dynasties of Egypt and later of Syria these places experienced a new era of political life and commercial prosperity. They had the right of self-government with their own assemblies, and many of them, such as Ptolemais, Gaza, Askalon, Joppa, and Damascus, had the right of minting coins. Such coins, indeed, are an important source of information concerning the political and cultural condition of the land during this time and in them the rulers of Palestine confront us in first-hand likenesses.

On the evidence of these coins it may be stated that, though Hellenistic architecture and institutions prevailed in the autonomous towns of the coast and plains of Palestine, in the sphere of religion the Greek deities did not supplant the native gods. Here as elsewhere the Greeks showed a broad tolerance for alien faiths and, where the native and Greek deities were not worshipped side by side, the old native deity was given the distinctive dress and attributes of his Greek counterpart. Thus Apollo was equated with Reshef, the old Semitic deity who slew men in mass, usually by war or pestilence, the Tyrian Baal Melqart, the power of providence in nature and the champion of order against chaos, with Heracles, whose labours also established order against the menace of chaos, Eshmun, the healer, with Asclepius, and the fertility-goddess Astarte with Aphrodite.

Up in the mountains round Jerusalem and the old Persian province of Jehud it is natural that the prevailing Hellenism should have been viewed with suspicion. The rulers of Egypt had shown favour to the Jewish communities in Egypt, particularly in Alexandria, but it was not difficult to give offence to the scruples of the more exclusive elements among the Jews. In 217 B.C., for instance, after his unexpected success against Antiochus III at Raphia, Ptolemy Philopator visited Jerusalem and, giving thanks to Yahweh, sought to enter the Holy of Holies. This occasioned a riot, which the king suppressed with severity, which naturally alienated the sympathies of the Jews. It is a measure of the extent of Hellenisation in the non-Jewish regions of Palestine that on this occasion the local inhabitants are said to have greeted Ptolemy with all kinds of adulation, sacrificing in his honour, dedicating altars, and offering him crowns.[1]

The sphere of Greek influence in the eastern part of Alexander's empire which had fallen to the share of Seleucus had been seriously limited by the nascent power of the Parthians.

[1] *Polybius* v, 84

Now the centre of administration was shifted from Babylon to Syria and the power of the state was consolidated under the House of Seleucus. Thus there were two powers in Syria and Egypt, both Greek in character and administrative personnel, yet each rapidly developing a strong national self-consciousness, and claiming Palestine as the natural adjunct to their homeland. For the rest of the time until the exhaustion of both, when Rome laid her strong hand on Palestine, Palestine was a Debatable Land.

Soon after the Battle of Raphia, Ptolemy Philopator died and was succeeded by his infant son, and again Antiochus asserted his claim to Palestine. Egypt disputed his claim and the two powers met in battle at Banias in the foothills of Hermon. The battle, fought in 198 B.C., was a triumph for Syria. Antiochus now occupied Palestine, and Josephus states that when he came to Jerusalem the Jews helped him to eject the Egyptian garrison. Antiochus on his part granted the Jews a rebate of taxes, provided for the repair of the Temple and the maintainance of the services out of imperial revenues, and granted total absolution from taxation to cultic personnel and to the council of elders, and to the scribes.[1]

Events in the next phase of the history of Palestine are largely conditioned by the economic situation in the Seleucid kingdom. Antiochus had tried issues with Rome and had been inflicted with the burden of a heavy indemnity. Though Antiochus was too wise a ruler to antagonise his newly acquired subjects by undue extortion, his successors had less scruple and resorted to extraordinary levies on whatever funds were thought to be at their disposal in the various communities in the empire. Under these men Jerusalem was one of the potential victims of the bankrupt House of Seleucus and soon experienced not only the cancellation of the concessions of Antiochus III, but increased taxation and even the plunder of the Temple treasury.

In this new involvement of the ancient East in Greek politics and culture the Jewish community underwent a crisis. Some favoured the new Hellenistic manners and thought, not objecting to be in the mainstream of the world's culture ; others saw in these a menace to the ancestral faith and conduct. Some, with happy recollections of the beneficent rule of Persia,

---

[1] Josephus, *Antiquities* xii, iii, 138–44. These concessions are not otherwise attested, but it will be recalled that a similar policy was adopted by the Persian administration in favour of the Jews (Ezr. 6:8–9).

did not resent Seleucid rule, being willing to collaborate, no doubt to their own personal advantage, as local administrators and fiscal officers ; others again resisted all encroachments on their political and religious liberties. Other rifts in the Jewish community were due to family, and even personal, rivalries, and the office of the high priest was a bone of contention. When finally Antiochus IV appointed one Jason, then Menelaus, high priest a decisive breach was imminent between the orthodox and the Seleucid king and Jewish collaborators, who had not scrupled to receive the holiest office in Judaism from the hand of a gentile.

Under Antiochus IV, whose hostility to the recalcitrant Jews was aggravated by the trouble which he constantly apprehended from Egypt and by frequent frustration, persecution and atrocity in Judah rose in high crescendo until in 168 B.C. Jerusalem was attacked and suffered plunder and massacre. The fortifications were dismantled, a fortress built for a Seleucid garrison, the famous Akra on the north part of the Ophel, Judaism suppressed by decree, and the cult of Olympian Zeus instituted in Jerusalem. The pagan altar occupied the site of the altar of Yahweh, and the image of Olympian Zeus, the Greek counterpart of Baal of the Heavens (*Baal Shamaim* [1]), was the final affront to Judaism. In the province also Judaism was suppressed, pagan altars were set up, on which sacrifice by the Jews was demanded as a test of loyalty. This policy was but too effective, until at Modein in the Judaean foothills some six miles east of Lydda, Mattathias, of a minor priestly family, dared to slay the local commissioner and a Jew who was sacrificing, and so raised the standard of open revolt in 166 B.C.

This was the act of a desperate man and not a preconcerted revolt of a party. Now Mattathias and his sons took to the hills, where they were joined by others whom persecution had rendered desperate. They ranged the country, making sudden descents upon the villages, destroying pagan altars, killing apostates, and circumcising Jewish boys. Their forces grew after they had, under Judas the son of Mattathias, beaten Syrian forces at Beth Horon in the famous pass from the coastal plain to the mountains north of Jerusalem, Emmaus in the valley of Ajalon, the base of operations against Jerusalem by way of the ' ascent of Beth Horon ', the Wadi Aly, or the valley of Sorek (Wadi Ṣurar), and at Bethsur, where the Vale of Elah gives access to

---

[1] *Baal Shamaim* is parodied by *hashshiqquṣ meshômēm*, ' the abomination which maketh desolate ' (Dan. 11:31).

the mountains north of Hebron. The orthodox, not at first actively supporting the revolt, eventually did so when it became apparent that passive resistance was suicidal, and as a result of the victory of Bethsur the Temple was cleansed and rededicated in December 164 B.C., to which the Feast of Hanukkah traditionally relates, and Bethsur was fortified.

It is not the purpose of the present work to describe fully the struggle of the Jewish patriots for faith and freedom as that is detailed in the Books of the Maccabees and the *Antiquities* of Josephus. It was a fluctuating conflict, Jewish success being made possible by the terrain, the fact that the financial embarrassment of the Seleucids and their political involvement with the Parthians in the east obliged them to send only inferior provincial troops to Palestine, and by dynastic troubles in the Seleucid House. Repeatedly disastrous situations were redeemed for the Jews by the outbreak of some such trouble. This occurred notably in 163 B.C., when the forces of Judas were forced back on their last defences in Jerusalem. On that occasion the Syrians were glad to reach a *modus vivendi*, and agreed to a revocation of the oppressive decrees of Antiochus IV. With this it seemed that Judas and his followers had won what they were fighting for. This success, however, opened two new rifts in the Jewish community. Judas and his brothers had already undertaken campaigns beyond the province of Judah and had had a taste of conquest, but there were many of the orthodox who had fought only for spiritual liberty and had no desire to further the secular ambitions of the Hasmonaean family. These accordingly dissociated themselves from Judas, hence the name ' Pharisees ' (' Those who separated themselves '). Again, in spite of the revocation of the decrees of Antiochus IV, the Seleucid king still reserved the right to appoint the high priest. Some, as formerly, were content to acquiesce, notably the incumbent in the high priestly office, held to be reserved for the descendents of Sadoq, the high priest in the days of Solomon. The supporters of this order were consequently termed Sadducees. To others, again, this was intolerable. These divisions became more acute as the secular ambitions of the Hasmonaeans became more apparent in the political opportunism of Jonathan, the brother of Judas, and under the later Hasmonaeans, especially Alexander Jannaeus, who was the first of the family to use the title ' King ' on his coins.

Archaeological evidence of the Hasmonaean struggles and

ascendancy is not abundant. There are many references in the Books of the Maccabees and the *Antiquities* of Josephus to their buildings and fortresses. Their palace was on a spur of the West Hill of Jerusalem over against the Temple towards the south-west corner of the sacred area,[1] and at the north-west of the sacred area they built the fortress Baris,[2] the site of the better-known Antonia of Herod the Great, where Jesus was condemned before Pilate. In the time of the Hasmonaeans the occupation of Jerusalem shifted generally north and west, no doubt because of the Syrian occupation of the Akra, or fortress, on the Ophel Hill, which the Seleucids held till 141 B.C. This fortress was then demolished, the Ophel itself deliberately truncated, and the depression between it and the West Hill partly filled with the debris. With this demolition all traces of the palace of the kings of the House of David no doubt disappeared. Other notable demolitions at this time were Samaria and the Samaritan temple on Mount Gerizzim, which were destroyed by John Hyrcanus (135–104 B.C.). Outside Jerusalem there were Hasmonaean fortresses, such as Hyrcania (Ḥirbet Mird) in the desert between Bethlehem and the Dead Sea, Alexandreion (Qarn Sarṭaba) in similar country fifteen miles south-east of Nablus, and Machaerus (Ḥirbet el-Mukawwar) east of the Dead Sea, but these and the Hasmonaean buildings in Jerusalem were, with the exception of the Alexandreion, completely rebuilt by Herod the Great (37–4 B.C.). A notable exception is Bethsur (Ḥirbet et-Ṭubeiqeh), where the evidence of coins of the period taken in conjunction with the detailed accounts of the Maccabaean campaigns makes it possible to reinterpret the archaeological remains rather accurately.[3] This place, a Jewish fortress between the Persian administrative districts of Jehud and Arabia, assumed a new significance now owing to its strategic situation at the head of one of the few passes from the coastal plain to the interior by the famous valley of Elah. Now it had its fortifications rebuilt and extended in the 2nd century B.C. This is almost certainly the work of Judas Maccabaeus in the initial success of the Jewish revolt in 165–163 B.C. (1 Mac. 7:7). The destruction of these fortifications and their subsequent reconstruction may be the work of the Seleucid general Bacchides in 161 B.C. (1 Mac. 9:52). Handles of wine-jars stamped with names of the high priests of

[1] Josephus, *Antiquities* xx, viii, 11 ; J. Simon, *Jerusalem in the Old Testament* (1952), 152   [2] Josephus, *Antiquities* xv, xi, 4
[3] O. R. Sellers, *The Citadel of Beth Sur* (1933)

Rhodes probably indicate occupation by Seleucid garrisons until, with the establishment of native Jewish rule, the place ceased to serve as a fortress commanding access to Judah, and, on the evidence of coins, was abandoned *c.*100 B.C. Other settlements which had a similar history until the extension of Jewish rule beyond the mountains of Judah made them strategically insignificant were Samaria, Gezer commanding access to Jerusalem by the valleys of Aijalon and Sorek, and Marissa (Tell es-Sandaḥannah) near old Lachish commanding the approach to Hebron by Wadi 'l-Afranj (Crusaders' Wadi).

Marissa is an interesting instance of a provincial Hellenistic town in Palestine. Its town plan is much more systematic than in the Oriental period ; its houses are arranged in blocks and its streets mostly at right angles and much more spacious than in towns of the preceding ages in Palestine. Here scores of Rhodian jar-handles were found, testifying to trade with the Aegean and probably to occupation by garrisons of the Ptolemies of Egypt and the Seleucids of Syria until the district was incorporated in the native Jewish state under the Hasmonaean prince John Hyrcanus. In the Ptolemaic period in the 3rd century B.C. a number of family tombs cut in the soft limestone reveals a colony of Phoenicians from Sidon.[1] Their business at Marissa is not revealed by the Greek and Aramaic inscriptions in the tombs, but theophoric names containing the name of Kos, the national deity of Edom, point to association with the Edomites, who by this time occupied the south of Palestine, and may possibly point to an interest in the caravan trade from Arabia via Aqaba to the markets of Gaza, where there was another Sidonian settlement dating from the 5th century B.C.

The development of the power and status of the Hasmonaean family may be traced in the coins which they issued. Jonathan, the brother of Judas Maccabaeus, had been invested with the high-priestly office in 152 B.C. as a political bribe by the Syrian pretender Alexander Balas, and his brother Simon and his descendants continued to enjoy the office independent of the favour of the Syrians. The son of Simon, John Hyrcanus (135–104 B.C.), who ruled as an independent prince, but with the authority of high priest, was the first to issue coinage, with the legend in proto-Hebraic characters ' *Jehohanan the High Priest and the Community of the Jews* '. The son of John, Alexander Jannaeus, whose Hebrew name was Jonathan (103–76 B.C.) was

[1] J. H. Peters and H. Thiersch, *Painted Tombs of Marissa* (1905)

the first to use the title ' King ' on his coins, which bore the legend ' *Jonathan the King* '. Though he used the proto-Hebraic script, he used also Greek letters on certain coins, which reflected the extension of his authority as the result of his conquests beyond the pale of the province of Judah in gentile Samaria, Galilee, the south of Palestine, and even beyond Jordan, regions which had already been open to Greek influences of all kinds. The coins of his sons, John Hyrcanus II (67 and 63–40 B.C.) and Antigonus, whose Hebrew name was Mattathias (40–37 B.C.), belong to the Roman period. In the case of the former the high-priestly title alone is used, indicating a curtailment of native power by Rome, and in certain coins of the latter both Greek and Hebrew legends are used, the latter mentioning only the high-priestly office in deference to native opinion, and the former bearing the royal title in defiance of Rome. The Hasmonaean princes, however, in spite of their worldly ambitions, so far respected native scruples as to avoid the use of their personal images and confine themselves to such symbols as laurel wreaths, cornucopiae, flowers, and the seven-branched candlestick, which first appears on a coin of Antigonus-Mattathias. The first Jewish king whose features are known to us is Herod Agrippa I (A.D. 37–44), the contemporary of St Paul.

In contrast to the many sites dismantled at this time, a settlement which assumed a new significance now was that of Hirbet Qumran overlooking the Dead Sea from the north-west, some eight miles south of Jericho. Some traces have been found of an earlier settlement there in the 8th and 7th centuries B.C., perhaps associated with desert settlements attributed to Jotham, the son and co-regent of Uzziah (2 Chr. 27:4), and possibly ' the City of Salt ' (Jos. 15:62), as suggested by Professor Noth. The excavation of this site by the Jordan Department of Antiquities, L'École Archéologique Française, and the Palestine Archaeological Museum under G. L. Harding and Père R. De Vaux in five campaigns between 1951 and 1956 revealed three main phases of occupation, the first two by the Sect, or Community, of the New Covenant, as they called themselves. It is not possible to determine, either from the excavations or from the documents so far deciphered, when and in what circumstances the Sect took its origin. The whole period of occupation by the Sect is well delimited by coins, and the fact that these, so far as they have been cleaned and deciphered, begin in the time of John Hyrcanus (135–104 B.C.) suggests that the settlement dates from about this time, the Sect having taken its origin a little earlier, perhaps in protest at the assumption of the high-priesthood by Jonathan as a political bribe at the hands of the Seleucid pretender Alexander Balas in 152 B.C., or perhaps a decade earlier, when Jason (2 Mac. 4:7 ff.), Menelaus (2 Mac. 4:23), and Alkimos (Josephus, *Antiquities* XII, ix, 7) were created high priests. Non-biblical texts, at any rate, such as the Manual of Discipline of the Sect and particularly the ' commentary ' on the first two chapters of the Book of Habakkuk, show that for the Sect the legitimacy of the priesthood was a controversial issue. The exploration of caves in the escarpment behind the settlement indicates that probably the community lived in tents with caves as storehouses and dwellings in the winter rains, which are rare enough in that region of rain-shadow. The buildings excavated were a watch-tower, the public meeting-houses, refectory with kitchen and pantries, scriptorium, common bakery, pottery, and other work-shops, together with the vital conduits and cisterns, most of which were used for storage of water rather than for ceremonial ablution, which we know from the Manual of Discipline to have been one of their important rites. There is good evidence that this somewhat modest settlement was disrupted by earthquake. From coins of Herod the Great (37–4 B.C.), which are the last precisely datable evidence from this level, Père de Vaux connects the earthquake with that noted by Josephus in the reign of Herod in 31 B.C. The second phase of occupation begins, after a period of dereliction, in the time of Herod's son Archelaus (4 B.C.–A.D. 6) and, on the evidence of coins, continues to the second year of the Jewish Revolt (A.D. 66). Again Josephus may enable us to par-ticularise, since he records that in that year, in his systematic isolation of Jerusalem, Vespasian brought the Xth Legion down the Jordan Valley to Jericho. This phase of the settlement of Qumran ended in conflagration, and iron arrow-heads indicate violence. This is the time when the Scriptures of the Sect were secreted in the caves as the archaeological evidence from Cave I suggests.[1] After this a limited area of the site was occupied as a garrison-post by troops apparently of the Xth Legion, who were engaged in the Judaean desert in mopping up rebels after the fall

---

[1] This consisted of tall jars, in which the scrolls were found, their lids, a juglet, some lamps, and a cooking-pot. The jars have no exact parallel in Palestine, except in the Hasmonaean period at Bethsur, but are similar in form and purpose to jars used in Egypt in the 2nd century B.C. The lamps may be late Hellenistic or early Roman, and the rest of the pottery is similar to that found in Jewish tombs about Jerusalem in the 1st century A.D.

of Jerusalem in A.D. 70.[1] The site was again abandoned towards the end of the 1st century A.D., but was reoccupied by the Jewish insurgents in the Revolt of Bar Cochba (A.D. 132–5). On the suppression of this revolt Qumran was finally abandoned except by periodic squatters, who left a few coins from the Byzantine (till the 7th century A.D.) and Arab (after A.D. 636) periods.

In the period of occupation by the Sect the identification of buildings, in so far as that was not suggested by material evidence, was facilitated by the documents found in Cave 1. Obviously much copying of manuscripts was done, and the scriptorium was indicated by a room with long stone benches and stone tables with inkwells of brass and pottery. The Manual of Discipline of the Sect mentions communal meals, and a certain large room with kitchen and pantry with a great store of various dishes obviously served such a purpose. The careful burial of bones of domestic animals almost certainly indicates the disposal of the remains of such meals. The adjoining cemetery is also interesting. Burials were orientated southwards and there was no grave furniture. Coins were found only in the area of the public buildings and not in the caves, certain of which show signs of habitation. This agrees with the Manual of Discipline, which makes it clear that there was no private property in the Sect, but all money brought by novices or subsequently earned was paid into a common fund. The documentary evidence for the way of life of the Sect belongs strictly to the latter phase of their settlement (31 B.C.–A.D. 68), but it is highly probable that their Manual of Discipline records habits already fixed in the Hasmonaean age.

Apart from the Manual of Discipline, fragments of eleven copies of which are so far attested, the most significant documents are tendentious commentaries on the Prophets and Psalms, the scroll entitled 'The War of the Sons of Light against the Sons of Darkness', and Hymns, which in spite of their echoes of Scriptural phraseology, introduce us to the intimate spiritual experience of the Sect.

The 'commentaries' consist of the application of Scripture to topical affairs and personalities. It might be expected that these would afford a clue to the date and circumstances of the origin

---

[1] This was the legion which was quartered in the ruins of Jerusalem after A.D. 70, where tiles have been found with the stamp of the legion, LEG X F (i.e. Fretensis). A coin found at Qumran counterstamped with X is probably a relic of their occupation.

of the Sect, and indeed, we believe, they do. The allusions, however, are designedly cryptic, and, to modern knowledge, often ambiguous, so that there is great disagreement among scholars. We believe that the Habakkuk Commentary gives the surest clue to the question of the date and origin of the Sect. There is repeated reference to the opposition of a figure *Môreh ha-Ṣedheq*, which, with T. H. Gaster, we believe to mean ' the legitimate dispenser of the Tôrah ' or, as Gaster suggests,[1] ' the true interpreter of the Law ', and ' the evil priest ' (*ha-Kôhen ha-rashaʿ*), which we take to be a parody of ' the high priest ' (*ha-kôhēn ha-gādhôl*). Though we think that the political circumstances indicated in the text refer to the early Roman period in the history of Palestine, the references, in our opinion, cover a longer period and reach back to Hellenistic times. The controversy over the legitimacy of the priesthood was not limited to a particular priest but concerned the high-priesthood of the Hasmonaean House, the legitimacy of which was vitiated at the outset by the office being conferred upon Jonathan by the pretender to the Seleucid throne, of whom it might thus be said, in the words of the Commentary on Habakkuk (col. viii, 8–10) that ' he was called against the name of faith in the beginning of his establishment '. The text goes on to condemn ' the Wicked Priest ' for ' amassing wealth of the peoples '. It is well known that Jonathan owed his elevation to his astute exploitation of dynastic rivalries of the decadent Seleucid House, both parties of which vied with each other in courting his support by distinctions and wealth. The whole period of the Hasmonaean high-priesthood, however, is passed in review until, with ' the last priests ', their ill-gotten gains would be given over to the ' Kittians ' (col. ix, 4–7 on Hab. 2:8), the gentiles, who were, in our opinion, the Romans. In the ' commentary ' on Nahum there is a clear reference to the Seleucid period, and probably also to the gruesome incident when Alexander Jannaeus crucified eight hundred Pharisees who had withdrawn their support in 88 B.C.[2] Nevertheless, we applaud the caution of T. H. Gaster in seeing in many cases where some have sought particular references rather general references to offices rather than to personalities.[3] Thus ' The Legitimate Dispenser of the Law ' (*Môreh ha-ṣedeq*) denotes the office rather than the person. Against the tendency

---

[1] T. H. Gaster, *The Scriptures of the Dead Sea Sect* (1957), 15
[2] J. M. Allegro, ' Further Light on the History of the Qumran Sect ', *Journal of Biblical Literature* LXXV (1956), 89–93   [3] Gaster, op. cit., 33 ff.

to find particular references to actual historical events and conditions Gaster again does well to remind us that the Sect did not withdraw to the desert merely under stress of political circumstances, but chose the desert as symbolic of the life of concentration on the Law apart from mundane preoccupations and as conducive to the experience of the mystic.[1] Needless to say, this view is supported by ample evidence from the texts, particularly from the Hymns of the Sect, and in the Manual of Discipline the withdrawal from worldly men is specifically related to the text ' Prepare in the desert a highway for our God ' (Isa. 40:3).

In those stirring times, when Israel was fighting desperately in defence of the faith of her fathers, men recalled the mighty and marvellous acts of God in the history of the race, and in face of persecution and struggle against the superior arms and numbers of the Seleucid forces they were nerved to endure by a lively expectation of the intervention of God. Not only were the stories of the Exodus, the Conquest, and the Judges retold, but newer traditions became current, the story, for instance, of the fortitude of Daniel in Babylon, perhaps originally current in the Exile in an Aramaic form.[2]

The second half of the Book of Daniel introduces us to apocalyptic, that is to say revelation in terms and imagery to be understood by those who had the key to the meaning of God's working out of his people's destiny. The imagery of this type of literature is to the uninitiated bizarre and baffling, mythological matter being freely employed on purpose to disguise references to powers and personalities dangerous to offend, or in order to increase men's sense of awe before the mighty, mysterious, and ineffable power of God. Often the metaphysical speculation of the writers is a further complication. Nevertheless apocalyptic was born of a practical need ; it was the vivid presentation of a hope to sustain the faith of men under persecution. The apocalyptic matter in the Book of Daniel (chs. 8–9) introduces us at once to the practical problems of the Hasmonaeans and their followers and to the vivid hopes which they entertained of

[1] Gaster, op. cit., 16 ff. The desert in the texts is often figurative and symbolic and the Zadokite Fragments, which relate also to the Sect, legislate for urban communities of sectaries as well as those who live in ' camps ' like the Qumran community.

[2] A fragment of the Book of Daniel from Qumran, where the prayer of Nebuchadrezzar (Dan. 4:34–7) is attributed to Nabona'id, who is otherwise not mentioned in the book, suggests another, possibly Mesopotamian and so more accurate, tradition of the stories in Dan. 1–7 (D. N. Freedman, ' The Prayer of Nabonidus ', Bulletin of the American Schools of Archaeology 145 (1957), 32.

deliverance by God's breaking into history. No part of the Old Testament is more topical, yet practical wisdom and resolution is impregnated with the sanguine expectation that this world order was soon to pass away and the Reign of God to be manifestly established. There is a similar blending of topical allusions with eschatological hopes of the immediate triumph of God in the second part of the Book of Zechariah (chs. 9–14), most of which relates most probably to the struggles of Judas and his brother Jonathan and to the success of Simon [1] and possibly also his sons. The writings of the Qumran community also show this interest in topical events and personalities, on which they affected to find animadversions in Scripture, particularly, to judge from the extant material, in the Prophets and Psalms. They also believed that they were an elect community, the true Israel, ' preparing in the desert a highway for their God ', and disciplining themselves in view of a final struggle against the powers of evil, hence their systematic organisation in peace (cf. Manual of Discipline) and war (cf. The War of the Children of Light against the Children of Darkness). Their community was ' the camp ', and they visualised a final ' showdown ' with the armies of evil, ' the children of darkness ' led by Belial (' Worthlessness '), now personified as the personal head of all that militates against God's good order. The latter text in fact is well characterised by T. H. Gaster [2] as ' a kind of G.H.Q. manual for the guidance of the Brotherhood at Armageddon '. This strange document, with all the military organisation and etiquette of a veritable Salvation Army, anticipates a forty years' war ; fortunes will fluctuate ; thrice Belial will be defeated, thrice he will conquer ; but in the seventh engagement he will be finally routed and the triumph of God secured to all eternity.[3] In the conflict the Sect was very conscious of the fact that the angelic hosts were on their side :

For Thou, O Lord, art (terrible ?) in Thy royal glory,
And the cengregation of the Holy Ones is in our midst as an
    eternal succour.
So we have put shame upon kings,
Scorn and reproach upon mighty men.
For holy is our God,

---

[1] Simon may be named in Zech. 12:13, where the Septuagint version reads *Shime'on* for the Hebrew *Shime'i*.   [2] *The Scriptures of the Dead Sea Sect* (1957)

[3] *The War of the Children of Light against the Children of Darkness*, col. i, 13–15. The text is published by Y. Yadin with a commentary in Hebrew, *Me͏ghillath be͏ne 'ôr bibhe͏ne ḥôshekh* (1955). A slightly different reading is given by A. M. Habermann, *Me͏gilloth Midhbar Ye͏huda*, in Hebrew (1959).

Plate 22   The Monastery of Qumran looking towards the mouth
of the Jordan

Plate 23 Masada, a fortress of the Hasmonaean princes and of Herod the Great, and the last stronghold of the Jewish insurgents in the revolt of A.D. 66–70, from the north-east. At the bottom of the picture is the Roman circumvallation.

And the King of glory is with us together with His Holy Ones,
Mighty Ones and the army of angels are in our musterings,
And he that is mighty is in our congregation,
The army of his spirits is with our marching and deploying,
Even as clouds or as banks of dew covering the ground,
Or as rain-showers watering all that sprouts thereupon.[1]

The Prince of Light, the Archangel Michael himself, was engaged
with those warrior-saints, a confidence echoed in the Book of
Daniel (12:1). The military organisation and the tactics described
in the War text have been shown by the first editor of the text,
General Yadin, to be based on that of the Romans, so that in its
present state the text post-dates the Hasmonaean period. The
theological conceptions, however, in the light of relevant passages
in Daniel and Zechariah, may be said to be a legacy of those
critical times.

We have already expressed our belief that the Sect was led to
organise itself and, at least as far as concerned the Qumran
community, to withdraw to the desert not so much under political pressure as owing to a positive quietist tendency. Such
movements are not uncommon in periods of divided political
allegiance and party strife, and in an age when Judaism was
divided and Pharisees bitterly opposed Sadducees many found a
more congenial climate in the cultivation of the life of the soul.
Such were the Essenes, with whom we believe the Qumran Sect
to be identical.

After describing the deposition of Archelaus, the son of Herod
the Great, from his rule of Judea, Josephus (War II, viii)
makes a digression and gives us the fullest information we possess
of the Sect of the Essenes, which he classifies as a third philo-
sophical sect with the better-known Pharisees and Sadducees.
He does not give any indication of the nature and date of their
origin, but from an anecdote which he records of Simon the
Essene at this time (War II, vii, 3) it is apparent that the
Sect was already well established before the deposition of Archelaus
(A.D. 6). A detailed consideration of Josephus' account of the
Essenes in the light of the Qumran documents suggests that the
Qumran community, if not exactly conforming to the regulations
attributed by Josephus to the Essenes, agrees with them in most,
and these the essential, particulars. Disagreements may be due
to the fact that a principle of the Sect was secrecy, so that

[1] ibid., col. xii, 6–9

15

Josephus, for all his evident sympathy and information gathered in his three years' sojourn with the desert hermit Banus,[1] had the disadvantage of observation *ab extra*.

Josephus witnesses to the amity of the Essenes and their abstemious life. No community which lived at Qumran could be other than abstemious ; and, as for the amity of the community, this was almost compelled by the regulations in the Manual of Discipline against wrangling in council, and in daily life it is stated :

> And whoever answers his neighbour defiantly or speaks brusquely so as to disrupt his social amity and in so doing flouts the orders of one who is registered as his superior . . . he is to be mulcted for one year. . . .[2]

Or again :

> And whoever harbours a grudge against his neighbour without legitimate cause he is to be mulcted for one year, so also anyone who takes personal revenge on his neighbour in any respect.[3]

Josephus notes the community of property among the Essenes, the affairs of the community being administered by stewards. The Essenes, according to Josephus, speak no profane word before sunrise, but engage in prayer, after which they work till the fifth hour, then assemble for ablution clad in ceremonial white robes, then dine in the common dining-hall after a priest has said grace ; ritual ablution and common meals are a regular part of the way of life of the Qumran Sect. The food of each individual Essene is rationed, a practice which is explicitly attested in the Qumran Manual of Discipline :

> If there be found among them one who consciously lies in the matter of his wealth he is to be regarded as outside the state of purity of the assembly for one year, and he is to be mulcted of one-fourth of his food ration.[4]

Josephus states that the Essenes do not swear oaths, but let their Yea be Yea and their Nay be Nay ; in the Manual of Discipline the only mention of an oath is the pledge of the initiant of

---

[1] Josephus, *Life*, §§ 10–12

[2] *Manual of Discipline*, col. vi, 23 ff. The text is published by M. Burrows, J. C. Trever, and W. H. Brownlee, *The Dead Sea Scrolls of St Mark's Monastery* II, fascicle 2 (1951) ; also accessible in Habermann, op. cit.

[3] Burrows, *Manual of Discipline*, col. vii, 8 ff.   [4] ibid., col. vi, 23 ff.

allegiance to God and the community.[1] The Essenes, like the Qumran community, did not seek converts. Any who wished to join the Sect, according to Josephus, spent a probationary year outside the Sect, after which he was admitted to the rite of ablution and engaged on a further two years until he was finally admitted into the society and to the common meals after taking an oath of allegiance to God and the community. This involved a pledge to keep the secret lore of the Sect. The content of the oath is essentially the same as that in the opening of the Manual of Discipline. The Manual of Discipline also prescribes a probationary year for the person who wishes to join the Sect. He is examined ' as to his intelligence and his actions ' and is instructed by the superintendent of the community. After the year, if the candidate is approved by the general assembly, he is admitted to the rite of ablution and, if approved after his second year within the community, he is admitted as a full member, which is signalised by his admission to the common meal. He is then assigned his due rank in the society,[2] according to which he is bound to defer to his seniors in council, a detail which Josephus notes in the conduct of the Essenes. Finally Josephus states that the Essenes divine the future by the study of holy books, being ' perpetually conversant with the discourses of the Prophets ',[3] a statement which, if not quite accurate of the Qumran community, certainly reflects their preoccupation with the Prophets and their topical application of them. There are other details in Josephus' account which correspond strikingly with what is known of the Qumran community, so that there seems little doubt that the austere covenanters of Qumran were a branch of the Essenes.

From the attention that Josephus devotes to them in proportion to the space he devotes to the Pharisees and Sadducees, it is obvious that the Essenes were so considerable and their system so commendable that they commanded his admiration. We would make the further suggestion that, albeit pledged to an oath of secrecy in certain fundamental matters concerning the Sect, the saints of Qumran and other such settlements visualised in the kindred Zadokite Fragments [4] played no small role in preparing the ground for the Gospel.

[1] ibid., col. i, 1 ff.   [2] ibid., col. vi, 13 ff.   [3] Josephus, *War* II, viii, 159
[4] These were published by L. Rost, *Die Damaskusschrift* (H. Lietzmann's *Kleine Texte für Vorlesungen und Übungen*) (1933). See more recently H. H. Rowley, *The Zadokite Fragments and the Dead Sea Scrolls* (1952). For a translation of the Qumran material and the Zadokite Fragments see T. H. Gaster, op. cit.

XIII The Point of Fulfilment

IT was one of the major tragedies of Jewish history that the House of Hashmon which had won Jewish independence in the days of Seleucid oppression was directly responsible for its loss and the imposition of the iron rule of Rome. The personal ambitions of these stalwart defenders of the faith had already split Judaism since the days of Judas Maccabaeus ; now on the death of Alexander Jannaeus, under whom the new Jewish kingdom reached its apogee, and of his widow Salome, to whom he bequeathed his secular power, the ruin of the state was precipitated by the domineering ambition of their younger son Aristobulus. Aristobulus beyond doubt was much fitter to rule than his elder brother John Hyrcanus II, who held the office of high priest during the regency of his mother, succeeding to the secular authority on her death in 67 B.C. The whole policy of Salome, also called Alexandra, had been directed to winning the support of the Pharisees, whom already at his death Alexander Jannaeus, in spite of his Sadducee sympathies, had recognised as the stronger and more popular party, to be placated rather than antagonised. Already in the days of Alexander Jannaeus, Pharisaic opposition to the secularism of the ruling house had been so strong as to occasion civil war. Now under the regency of Salome and the high-priesthood of the supine John Hyrcanus the Pharisees were paramount in the state. Their vindictive policy towards their Sadducee opponents drove the latter to desperation, thus creating a situation which was exploited to the full by pretenders to the throne of the Hasmonaeans. So Aristobulus demanded the authority of his brother, and the two, encouraged by these hostile forces in sworn opposition, came to open war, and Hyrcanus was defeated in battle by Jericho, abdicating both royal and priestly office in favour of Aristobulus.

The issue, however, was opened up afresh by the machinations of Antipater, the governor of Idumaea, the southern district of Palestine, and the grandfather of Herod the Great, who persuaded the weak Hyrcanus to take the field again, having involved the Nabataean king Aretas III in the struggle. Aristobulus was thrown back on the defensive in Jerusalem and was extricated from his difficulties only by the intervention of M. Aemilius Scaurus, the Roman governor of Syria, in 64 B.C., the hostile brothers vying with each other with bribes to secure the intervention of Rome in a situation of itself too inviting for any imperialist power to neglect. The following year, after the suppression of Mithradates and Tigranes in Asia Minor and Syria, Pompey heard the case of Hyrcanus and Aristobulus in Damascus. The latter, suspecting that Rome would favour his more amenable brother, made a final desperate appeal to the sword and occupied Jerusalem. Pompey reduced the city, and Judaea, now stripped of the cities of the coastal plain, Samaria, and in Transjordan, was incorporated as a province in the Roman Empire. Hyrcanus was allowed to rule as high priest and ethnarch, the title of king being abolished. Kings were yet to rule in Jerusalem, but they reigned by grace of Rome, with the exception of the rebel Antigonus, the son of Aristobulus (40–37 B.C.) who became king by the support of the Parthians, exploiting the embarrassment of Rome in the civil wars after the death of Julius Caesar.

Now began a veritable revolution in the life and culture of Palestine ; the westernising tendency which was already since the conquests of Alexander the Great in full process in all but the immediate vicinity of Jerusalem, and was even present there, now received a decisive stimulus which set the pattern of culture for seven hundred years until the Arab Conquest. In the Roman civil wars which brought first Julius Caesar, then Octavian, to supreme power Roman troops were in Palestine, and local notables were involved in Roman politics. Herod the Great (37–4 B.C.) became king of almost the whole of Palestine not by the popular acclaim of his native subjects, but by the decree of the Senate at Rome. His settlement of his authority on his sons —Archelaus in Judaea, Herod Antipas in Galilee and part of Transjordan, and Philip in Ituraea north-east of the Lake of Galilee—was subject to the ratification of the Emperor. In A.D. 6 the incompetent Archelaus was deposed and Judaea thereafter, except during the brief reign of Herod Agrippa I (A.D. 37–44), a protégé of the Roman Imperial House, was administered from Caesarea by Roman procurators under the authority of the imperial legate of Syria, a situation reflected in the Lucan birth-narrative (Lk. 2:2). The best-known of the procurators of Judaea is Pontius Pilate (A.D. 26–36).

This situation is strikingly reflected by the material remains in the various sites excavated in Palestine, which are more and

more typical of the Graeco-Roman world rather than of the East.
In Herod's time western types predominate in art, architecture,
and building technique with marginal-drafted masonry, and all
but the simplest pottery. The extent of westernisation is indicated by inscriptions on public buildings, which are in Greek, and
it is significant that an inscription from the Temple court warning
gentiles to proceed no farther on pain of death was only in
Greek [1] : ' Let no foreigner enter within the screen and precincts.
Whosoever is taken will be responsible for death overtaking him.'
So too the inscription from a synagogue in Jerusalem, probably
that of the Freedmen (Ac. 6:9). This inscription from the Ophel
Hill of Jerusalem may be translated : ' Theodotos, son of
Vettenus, priest and archisynagogos, son of an archisynagogos,
grandson of an archisynagogos, built the synagogue for the
reading of the Law and for the teaching of the Commandments ;
furthermore, the hospice and the chambers and the water con-
veniences for lodging of needy strangers. The foundation stone
thereof had been laid by his fathers and the elders and Simonides.'
Local coins too from the time of Herod the Great use Greek
legends, and those of Herod Agrippa I from Caesarea are actually
stamped with his effigy, the first actual portrait of a Jewish king.
A further indication of the same cultural trend are various Greek
versions of the Old Testament (besides the four already known [2])
recently discovered in caves in the Wadi Murabba'at, some ten
miles south of Qumran. On palaeographic grounds these are
dated not later than the middle of the 1st century A.D. Palestine
from this time forward was culturally and politically a province
of the Roman Empire, and even the synagogues, the earliest
remains of which are from c.A.D. 200, are Roman in architecture
and decoration.[3]

East of the Dead Sea, however, in the region occupied by the
Nabataeans, who had come from the oases of the Hejaz and had
settled the country formerly occupied by the Edomites, a distinctively native tradition in architecture and ceramics flourished,
though here too from the 1st century B.C. till the incorporation of
the Nabataean kingdom in the Roman Empire in 106 A.D.
Graeco-Roman influences may be detected. Coins of this

---

[1] Facsimile and Greek text in A. Deissmann, *Light from the Ancient East*
(ET, L. R. M. Strachan, 1929)

[2] These are the Septuagint begun c.250 B.C. in Alexandria, and the versions
of Aquila (c.A.D. 130), Theodotion (later in 2nd century), and Symmachus
(early 3rd century)

[3] These include the remains of synagogues at Capernaum and Chorazin.

flourishing mercantile kingdom are found, the most interesting being those which bear the image of Aretas IV, the contemporary of Herod the Great and St Paul (2 C. 11:32) and the father-in-law and later conqueror of Herod Antipas. The best-known city of this kingdom is its capital, the fabulous Petra in an impressive sandstone canyon in the heart of Mount Seir (Jebel Sherra). The actual buildings of Nabataean Petra have all disappeared. ' High places ', or open-air sanctuaries, are extant, hewn out of the living rock, with characteristic features of stepped altars for sacrifice, basins for blood and water, and standing stone pillars, which probably signified the presence of the deity, locally known as Dusares (*Dhu Sharra*, Lord of Seir). The great rock-hewn façades with their extremely plain interior are probably tombs combined with mortuary chapels rather than temples, and may have housed the remains of the Nabataean kings. These and other rock-cut tombs, together with a theatre and amphitheatre, show many Graeco-Roman features and so pose the problem of date. Those keen Nabataean merchants controlled a wide net-work of caravan routes from Arabia to the north and in the Negeb, or south of Palestine, between Aqaba and Gaza, securing all strategic points, where they encouraged settlement by diligent agriculture, traces of which survive to the present time in cisterns, plaster-lined and often vaulted to prevent evaporation, channel-ing of cliff faces to catch flash showers, damming of wadis and terracing of hillsides to prevent erosion of soil. It is possible that the ' Arabians ' to whom the Apostles spoke at Pentecost (Ac. 2:11) may have been Jewish merchants from some of these caravan cities, and it is not improbable that it was in the Nabataean kingdom that Paul spent his sojourn in ' Arabia ' (Gal. 1:17), which was in fact the designation of the region when it was incorporated in the Roman Empire by Trajan in A.D. 106.

In the Roman period in Palestine we have the advantage of accurate and detailed history, particularly that of Josephus in his record of the events leading up to and culminating in the great Jewish Revolt of A.D. 66–70. In the light of those intimate records it is possible to give a very full interpretation of the remains of the period, many of which are still conspicuous monuments visible without actual excavation. On these monu-ments inscriptions often permit particularisation, and in stratified excavation coins of Herod the Great and his family and the Roman procurators of Judaea make precise dating possible within narrow limits.

Herod the Great, who became king over most of Palestine by decree of the Senate in Rome in 40 B.C. and effectively assumed his rule in 37 B.C., has left many monuments in the Graeco-Roman style.   Samaria was given to Herod as a personal estate by the Roman Emperor Augustus in 30 B.C. and was rebuilt with more extensive walls, a stadium, and a forum.   On the top of the mound, above the former Israelite palaces, a temple was erected to Augustus, the steps and platform of which partially remain.   Caesarea was also built between 25 and 13 B.C. on the site of the Phoenician settlement of Straton's Tower.   This city, which was the Roman administrative centre, was also equipped with the typical institutions of Graeco-Roman culture, forum, stadium, amphitheatre, and theatre, all on a grand scale, and a temple to Augustus, with a statue of the emperor.   Marble statuary in the Graeco-Roman style is now commonly found in Palestine.   Caesarea, like modern Haifa, was made into a considerable seaport by the construction of two great moles, remains of which may still be seen.   Indeed all the features we have mentioned at Caesarea are plainly visible from the air and even from the ground.

From these well-known monuments Herodian work may be detected where it is incorporated into later building as at Jerusalem, Hebron in the mosque which encloses the traditional cave of Machpelah, and at the reputed site of the oaks of Mamre at Ramat el-Ḥalil two miles north of Hebron.

As is well known, Herod rebuilt the Temple at Jerusalem. Nothing indeed survives of the building itself, but Herod's southern extension of the sacred area remains supported by the vaults popularly known since the time of the Crusades as ' Solomon's Stables ', and the lower courses of colossal masonry in the West Wall are thought to be his work.   The pavement of the fortress which commanded the sacred area from the north-west, called Antonia after Herod's patron Mark Antony, may still be seen under the modern Convent of the Sisters of Zion. The foundations of one of the three great towers, Hippicos, Mariamne, and Phasael, at the western angle of Herod's north wall have been discovered under the Turkish citadel of the city. Other monuments of Herod the Great are the striking desert fortresses, the Herodium, where Herod desired to be buried, on that isolated peak south of Bethlehem which resembles an extinct volcano, Qarn Sarṭaba, built on a former Hasmonaean fortress Alexandreion, fifteen miles south-east of Nablus, Masada, overlooking the south of the Dead Sea, where the last remnants of the Jewish resistance forces perished by their own hand in A.D. 73, and Machaerus, overlooking the north of the Dead Sea from the east, where, possibly, John the Baptist was beheaded. None of these sites, however, except Masada, has been excavated, though surface remains are typical of Herod's building. Another building recently excavated, which was associated either with Herod or Archelaus, is the palace situated on the south bank of the Wadi Qilt just west of modern Jericho. This in its day must have been a pleasant seat with its ornamental gardens sloping down to the wadi. If it belongs to Herod it is probably the palace at Jericho where he died and where also he disposed of the last Hasmonaean high priest, his young brother-in-law, whom he had drowned in a bath. A building, which is probably a bath-house, has been excavated in the immediate vicinity of the palace.

Those buildings were part of the Palestine which our Lord knew. He passed close by the palace at Jericho on his last journey to Jerusalem by the old road up the Wadi Qilt. In Galilee the town and palace at Tiberias built by Herod Antipas was contemporary with Jesus, though there is no record of his actually being in the town. The site of Cana of Galilee also may still be identified at Ḥirbet Qana about eight miles north of Nazareth on the northern edge of the Plain of Battuf; a conspicuous feature is plaster-lined cisterns. Jerusalem of Jesus' time was the city with its Temple as built by Herod the Great. The actual localities associated with incidents in the ministry of Jesus, of course, are highly controversial, and most can at the best be located only generally. The reputed site of the Holy Sepulchre is a case in point, there being no unanimity among archaeologists as to the position of the second and third walls on the north of the city mentioned by Josephus in his account of the Jewish Revolt. The traditional site, however, was certainly an ancient burial-place, and, if the second city-wall ran from Herod's palace-fort at the Turkish citadel to the Antonia, as is certain, then the traditional site of the Holy Sepulchre might well have been outside the city-wall. Recent excavation and surface exploration at the traditional site of the Shepherds' Fields by Bethlehem and in caves in the vicinity have shown evidence, in pottery and coins, of occupation in the Herodian period and subsequently to A.D. 66–70. Another point of contact with the Gospel story is an aqueduct constructed by Pontius Pilate to bring water from Ain Arrub, nine miles south-south-east of Bethlehem, to the Temple area in Jerusalem. This is now conveniently visible by the side of the new road from Jerusalem to Bethlehem. The sites of Capernahum (Tell Hum), and Chorazin (Ḥirbet Kerazeh), Bethsaida (Eṭ-Ṭabghah), and other localities around the Lake of Galilee are also fairly certainly identified, but the remaining monuments, except at Tiberias, are of a later date.

In the vicinity of Jerusalem many family tombs have been cleared, especially from the 1st century B.C. to the 2nd century A.D., and a great number of ossuaries, or bone-caskets, found. Among these the most interesting was one which was inscribed in Aramaic to the effect that it contained the bones of King Uzziah. This king, who died a leper, had been buried outside the city, and at some later time, when his tomb was used for burial, his bones had been collected and deposited in the ossuary. Other ossuaries more recently found on the site of the new Franciscan church on the slopes of the Mount of Olives bear names familiar in the New Testament, such as Jairus, Miriam (Mary), Martha, Simon bar Jonah, etc. Not only so but some of them are marked with the sign of the cross. The fact that these ossuaries do not occur in the vicinity of Jerusalem after the 2nd century A.D. make it feasible that this is a cemetery in which Christian families of the district had been buried, possibly since the first generation of believers.

An important feature of Roman Palestine was the life and doctrine of the Sect of the New Covenant as that has now been revealed by the discoveries at Qumran. If, as seems probable on the combined evidence of Josephus, Pliny the Elder, and Philo of Alexandria, the covenanters of Qumran were Essenes, then, on the statement of Josephus, their numbers were not confined to the settlement by the Dead Sea, but they were found throughout the country to such an extent that ' many of them dwell in every city '.[1] It was for such communities apparently that the Qumran Manual of Discipline legislated in the enactment that wherever there were ten of the Sect the number must include a priest, whose presence secured orthodoxy. Now that the high, if somewhat austere, ethic of the Sect is known, these Essene communities with their brotherly love and simple piety must have been a very effective *praeparatio evangelii*. It seems inconceivable that such men could not be interested in the work

[1] Josephus, *War* II, vii, 4, trans. Whiston

and teaching of Jesus. Seeking as they did to order their lives according to the plain truth of Scripture in contrast to the pedantic subtleties of Pharisaic interpretation, they must surely have welcomed the Gospel of him who taught ' with authority and not as the scribes '. It may well be that much of Jesus' teaching was consciously directed to those men who had renounced the world ' for righteousness' sake '. The Sermon on the Mount would have had a strong appeal to the poor saints of the New Covenant, and Jesus' reference to ' the fields white unto harvest ' could refer to the Essenes, whose uniform was a white robe.

The Qumran documents, particularly the Manual of Discipline, the War of the Children of Light against the Children of Darkness, and the Hymns, reveal many striking affinities between the Sect of the New Covenant and the early Christian Church in quasi-technical phraseology, doctrine, and organisation. These have been held by certain scholars to be more intimate and extensive than we should personally admit, and already sensational statements have been made concerning Qumran and Christian origins. Nevertheless the affinities are such as to challenge serious consideration.

The men of Qumran believed that men were in the power of one of two spirits, which were created by God in the beginning, that of the Good or Light, and that of Evil or Darkness. The latter is known as Belial, and is personified, as in the New Testament. These with the men in their power wage inveterate warfare, which, however, was soon to culminate in a critical series of battles, seven in number, resulting in the ultimate victory of the Prince of Light and his followers, including the Sect of Qumran. This cosmic and ethical conflict between Light and Darkness is the background of the prologue to the Fourth Gospel, and is expressed again in the First Epistle of John (1:5-7 ; 2:8-11), and Jesus himself referred to himself as ' the light of the world '. The imagery of light as opposed to darkness, expressing the reign of God in conflict with all powers of chaos, is already familiar in the Old Testament (e.g. Am. 5:18 ; Isa. 9:2 ; 60:1-3), and in this as in other points of affinity between the Qumran Scriptures and the New Testament we should be ready to recognise that both drew on a common source in the Old Testament. Nevertheless the doctrine of the prologue to the Gospel according to St John suggests an affinity which goes beyond the use of a common source in the Old Testament. There has for some time been a growing conviction that this Gospel reflects a genuine old local tradition, especially from southern Palestine.[1] Now the recovery of the Qumran documents shows that in its philosophic interpretation of the life and teaching of Jesus the Gospel reflects not the gnostic tendencies of a Greek milieu, as used to be generally held, but the genuine theological climate of an important section of local Judaism.

The establishment of the régime of God after conflict with the powers of chaos is a well-known theme in the Old Testament and has a much longer history in Near Eastern myth and ritual, and in the Gospels it is developed in the parables of the kingdom, notably in that of the strong man overcome in the famous Beelzebub controversy (Mt. 12:25 ff.; Mk. 3:23 ff.; Lk. 11:17 ff.). The War of the Children of Light against the Children of Darkness in the Qumran scriptures, however, reflects a new urgency and sense of personal involvement in an imminent struggle, which was much more vividly visualised than anything of the kind before. This is the nature of the conflict visualised in the Book of Revelation.

In their involvement in this conflict ' the Children of Light ' of Qumran were convinced of their membership in the eternal community of God and the celestials, a conviction shared by the early Christians, who regarded themselves as ' fellow-citizens of the saints and of the household of God '. Both Christians and the men of Qumran, moreover, thought of themselves as ' a building of God . . . eternal in the heavens ' (cf. 2 C. 5:1), a striking figure, which can hardly be a fortuitous correspondence.

Predestination too was a doctrine of the Qumran Sect : ' all that is and ever was comes from the God of knowledge. Before things came into existence he determined the plan of them '.[2] This doctrine finds a place in the Pauline theology, the *locus classicus* being Romans 8:28 ff. The Qumran statement of the doctrine in the Sect's Manual of Discipline suggests determinism rather than predestination, but the life of strenuous piety of the brethren, with the ever-present possibility of a fall from grace, suggests that practically they held a belief in this matter closer to the Pauline doctrine of predestination. Their belief too in reward and retribution in the hereafter, ' a crown of glory ' (cf. 1 Pet. 5:4) and ' a robe of honour ' (cf. Rev. 6:11) on the one

---

[1] C. H. Dodd, *The Interpretation of the Fourth Gospel* (1953), 453 ff.
[2] cf. Josephus' statement that the Essenes are fatalists (*Antiquities* XIII, v, 9)

hand and ' damnation in the fire eternal ' on the other (cf. Mt. 18:9), is reflected in the doctrine of the early Church.

There are many other instances of affinities in language between Qumran and the early Church which, when taken cumulatively, make a very impressive case for the regard which Jesus and the first generation of his followers paid to contemporary thought illustrated by the Qumran scriptures, as apart from current Rabbinical thought. In organisation too there are striking parallels. The Qumran Sect and the early Church both practised community of property, the Qumran Manual of Discipline declaring that ' if a man lie regarding his property he shall be excommunicated for one year, his rations being reduced by a quarter for one year '. The communities of the Qumran Sect were under overseers, who presided over the councils of the brethren. This is thought, on insufficient grounds, we think, to suggest the office of the Christian overseer, *episcopos*, or bishop. The supreme council of Qumran consisted of twelve, either excluding or including three priests as authorities in the Law and its interpretation. It is submitted that this suggested to Jesus the twelve apostles, of which Peter, James, and John correspond to the three priests of the Qumran council. We think it more likely that in both cases the number was symbolic of the twelve tribes of Israel. It is difficult again to visualise the three apostles, provincial Galileans and fishermen, as legal experts, though it must be admitted that their status was owing to the fact that they had special insight into the mind of Jesus, who had come ' to fulfil the Law ', and they were undoubtedly accorded an authoritative place as ' pillars ' in the Jerusalem community (Gal. 2:9). Here again the peculiar conjunction of language and doctrine in both communities is suggestive. The Qumran Manual of Discipline declares that the three priests will be a ' holy of holies ' of the sanctuary, with which we may compare Paul's ' Ye are a temple of God, and the Spirit of God dwelleth within you ' (1 C. 3:16 ; cf. 2 C. 6:16), ' built upon the foundation of the apostles and prophets, Jesus Christ himself being the chief corner-stone, in whom all the building fitly framed together groweth into an holy temple in the Lord, in whom ye also are builded together for an habitation of God through the Spirit ' (Eph. 2:20–2).

These similarities, striking as they admittedly are, do not prove the close connection between Christianity and the Qumran Sect which has been asserted. We venture to suggest, however, that they indicate the great importance of that Sect, which we take to be Essene, in the Palestine of our Lord's day, and maintain that the Jewish substratum of the Gospels must be sought in the life and doctrine of this Sect and others, whose thought finds expression in the Apocrypha, rather than in the orthodox Rabbinic Judaism illustrated by the Talmud.

The Christian Church was more than the development of any one of these Jewish sects, however, and indeed differed fundamentally from the Qumran Sect. Like the Christian Church, the Qumran Sect was 'the Sect of the New Covenant', but the saints of Qumran lacked the missionary impulse of the Church. They were at pains to segregate themselves from worldly men, and even avoided discussion with others ; Jesus sat at meat with 'publicans and sinners'. Indeed it was probably on the issue of a positive mission to the world that John the Baptist may have left the Sect, with whom he had apparently so much in common. John certainly could not fail to know the Sect, since he baptised in the wilderness of Judaea on the lower Jordan, but a few miles from Qumran. The attitude of the Sect to those opposed to their own views and to those of their own number who failed to keep the covenant is expressed in the formal curse of their priests, which is the contrary of the high-priestly blessing. This amounts to an irrevocable curse, which is quite alien to the spirit of Christianity. The two communities differed radically in the doctrine of atonement too. The Qumran saints regarded themselves as atoning for the sins of Israel by their own practice of righteousness ; the Christian Church is conscious of its dependence on the atoning work of Jesus Christ. It has been thought that the so-called 'Teacher of Righteousness', whose sufferings are mentioned in the Qumran Commentary on Habakkuk and whose death is mentioned in the Zadokite Fragments, is a figure in the Sect comparable to Jesus in the Church. This figure, however, whom we regard as a priestly figure, 'the legitimate dispenser of the Tôrah', is, we feel sure with T. H. Gaster, not a single individual like Jesus but a succession of persons holding priestly office, the title denoting the office rather than the person. Nor is there any evidence that any one of the holders of this office at Qumran ever wrought atonement by his sufferings and death. The Sect looked to the coming of a Messiah, indeed of two Messiahs, and had compiled catenae of Messianic prooftexts from Scripture, such as the early Church also probably used. The two Messiahs mentioned in the Qumran Texts, however, are simply the anointed king and the anointed priest of a rehabilitated Israel. Of these the priest is to take the precedence, it being stated that where the two sat down to a meal, where the Sect observed due order and rank, the priest, ' the Messiah of Aaron ', should take precedence over the king, 'the Messiah of David'. This is the illustration of a general principle, however, and not a reference to the supernatural Messianic banquet of Jewish apocalyptic.

In ritual too it has been stated that the ritual bathing of the Sect corresponded to Christian baptism just as the ceremonial meals corresponded to the Eucharist. The correspondence is more apparent than real. The Christian baptism was a rite of initiation, whereas in the Sect bathing was a daily ceremony, and there is no suggestion of a sacrament in the meals of the Qumran Sect, which were rather expressions of fellowship.

Nevertheless the worth of the Qumran discoveries for Biblical study is immense. In the department of Old Testament scholarship their value is limited to the study of the transmission of the tradition of the Hebrew text. In view of the relatively late manuscript authority for the Old Testament in Hebrew the Greek version of Alexandria (Septuagint) has been greatly valued, particularly where it is at variance with the accepted Hebrew text, for manuscripts of this version of the whole Old Testament, Codex Sinaiticus (א) and Codex Vaticanus (B), antedate the oldest Hebrew manuscripts by over half a millennium. Now the Biblical manuscripts of Qumran carry the tradition of the Hebrew text back two and a half centuries at least before even the codices Sinaiticus and Vaticanus. The Hebrew texts of Qumran substantiate, though they do not absolutely agree with, the Hebrew accepted text (the Masoretic text).

The first Biblical scrolls to be discovered, the Isaiah Scrolls, do not reproduce the Masoretic text accurately, but the minor nature of the variants, which in the main amount to little more than copyists' errors and orthography, is itself strong testimony to the fact that the standard text was well established, as Burrows argues.[1] Fragments later discovered in Cave 4, however, reveal a more fluid state of the text, though here too the trend towards a standard text was well advanced. Certain fragments, for instance, especially from the Books of Samuel, agree with the Septuagint where it differs from the Masoretic text.[2] Fragments

[1] Millar Burrows, *The Dead Sea Scrolls* (1956), 304
[2] F. M. Cross, ' A Report on the Biblical Fragments of Cave Four in the Wadi Qumran ', *Bulletin of the American School of Oriental Research* 141 (1956), 9–13

from the Song of Moses in Deuteronomy 32 are actually arranged in verse-form in a style which was not permitted once the scribal tradition of the Old Testament with which we are familiar from later manuscripts was firmly established. The comparative fluidity of tradition is again illustrated by certain fragments of Exodus from the same cave which, often with the support of the Septuagint, confirm variations and even expansions of the text found in the Samaritan Pentateuch of the 11th century A.D., still preserved in the Samaritan synagogue on Mount Gerizzim above Nablus.[1]

Not the least service done by the new Biblical texts, especially those from Cave 4, is to enable us to determine the worth of ancient versions such as the Septuagint. Such versions, particularly the Aramaic Targums, have occasionally a tendency to paraphrase, and may even reflect the theological climate of the times of the translation rather than render faithfully the words of Scripture. Though Hebrew texts of Scripture from Qumran which support the Septuagint may themselves adapt the text in the interests of local interpretation, they do supply the instrument whereby we may control the Greek version and so determine what represents an actual Hebrew text and what is in the nature of a paraphrase. The agreement of certain of the Qumran Hebrew fragments with the Pentateuch of the Samaritans, who were regarded with horror as schismatics during the whole period of the occupation of Qumran, is very impressive testimony to the genuine significance of early Hebrew variant texts. It must, however, be reiterated that interesting though such variants may be, they do not materially affect the meaning of Scripture, and no revision of doctrine will be necessitated by the discoveries of Qumran.

The real value of the texts, however, is, in our opinion, in the field of the New Testament. They illustrate the immediate background of the Gospels. It goes without saying that the New Testament must be understood primarily in the light of the Old Testament. Revelation, however, is not a static deposit but a developing experience, and already in the Old Testament the latter part of the Book of Daniel and Zechariah chs. 9–14 mark a new departure in theological speculation. This new development in the faith of ancient Israel, which finds expression notably in the apocalypses of the Apocrypha, was a not insignificant part

---

[1] P. W. Skehan, 'Exodus in the Samaritan Recension from Qumran', *Journal of Biblical Literature* 74 (1955), 182–7

Plate 24 The podium of the temple of Herod the Great to Augustus at
Samaria, looking south-west

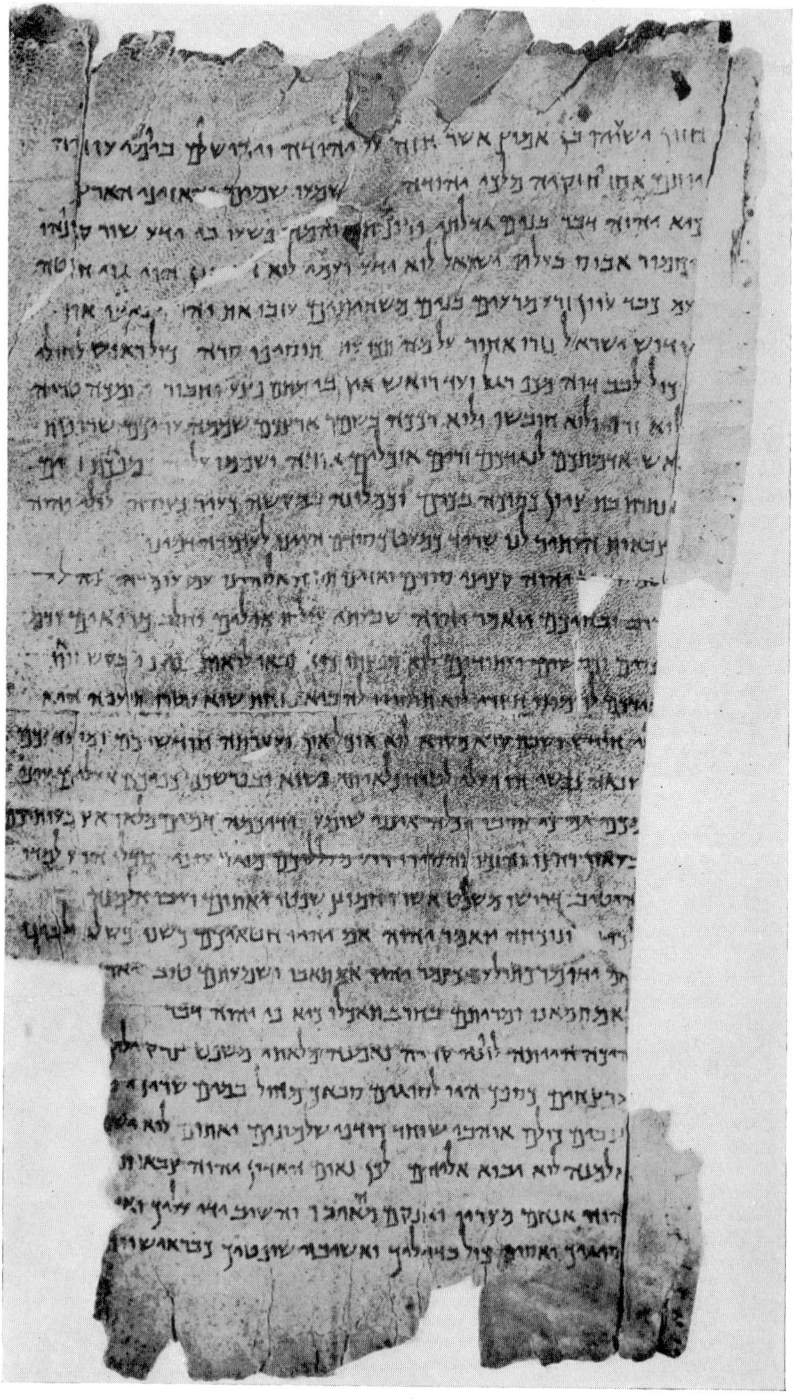

Plate 25 Manuscript of Isaiah 1:1–26 from the first cave to be discovered at Qumran

of the ground on which the seed of the Gospel was sown. Of this important background of the Gospel the Qumran discoveries bring new and striking illustration. There are naturally many cases of correspondence in creed and conduct between the Qumran Sect and the early Church. Many of the beliefs of early Christianity which strike us as strange and bizarre, especially in the realm of angelology and apocalyptic, are seen more clearly than ever in the light of the Qumran Texts to be signs of the local and temporal limitations of the Gospel. What most impresses us from a study of the Qumran Texts is the extent to which the Spirit of God transcends these limitations. All that was best in Judaism, all that the saints of Qumran legitimately valued, was brought to fulfilment in the Christian faith, but in such a manner that all things were made new.

16

Selected Bibliography

The following bibliography is of more general significance than the specialised studies quoted in the footnotes to the text, and is designed primarily for the non-specialist.

Chapter I
ABEL, F. M.   *Géographie de la Palestine* (Paris, 1933–8)
BALY, D.   *The Geography of the Bible* (New York, 1957)
BELL, G. L.   *Syria, the Desert and the Sown* (1908)
DALMAN, G.   *Arbeit und Sitte in Palästina* (Gütersloh, 1928–37)
DRIVER, G. R.   *Semitic Writing* (1948)
DUSSAUD, R.   *Topographie historique de la Syrie antique et mediévale* (Paris, 1927)
GLUECK, N.   *The Other Side of the Jordan* (New Haven, 1940) ;   *The River Jordan* (Philadelphia, 1946) ;   *Rivers in the Desert* (1959)
GROLLENBERG, L.   *Atlas of the Bible* (1956)
JARVIS, C. S.   *Yesterday and Today in Sinai* (1938)
JAUSSEN, A.   *Coutumes des Arabes au pays de Moab* (Paris, 1908)
LUKE, C. H. and KEITH-ROACH, E.   *The Handbook of Palestine and Transjordan* (1930)
NOTH, M.   *Die Welt des Alten Testaments* (Berlin, 1957)
NYSTRÖM, S.   *Beduinentum und Jahwismus* (1946)
PEDERSEN, J.   *Israel : its Life and Culture* (I–II, 1926 ; III–IV, 1947)
SMITH, G. A.   *A Historical Geography of the Holy Land* (26th ed., 1935)
SMITH, W. R.   *The Religion of the Semites*, rev. Cook, S. A. (1927)
WOOLLEY, C. L. and LAWRENCE, T. E.   *The Wilderness of Zin* (1914–15)

Chapter II
CONTENAU, G.   *Everyday Life in Babylon and Assyria* (1954)
DRIVER, G. R. and MILES, J.   *The Assyrian Laws* (1935) ;   *The Babylonian Laws* (I, 1952 ; II, 1955)
FRANKFORT, H.   *Kingship and the Gods* (1948)
HOOKE, S. H.   *Babylonian and Assyrian Religion* (1953)
JASTROW, M.   *The Religion of Babylonia and Assyria* (Boston, 1898)
LLOYD, S.   *Foundations in the Dust* (1947)
PRITCHARD, J. B. (ed.)   *Ancient Near Eastern Texts relating to the Old Testament* (1950) ;   *The Ancient Near East in Pictures* (1950) ;   *The Ancient Near East* (an abridgment of the preceding two vols.) (1958)
THOMAS, D. W. (ed.)   *Documents from Old Testament Times* (1958)
WISEMAN, D. J.   *Illustrations from Biblical Archaeology* (1958)

Chapter III
BREASTED, J. H.   *A History of Egypt* (1906)
CERNY, J.   *Ancient Egyptian Religion* (1952)
ERMAN, A.   *Egyptian Literature* (ET) (1927)
FRANKFORT, H., *op. cit.* (Ch. II)
GLANVILLE, S. R. K. (ed.)   *The Legacy of Egypt* (1942)
MONTET, P.   *L'Égypte et la Bible* (Neuchâtel, 1959)
PRITCHARD, J. B. (ed.), *op. cit.* (Ch. II)
THOMAS, D. W. (ed.), *op. cit.* (Ch. II)
WILSON, J. A.   *The Burden of Egypt* (Chicago, 1951)

Chapter IV
BRIGHT, J.   *A History of Israel* (1960)
DUPONT-SOMMER, A.   *Les Araméens* (Paris, 1949)
JIRKU, A.   *Die Welt der Bibel* (Stuttgart, 1957)
KENYON, K. M.   *Digging up Jericho* (1957) ;   *Archaeology in the Holy Land* (1960)
NOTH, M.   *The History of Israel* (ET) (1958)

O'CALLAGHAN, R. T.   *Aram Naharaim* (Rome, 1948)
ROWE, A.   *The Topography and History of Bethshan* (Philadelphia, 1930)
ROWLEY, H. H.   *From Joseph to Joshua* (1950)

Chapter V
CONTENAU, G.   *La Civilisation Phénicienne* (Paris, 1949)
COOK, S. A.   *The Religion of Ancient Palestine in the Light of Archaeology* (1930)
DRIVER, G. R.   *Canaanite Myths and Legends* (1956)
DUSSAUD, R.   *Les Découvertes de Ras Shamra et l'Ancien Testament* (Paris, 1937)
GASTER, T. H.   *Thespis* (New York, 1950)
GORDON, C. H.   *Ugaritic Literature* (Rome, 1949)
GRAY, J.   *The Legacy of Canaan* (Leiden, 1957)
HOOKE, S. H. (ed.)   *Myth, Ritual, and Kingship* (1958)
JACOB, E.   *Ras Shamra et l'Ancien Testament* (Neuchâtel, 1960)
KAPELRUD, A. S.   *Baal in the Ras Shamra Texts* (Copenhagen, 1952)
SCHAEFFER, C. F. A.   *The Cuneiform Texts of Ras Shamra-Ugarit* (1939)
VINCENT, H.   *Canaan d'après l'Exploration Récente* (1907)

Chapters VI–X
ALBRIGHT, W. F.   *The Archaeology of Palestine* (1949) ;   *Archaeology and the Religion of Israel* (3rd ed., 1953) ;   *From the Stone Age to Christianity* (rev.) New York, 1957)
BARROIS, A. G.   *Manuel d'Archéologie Biblique* (Paris, I, 1939 ; II, 1953)
BRIGHT, J., *op. cit.* (Ch. IV)
BURROWS, M.   *What Mean these Stones ?* (New Haven, 1941)
JACK, J. W.   *Samaria in Ahab's Time* (1929)
JOHNSON, A. R.   *Sacral Kingship in Ancient Israel* (1955)
KENYON, K. M., *op. cit.* (Ch. IV)
NOTH, M., *op. cit.* (Chs. I, IV)
PARROT, A.   *Nineveh and the Old Testament* (1956) ;   *The Temple of Jerusalem* (1957) ; *Samaria the Capital of the Kingdom of Israel* (1958)
WRIGHT, G. E.   *Biblical Archaeology* (1957)

Chapter XI
BRIGHT, J., *op. cit.* (Ch. IV)
WRIGHT, G. E. and FILSON, F. V., *op. cit.* (Chs. VI–X)
GROLLENBERG, L., *op. cit.* (Ch. I)
NOTH, M., *op. cit.* (Chs. I, IV)
THOMPSON, J. A.   *Archaeology and the pre-Christian Centuries* (Grand Rapids, 1958)

Chapters XII–XIII
ABEL, F. M.   *Histoire de la Palestine depuis la conquête d'Alexandre jusqu'à l'invasion arabe* (Paris, I, 1952)
ALLEGRO, J. M.   *The Dead Sea Scrolls* (1956)
BARTHÉLEMY, D. and MILIK, J. T.   *Discoveries in the Judaean Desert* I : *Qumran, Cave* I (1955)
BEVAN, E. R.   *The House of Seleucus* (1902) ;   *Jerusalem under the High Priests* (rev.) (1952)
BRIGHT, J., *op. cit.* (Ch. IV)
BLACK, M.   *The Scrolls and Christian Origins* (1961)
BURROWS, M.   *The Dead Sea Scrolls* (1955) ;   *More Light on the Dead Sea Scrolls* (1958)
CROSS, F. M.   *The Ancient Library at Qumran* (1958)
DUPONT-SOMMER, A.   *Aperçus préliminaires sur les manuscrits de la Mer Morte* (Paris, 1950) ; *The Jewish Sect of Qumran and the Essenes* (1954)
GASTER, T. H.   *The Scriptures of the Dead Sea Sect* (1957)
MILIK, J. T.   *Ten Years of Discovery in the Wilderness of Judah* (1957)
ROWLEY, H. H.   *The Zadokite Fragments and the Dead Sea Scrolls* (1952)

List of Maps

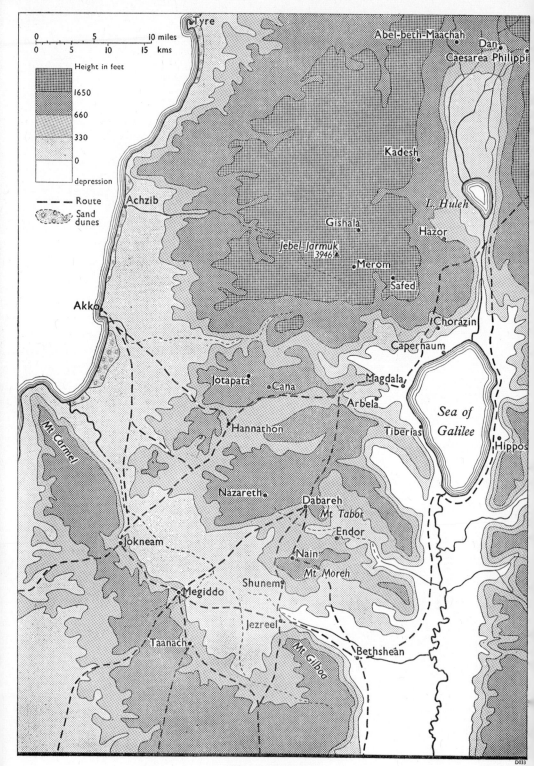

North Palestine
Strategic points and main trade routes

234

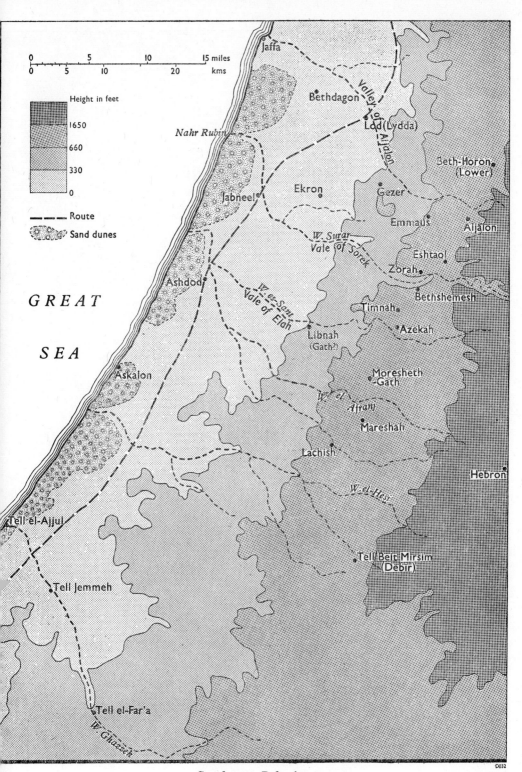

South-west Palestine
Main trade route and strategic points

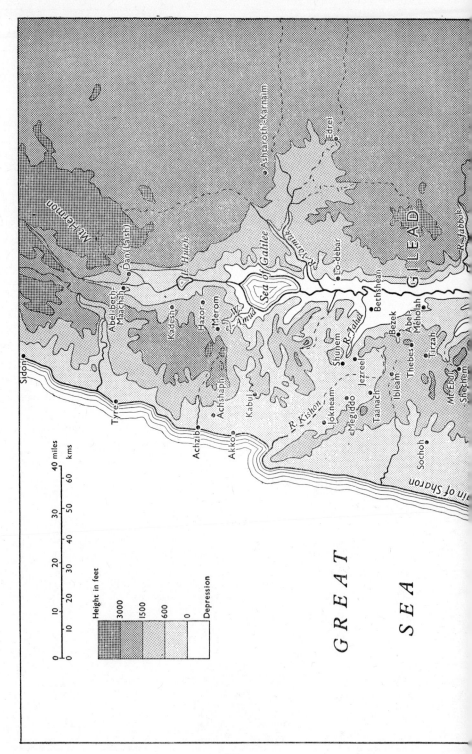

Palestine and the neighbouring lands in the Early Iron Age

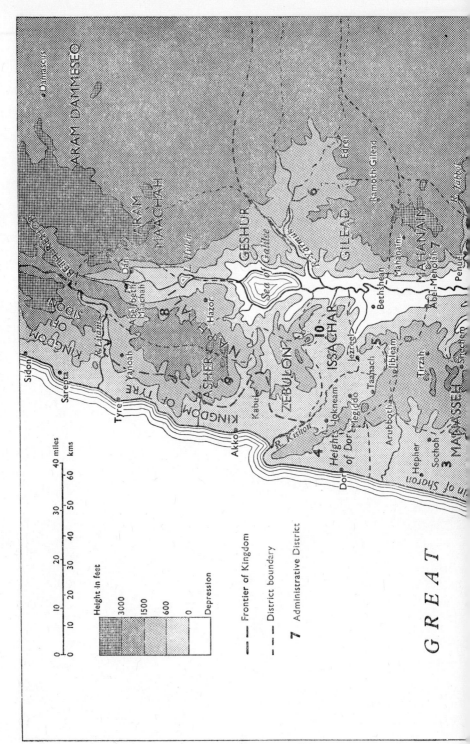

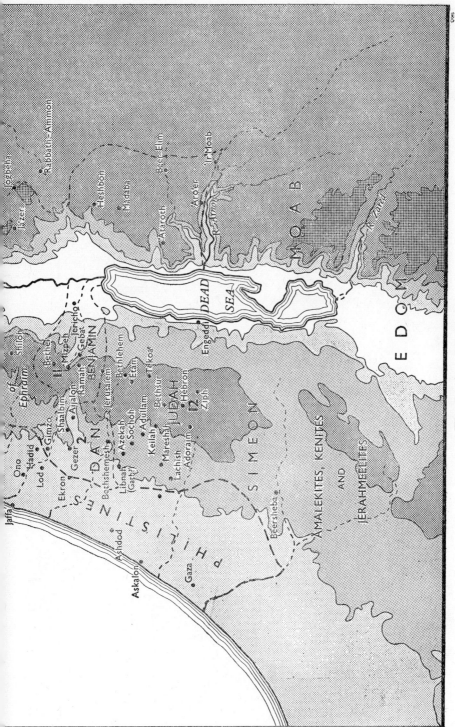

The Realm of Solomon

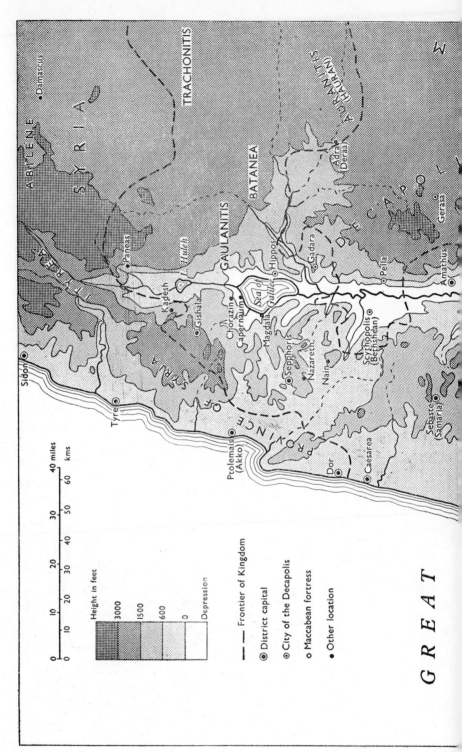

Height in feet

	3000
	1500
	600
	0
	Depression

——— Frontier of Kingdom

◉ District capital

⊙ City of the Decapolis

○ Maccabean fortress

• Other location

40 miles

kms

SYRIA

ABILENE

•Damascus

TRACHONITIS

(AURANITIS)

AURANITIS

BATANEA

GAULANITIS

ITURAEA

Paneas•

L. Huleh

Kadesh•

Gishala•

Chorazin•

Capernaum•

Sea of Galilee

Magdala•

Hippos⊙

Gadara⊙

Adra (Deraa)

D E C A P O L I S

Gerasa•

Pella⊙

Amathus•

Sidon◎

Tyre◎

Sepphoris•

Nazareth•

Nain•

Scythopolis (Beth-shean)⊙

P R O V I N C E   O F   S Y R I A

Ptolemais (Akko)◎

Dor•

Caesarea•

Sebaste (Samaria)◎

G R E A T

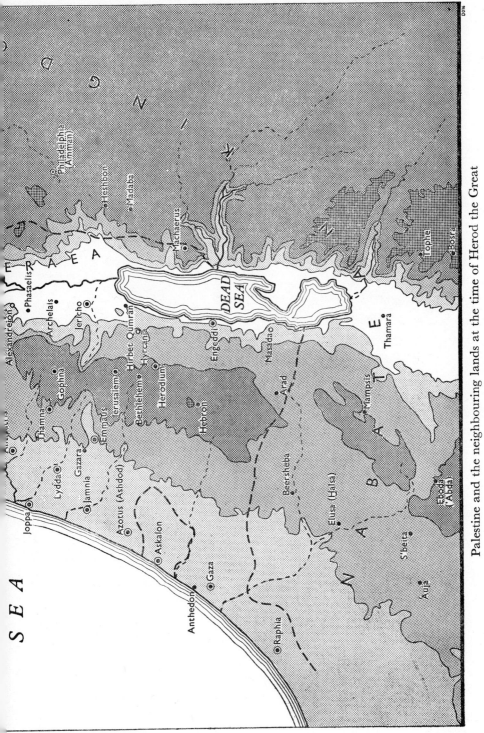

Palestine and the neighbouring lands at the time of Herod the Great

I General Index

II Index of Authors

III   Index of Scripture References

OLD TESTAMENT

253

THE APOCRYPHA

NEW TESTAMENT

Printed in Great Britain by
Thomas Nelson and Sons Ltd, Edinburgh